Guitar

Phil Capone

Exploring Jazz Guitar

*An introduction to jazz harmony, technique
and improvisation*

For my wife, Anita

www.schott-music.com

JUNE 2012

Mainz • London • Madrid • New York • Paris • Prague • Tokyo • Toronto

About The Author

Phil Capone (GDLM, LGSM) is a graduate of Newcastle College, Newcastle-upon-Tyne, and a postgraduate of the prestigious Guildhall School of Music in London. During this time he studied with the highly respected guitarists Phil Lee and Jim Mullen. His many years of experience as a professional guitarist and teacher give him a broad understanding of the world of the contemporary guitarist. Phil frequently performs on the London jazz circuit and enjoys a popular residency with his own quintet. He teaches at The Institute of Contemporary Music Performance (formerly The Guitar Institute), London and is a regular contributor to *Total Guitar* magazine. He is also the author of *The Guitar Player's Chord Bible*.

ED 12945
British Library Cataloguing-in-Publication Data.
A catalogue record for this book is available from the British Library.
ISMN M-2201-2591-1
ISBN 978-1-902455-90-7

© 2007 Schott Music Ltd, London

Project management and book layout by Artemis Music Ltd. (www.artemismusic.com)
Cover design by www.adamhaystudio.com
Copy-editing by Helen Peres da Costa

Photographs: Redferns Music Picture Library – Andrew Lepley (p. 34)/David Redfern (pp. 44, 108, 138 & 180)/Graham Knowles (p. 54)/Paul Bergen (p. 72)/Bob Huntbach (p. 98)/Stephan Engles (p. 118)/Max Jones Files (p. 170)

Printed in Germany S&Co.8241

Contents

Introduction

Starting Your Journey

If you're holding this book then you've already taken your first step on a fascinating journey – to become the jazz guitarist you've always wanted to be. This book will equip you with all of the essential tools that can help you to achieve your goal. Maybe you only want to enhance your playing with some cool jazzy flavours? I'm sure you will still find this is a useful resource that can be dipped in and out of as you wish. But, read from cover to cover, it will not only give you a solid grounding in jazz harmony and fingerboard geography, it will also de-mystify and thoroughly explain the art of improvisation.

You will learn many new chords, not by just being presented with a load of meaningless shapes, but with a full explanation of the harmony in 'guitar-friendly' terminology. In short, you will gain a rewarding insight into the art of jazz guitar that is sure to enhance your technique and harmonic knowledge, whatever style of music you play.

What Is Jazz?

It's believed by some that the world of jazz is a free and easy place where musicians just pluck random notes out of the air while consuming vast amounts of alcohol and illegal narcotics. Most jazz musicians these days only drink water when they're playing – just mention drugs and you'll be off the gig. Jazz has come of age – it's a serious music played by serious musicians.

There are many jokes about 'playing any old note – that's jazz'. Don't get me started. Yes, you can play any note, but it must be delivered with impeccable timing, it should be conceived and 'heard' in the musicians' mind before it is played, oh, and it must also be delivered within the context of a musical phrase. Random notes? I don't think so!

Jazz is a highly disciplined art form with a strict set of rules and a well-established vocabulary. It can't be bluffed, and it takes many years to become accomplished. However once you've got the bug, there is no cooler, more rewarding music on the planet, period. Jazz will take you to places you've never dreamed of. And because you can't fake it in jazz, the musicians are the most genuine cats on the planet. They have to be. Every solo has to come straight from the heart.

Notation

This book assumes a basic level of proficiency on the instrument. It is not intended for the beginner, but it is ideal for anyone who has mastered the basics. Maybe you've just got bored with your playing and you want to learn how to 'jazz it up'. So to make this book as accessible as possible TAB has been used throughout. However, conventional notation always appears above the TAB since this is still the best system for illustrating rhythmic content. If you don't read 'the dots' yet, it is well worth taking the time to at least familiarise yourself with the rhythmic information it contains. Although the tunes featured in each chapter are demonstrated on the accompanying CD, the musical examples are not. And the TAB can only tell half the story; without the rhythmic content you will be missing 50% of the information. I've added a quick reminder below (figure 1) to illustrate the values of the most frequently used notes and rests. If you can't read conventional notation at all, there are many good books (and internet sites) around that can help to get you started.

Fig 1 Note and rest values

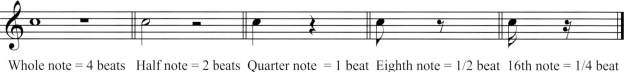

Whole note = 4 beats   Half note = 2 beats   Quarter note = 1 beat   Eighth note = 1/2 beat   16th note = 1/4 beat

Using A Metronome

One tool that you will definitely need is a metronome – and the electronic variety can now be purchased for little more than the price of a couple of sets of strings. I cannot stress the importance of practising with a metronome enough. All the pros do this obsessively. After all, what is the point of learning a super-cool lick if you can't play it in time?

Don't forget that the roots of jazz can be traced back to African music, which is based on complex polyrhythmic (two independent rhythms played simultaneously) drum patterns. So rhythm is arguably the most important element of jazz. The drummers' role in jazz is different too; they are not there to simply 'keep time' for the other musicians. The jazz drummer is free to improvise just as you are, and will commonly accent weak beats to 'hide' the first beat in the bar. This is what makes jazz exciting to listen to.

So it is imperative that you develop an independent, self-contained, sense of time. By this, I mean the ability to play without speeding up or slowing down, always knowing where the first beat is, and being able to count those bars going by. So get into the habit of playing with a metronome – it will optimise your practice sessions and accelerate your rate of progress.

Rhythm Workouts

You can work on enhancing your sense of rhythm away from the guitar, or you can start each practice session with a short rhythmic 'workout'. Try the following exercises starting slowly (80 b.p.m.) and gradually building the tempo (180–200 b.p.m.) by 'notching up' the metronome a little each day.

Counting the beats with '+' between them will help you to place the offbeat notes more accurately. Tap your foot on every beat and clap the rhythm with your hands. In this way you will be internalizing the groove – your foot maintains the pulse while your hands clap the rhythm – allowing you to 'feel' the syncopation. Use this method when learning any new piece of music – 'If you can't clap it, you can't play it'!

When playing at faster tempos, try setting the metronome to half the b.p.m. and counting the resulting pulse as beats 2 and 4. With your foot still tapping on every beat, the metronome will provide the illusion of a swinging 'backbeat' – beats 2 and 4 are exactly where the drummer plays the hi-hat. And don't forget that 'swing' means swing those eighth notes – think shuffle blues and you'll get the idea! For more exercises like these, buy a copy of Louis Bellson's *Modern Reading Text In 4/4* – it's an excellent book and has been used by jazz musicians for decades.

Fig 2 Rhythm workout

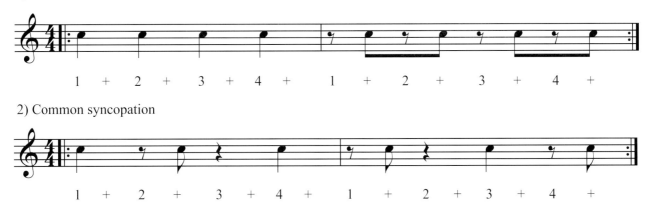

1) 'On' and 'off' the beat

2) Common syncopation

The 'CAGED' System

One philosophy that features heavily throughout the book is the 'CAGED' system. This is a concept that organises the guitar's fingerboard using the five basic open chord shapes C, A, G, E and D. By organising these five simple shapes into the same key, you will become the master of the guitar's fingerboard – it really is that empowering.

First, each of these shapes must be converted to moveable chord forms by barring with your first finger where the open strings would have been. This allows the five shapes to be placed in the same key. Let's start in the key of C (with the open C chord). As you will see in figure 3, the 'A shape' (each shape takes its name from the original open chord) sits in front of the C chord on the third fret. The 'G shape' then sits in front of that on the fifth fret. And so on until you reach the C shape an octave higher.

Fig 3 The 'CAGED' system in C major

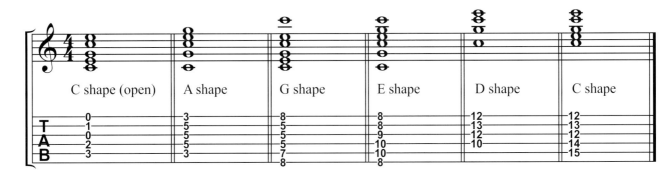

If this concept is completely new to you then it will be a welcome revelation. The 'CAGED' system organises the fingerboard into five manageable areas for every key and it will revolutionise your thinking. It is a system that all professional guitarists use. Obviously you won't just use the system for major chord shapes, it can be adapted to host arpeggios and scales too. In fact you can use it for any type of chord, scale, arpeggio, riff or lick. By learning every new lick in each of the five 'CAGED' shapes you will be able to play it in any key, anywhere on the neck.

Why 'EDCAG'?

As good as the 'CAGED' system is, it needs a little reshuffling to transform it into the perfect fretboard mapping system. The open E chord is the lowest open chord; its root is on the sixth string and it's the chord that the full six-string barre chord is based on. The first scale that guitarists generally learn is the E minor pentatonic scale, either open or in its moveable form. So it makes sense to reorganise the 'CAGED' system as the 'EDCAG' system with the 'E shape' forming shape one. Shape four (the 'A-shape') is the next most important since it forms the frequently used five-string barre. One major advantage of the 'EDCAG' system is that the confusing reference to the original chord shape can be dropped – each shape can be referred to numerically. Figure 4 illustrates the system in the key of F major (since it uses no open shapes it can be applied to any key).

Fig 4 **The 'EDCAG' system in F major**

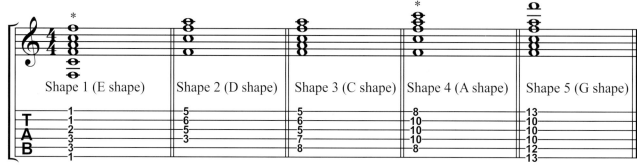

Shape 1 (E shape)   Shape 2 (D shape)   Shape 3 (C shape)   Shape 4 (A shape)   Shape 5 (G shape)

* principle shapes

Chapter Content

The first three chapters of this book concentrate on building a full understanding of the three chord types: major, minor and dominant seventh. For this reason they contain a lot of scales and chord voicings. These chapters are designed to build your fingerboard knowledge and equip you with all the essential scales, modes and arpeggios you will need – so be prepared for plenty of scale practice!

Unlike practically every other music theory book that has been written, I have taken the unprecedented step of starting with minor tonality. Although all harmony is essentially based on (and related to) the major scale, I felt that starting with major tonality would be too 'guitar-unfriendly'. All non-classical guitarists learn the minor pentatonic scale first. In fact I've had so many students over the years asking me how to improvise over major chords, that I felt the most comfortable starting point had to be with minor tonality. The guitar is inherently minor (strum the open strings and you get E minor11). The blues is all about superimposing minor thirds over major chords. Even the most accomplished jazz guitarists will still use the minor pentatonic to create those timeless, bluesy licks, often over a major chord. It's part of the jazz vocabulary. So, major tonality is not dealt with until the third chapter, by which time you will have built on your existing knowledge and will be better equipped to deal with major chords and scales.

Each chapter progressively builds your knowledge. But be prepared to return to material in earlier chapters. You'll probably find some useful stuff that you missed first time around. The learning process is most effective when it contains reinforcement and repetition. That's how we learn best. If you're struggling with a particular topic, jump ahead to the next section, tune or chapter. You can always review that subject later when it will probably just fall into place and all make perfect sense.

Backing Tracks

There are two original tunes in each chapter with a full backing track provided on the accompanying CD. In true jazz tradition, each of these tunes is based on the chord sequence of a popular jazz standard. So you don't waste time learning chord sequences that you'll never use again. Each tune is also designed to allow you to apply the material you have studied in the chapter to a real musical situation.

Every track has the tune panned left and the accompaniment panned right. By adjusting the balance control on your hi-fi system you will be able to eliminate either part and play it yourself. You will need to practise the tunes before you attempt to play them with the backing track – in this way you can start slowly and build up tempo. It is also recommended that you practise scales, arpeggios and improvising using this approach so that you can isolate particular sections and also build tempo where necessary.

Practice Environment

Try to keep an area of your living space dedicated to guitar practice. By this I mean you should have a guitar on a stand, an amplifier (if you need one), and a CD player all set up and ready to go. If you have to get your guitar out of its case, hunt around for the portable CD player, find a suitable chair etc. you won't practise as frequently. That's human nature. Make it easy just to grab your guitar and play – you don't have to practise for hours on end – short bursts are far more effective.

Remember that we learn best by using reinforcement and repetition. Try to avoid relying on your computer for practice sessions too for the same reasons. There are some fantastic tools available for the guitarist in software form: amp simulators, multi-track recording systems, tuners, drum sequencers, etc. They all have their uses but avoid using them for regular practice – if you have to boot up the computer and get the guitar out of its case you'll be less inclined to bother. Make it easy to practise.

The Guitar In Jazz

The guitar has been 'king' in popular music for many decades; it dominates every genre – every genre that is except for jazz. Ask anyone what instrument they associate with jazz and they'll probably mention the saxophone, a double bass or the piano (unless they're a jazz guitarist of course!).

There's no doubt that the guitar cannot compete harmonically with the piano, nor can it equal a saxophonist's soaring legato phrases and effortless flurries of notes. So a jazz guitarist has to be really exceptional if he or she is to make any impact on the jazz world. And there have been many exceptional players throughout the history of jazz. The

pioneering work of **Django Rheinhardt** and **Charlie Christian**; the cool, sophisticated sounds of **Wes Montgomery**; the post-**Hendrix** fusion style of players such as **Mike Stern** and **John Scofield**.

The world of jazz guitar is certainly diverse and whether you play acoustic or electric, solid body or semi-acoustic, there will be a style of jazz that will suit you. Practise hard, listen to as much jazz as you can lay your hands on, sit in on as many jam sessions as you can and who knows, you could be the next big name in the jazz guitar world...

1: Static Minor Chords

The Minor 7th Chord & Arpeggio

Most books that deal with music theory, be it jazz or classical, begin with the key of C major. It is after all, the logical place to start. But for us guitarists, who have to deal with a complicated fretboard system ruled by shapes and patterns, it is not an ideal starting point.

The ubiquitous minor pentatonic is the most widely used scale in the guitar world and so it seems more sensible to begin with a minor key. Minor tonality is also very 'guitar-friendly'; some players even 'think' in minor keys when playing over major or dominant seventh chords, an approach pioneered by the late, great Wes Montgomery and expanded by the legendary Blue Note guitarist Pat Martino.

Arpeggios are an indispensable element of jazz improvisation, so they will become a frequent ingredient of this book. An arpeggio is made up of the same notes as the chord it shares its name with, as illustrated in figure 1.1(a). The Amin7 arpeggio can also be viewed as the minor pentatonic with the third scale note omitted (the note in brackets).

Fig 1.1(a) **Amin7 arpeggio**

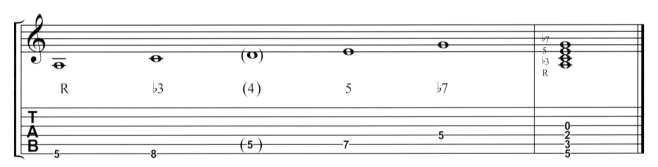

All intervals are defined in relation to the major scale – that's why all the intervals contained in the major scale are major or perfect. It follows that once you stray from the confines of major tonality you are more likely to encounter minor, augmented and diminished intervals.

In figure 1.1(b) a one octave chromatic scale is used to illustrate how these intervals transfer to the fretboard (by repeating the root note between each interval you will be able to hear the individual character of each).

Fig 1.1(b) **One octave chromatic scale**

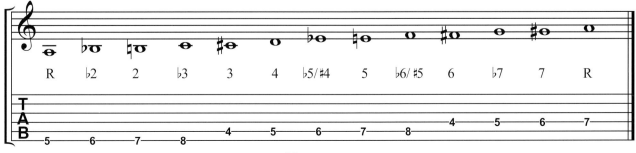

If all this is new to you, it's essential that you become accustomed to how each of these intervals sounds, and how they can be played from any point on the fretboard. (Note that some notes have two names; the correct name is governed by the musical context they are used in.)

By expanding the Amin7 arpeggio across the fingerboard, we get a much more useful note pool for improvising. Figure 1.2 spans just over two octaves (2 octaves + minor 3rd) and it's the first shape in the CAGED (EDCAG) system.

Fig 1.2 Amin7 arpeggio – shape one

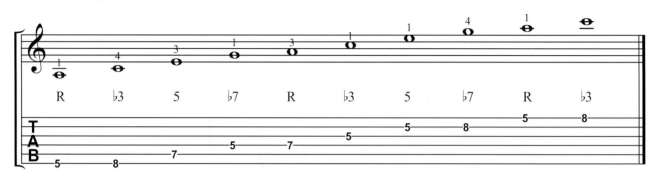

You may find this is a little tricky to play because of its similarity to the A minor pentatonic. If so, practise slowly and think of the interval names as you play. You could also try starting on a note other than the root to prevent your fingers from slipping into that familiar pentatonic pattern.

The minor seventh chord, when used in a jazz context, is usually paired down to a simple four-note voicing. This is because notes are seldom dou-

bled in jazz guitar voicings. More often than not, less important notes such as the fifth (and even the root) are omitted to allow additional tensions to be added. Figure 1.3 shows the five EDCAG shapes for an Amin7 chord. There are no doubled notes so make sure you damp unwanted notes (such as the open 5th string in the first shape) and avoid adding extra notes from familiar barre shapes (as in the fourth shape which does not include the first string).

Fig 1.3 Amin7 – four-note voicings

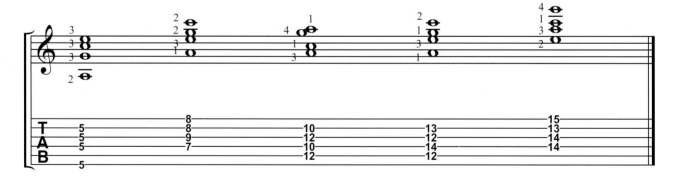

The Aeolian Mode (Natural Minor)

Modes play a big part in post-bop jazz; ever since **Miles Davis** turned the jazz world on its head with his revolutionary album *Kind Of Blue* in 1959, no self-respecting jazz musician can afford to ignore their importance.

By playing the major scale from a starting note other than the root, a new pattern of intervals is created and so a new scale, or mode, is born. Six major modes can be created in this way. Don't dwell too much on a mode's relationship to its parent major scale – it's more important to consider the scale on its own merits. The Aeolian mode is built from the sixth step of the major scale and so is often called the natural minor scale since it occurs in the relative minor key. Figure 1.4 below is the one octave scale with intervallic spelling.

Fig 1.4 **The Aeolian mode**

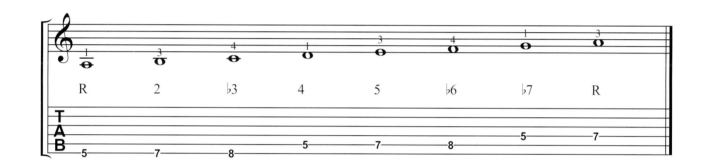

The Aeolian mode could also be viewed as the A minor pentatonic scale with two notes added. These two notes, along with the 4th, are the colour tones of the scale; they are non-chord tones and so will have a colouring effect when played over the parent chord. To familiarise yourself with the colour tones you should practise singing these notes against an Amin7 chord.

Just as we used numbers to describe the intervals of the Amin7 arpeggio, so we can number chords in the same way, using roman numerals when writing them to avoid any confusion. By using only the notes of the Aeolian mode we can create seven seventh chords by stacking thirds above each step of the scale. Chords built in this way are called diatonic chords since they only contain notes from the parent scale.

Figure 1.5 illustrates the diatonic Aeolian chords in close position voicings. By thinking of the chords numerically (as in the roman numerals below the stave), it will be easy to construct diatonic chords in another key, for example D Aeolian.

Fig 1.5 **Diatonic Aeolian chords**

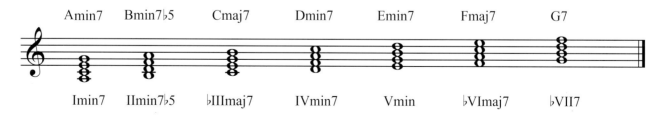

Close position piano-style chord voicings are extremely difficult on the guitar due to the large stretches required to play them. By raising the third an octave we can create more practical voicing (as used in the fourth EDCAG shape in figure 1.3).

In figure 1.5 all the chords are shape four voicings with the following interval formula:

R–5–♭7–♭3	=	min7
R–♭5–♭7–♭3	=	min7♭5
R–5–7–3	=	maj7
R–5–♭7–3	=	dom7

Although this may all seem rather mathematical, analysing the interval formula of every chord you play is actually extremely liberating, and is a far more musical approach to harmony than just learning a whole bunch of chord shapes.

Fig 1.5 Diatonic Aeolian chords – guitar voicings

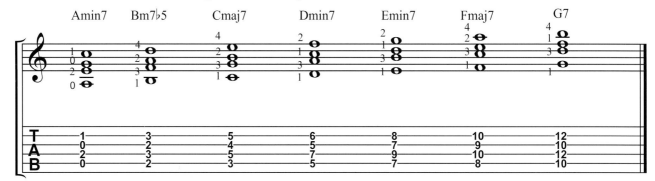

Figure 1.6 is the full shape one (EDCAG) of the Aeolian mode; notice that it spans just over two octaves, finishing on a high C (minor 3rd) which is the same span as the Amin7 arpeggio.

Practising the Amin7 arpeggio before the Aeolian mode helps to distinguish the chord tones from the colour tones – an essential skill for improvising.

Fig 1.6 Two octave Aeolian mode – shape one

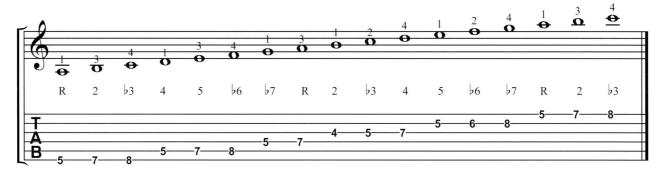

By learning all five EDCAG shapes each time you learn a new scale or mode you will be preparing yourself thoroughly for the technical demands of improvising. Figure 1.7 maps out the remaining four shapes of the Aeolian mode; only shape one

has the root as its lowest note (this is true of all EDCAG scale shapes). Once you are familiar with these shapes try omitting the colour tones (2nd, 4th & 6th) to obtain the four remaining Amin7 arpeggio shapes.

Fig 1.7(a) Two octave Aeolian mode – shape two

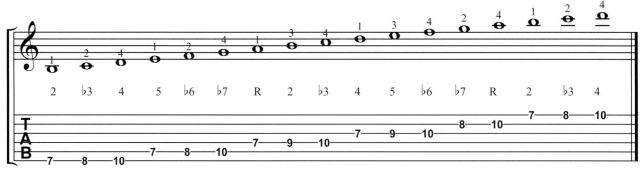

Fig 1.7(b) **Two octave Aeolian mode – shape three**

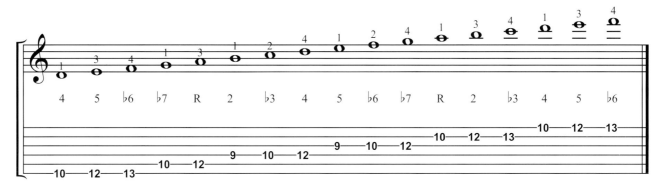

Fig 1.7(c) **Two octave Aeolian mode – shape four**

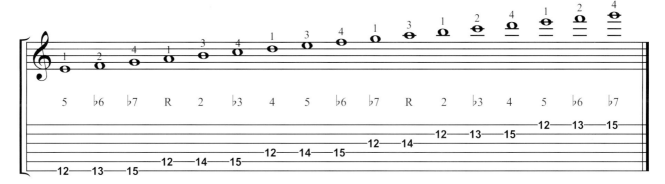

Fig 1.7(d) **Two octave Aeolian mode – shape five**

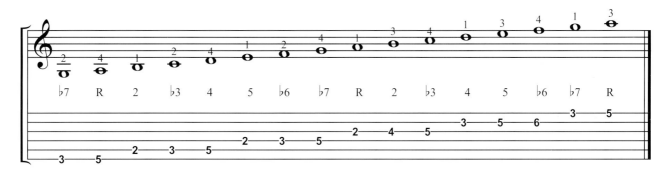

Remember that by learning the Aeolian mode in all five of the EDCAG shapes (the EDCAG system is fully explained in the Introduction if this philosophy is new to you), the entire fingerboard becomes one huge Aeolian scale – giving you the freedom to play wherever you want to on the neck.

The Dorian Mode

The Dorian and Aeolian modes are identical apart from the sixth step; in the Dorian this is major, a half-step higher than in the Aeolian. This may seem rather insignificant, yet this small change has a significant impact on the scale and its potential applications.

The Aeolian mode is generally used for soloing over the tonic chord in a minor key (e.g. Amin7 in the key of A minor), and although the Dorian is just as effective in this context, it is also widely used over non-tonic minor chords. The major sixth gives the mode a much brighter, funkier sound than its darker-sounding Aeolian cousin, and this makes it ideal for creating cool minor licks.

The major sixth interval will also 'sit' happily on top of a minor seventh chord; in fact many soloists will accentuate the major sixth by ending phrases on it instead of a chord tone. You will notice that in figure 1.8 below, an accidental now occurs on the sixth step in order to raise it a half-step. Most music written in the minor key contains accidentals, and since the same key signature is used for related major and minor keys, this is a good way to establish a tune's true tonality when reading music.

Fig 1.8 **The Dorian mode**

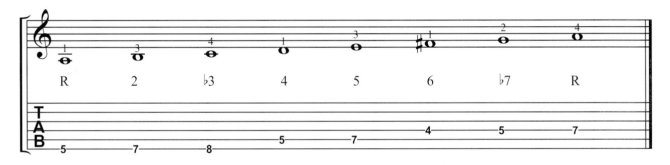

The raised sixth step of the Dorian also creates a different set of diatonic chords as you will see from figure 1.9(a). There are still three minor sevenths, two major sevenths, one dominant seventh and one minor seven flat five, however, with the exception of the tonic (Amin7), minor third (Cmaj7), and fifth (Emin7) chords, they occur on different notes of the scale.

Fig 1.9(a) **Diatonic Dorian chords**

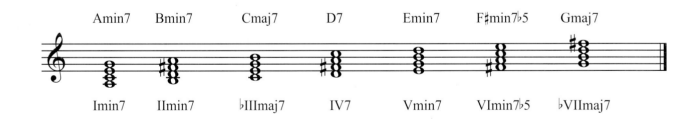

One of the great advantages of using the EDCAG system is that scale patterns and chord voicings will recur, albeit on different scale steps, in modes derived from the same parent scale. Even when comparing say, modes of the major scale with that of the melodic minor, there will still be some similarities with sometimes just one note being different. The more you know about the notes you are playing (i.e. which scale step you are on), the easier it becomes to adapt previously learnt material, and so your knowledge of the fingerboard will cumulatively broaden.

So in figure 1.9(b) below, all the four-note voicings are identical to the diatonic Aeolian chords, they just occur in a slightly different order. Try and modify the previously learnt Aeolian voicings by altering the relevant intervals, e.g. if you want to change Bmin7♭5 to Bmin7 simply identify the fifth and raise it a half-step.

Fig 1.9(b) Diatonic Dorian chords – guitar voicings

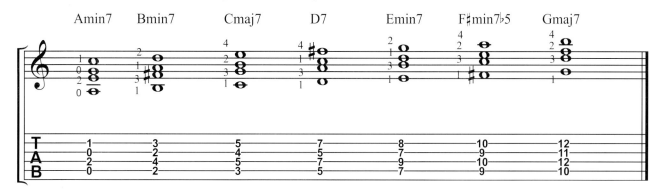

Shape one of the Dorian (figure 1.10) shifts between fifth and fourth positions and is almost symmetrical apart from the different note counts on the 2nd and 5th strings. This makes the pattern easier to memorise than the Aeolian shape one. It might also seem familiar since it's identical to the third shape of the Aeolian.

This shape ambiguity is rife in the EDCAG system, which is good news for learning new modes, but bad news if you don't practise the scale and arpeggio patterns together to identify the chord and colour tones (which do not transfer between modes).

Fig 1.10 Dorian mode – shape one

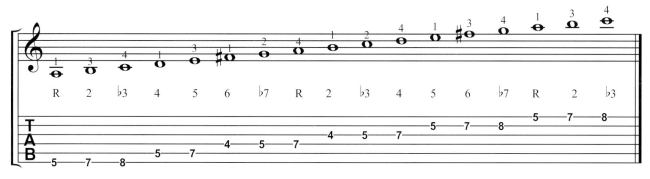

In figure 1.11 the remaining four Dorian shapes are annotated. As before, you should also learn the corresponding arpeggio shapes by omitting the colour tones (2nd, 4th & 6th steps).

Fig 1.11(a) Dorian mode – shape two

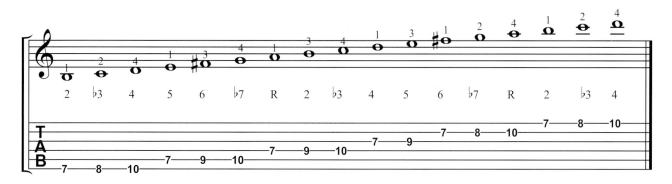

Fig 1.11(b) **Dorian mode – shape three**

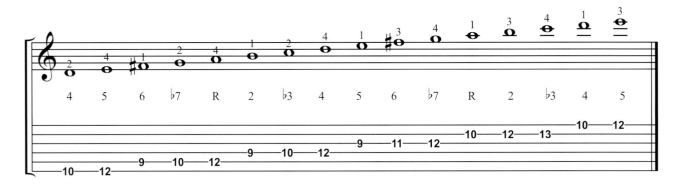

Fig 1.11(c) **Dorian mode – shape four**

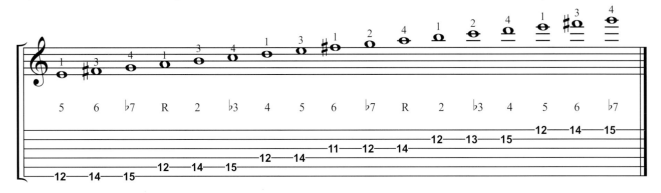

Fig 1.11(d) **Dorian mode – shape five**

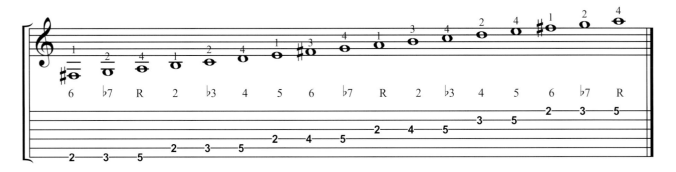

The following tune is a vehicle for you to practise your new improvising skills. The chord sequence uses two unrelated minor seventh chords, effectively creating two separate tonal centres (in other words both min7 chords function as tonic minors). This enables you to use either the Aeolian or Dorian mode when improvising.

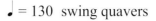**Minor Jam**

Phil Capone

♩ = 130 swing quavers

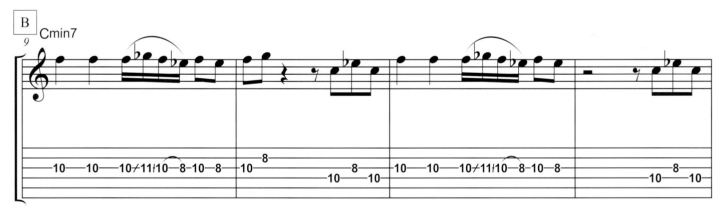

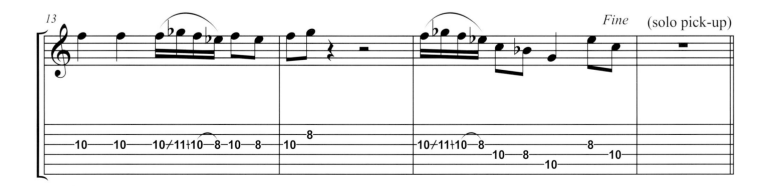

Minor Jam – solo

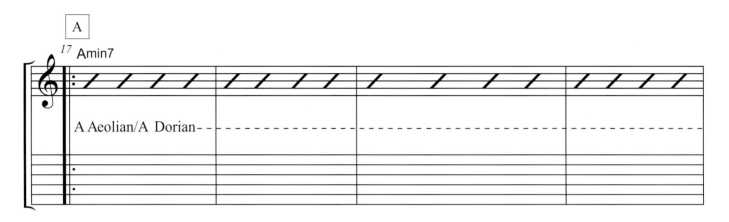

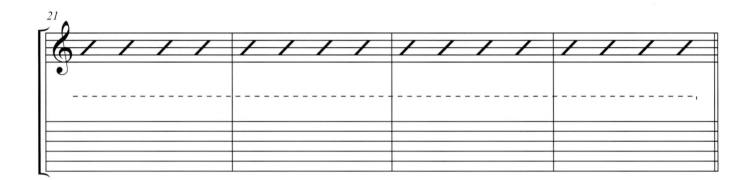

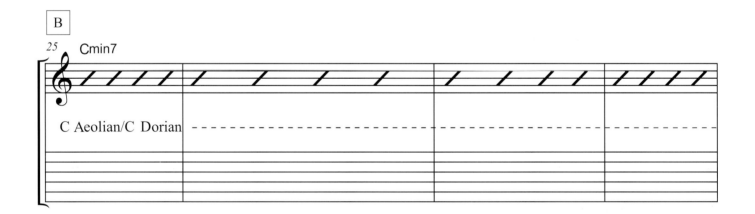

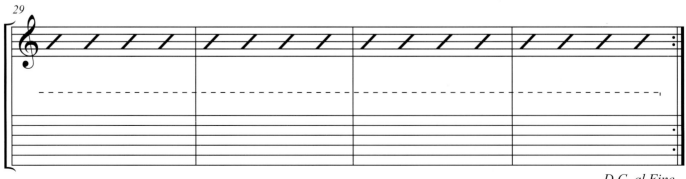

D.C. al Fine
(after repeat)

Checkpoint

Song Form

A very simple form has been used to construct this sixteen-bar tune: it's an eight-bar 'A' section followed by an eight-bar contrasting 'B' section (the boxed letters indicate the start of each section). With the exception of the twelve-bar blues, the majority of jazz tunes comprise eight-bar sections that are added together to build songs thirty-two bars in length.

The instruction **D.C.** (abbreviation of the Italian: *da capo*) **al Fine** sends you back to the beginning of the piece (after repeating the solo section) to play the tune one more time, finishing at the end of bar 15 at the instruction *Fine*.

Solo Choruses

All Jazz standards originally started life either as show tunes or popular songs of the day, and usually included a verse as well as a chorus. The verses were subsequently dropped when jazz musicians adopted them; hence the term chorus is used to describe a complete cycle of the chord sequence. Once the tune has been played (usually once through) the sequence is repeated for improvising: these are called solo choruses. It is common practice to play the tune at the beginning and end of the arrangement.

Ornamentation

Jazz musicians frequently add ornamentations to melody notes, often as a way of stamping the melody with their own personal signature. This tune has a written ornamentation that occurs on the third beat of each new phrase. The melody note (D), is followed by the note a half-step above (E♭ – the flattened fifth from the blues scale), a repeat of the melody note, and finally the note below (C).

In classical music this type of ornamentation is called a turn. The single slur line above the four notes in the top stave is translated into two slides and a pull-off to the final note (as indicated in the TAB), only the first note should be picked.

Swing Eighth Notes

It don't mean a thing if it ain't got that swing! **Duke Ellington**'s famous composition echoed the sentiment of the 30s swing era, but it remains equally relevant today.

Swing eighth notes are written as normal eighth notes, but it's understood that the musician will interpret the tune with a swing feel. The only clue is the 'swing quavers' or 'swing' indication written at the beginning of the tune (but not always). If you listen to the recording of 'Minor Jam' you will notice the eighth notes are not played evenly – the first note of a pair is actually longer than the second.

Below you can see how swing quavers are written and how they actually sound; just like the first and last note in a group of three triplets. It's a good idea to practise counting and clapping swing quavers frequently – this can be done any time you have a spare moment so that it doesn't eat into your practice time.

How to swing

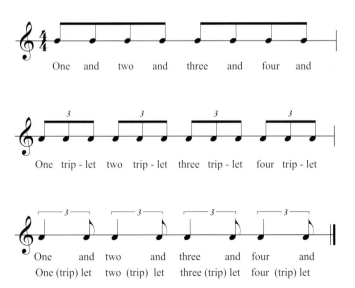

21

Assignments and Improvisation Tips

1. Arpeggios & scales. Remember that it's essential to be in control of the notes you are playing when you improvise, rather than just playing random sequences of notes. The best way to advance your technique is to practise everything in a strict sequence: chord/arpeggio/scale. So when practising shape three of the Dorian for example, play the shape three chord followed by the corresponding arpeggio and finally the scale pattern.

2. Colour tones are vital to improvisation. A skilled improviser can expertly juggle them with chord tones to create an exciting solo. Not only will you need to be able to hit colour tones 'on the fly' when improvising, you also need to know what they sound like before you play them. Practise singing the 2nd, 4th, min 6th/maj 6th intervals against a minor seventh chord – simply play the note and then copy it with your voice (don't forget to experiment with different octaves to find the best range for your voice).

Aeolian colour tones

Dorian colour tones

3. Using a metronome when you practise is vital and will help you to develop a strong sense of rhythm and time. It is not the drummer's job to simply keep time for the other musicians; he or she is an equal member of the ensemble and will simultaneously be improvising as you are.

You need to be an equally confident time-keeper and maintain the groove without speeding up, slowing down or losing track of the beat. It's a good idea to practise with your metronome at half tempo (so if you are playing at 140 b.p.m., set it to 70 b.p.m.) and count the metronome pulses as beats two and four, this simulates the drummer's backbeat hi-hat rhythm on beats two and four.

Pentatonic Superimposition

Some interesting modal textures can also be created by superimposing a minor pentatonic scale over a non-parent minor seventh chord (i.e. with a different root name). One advantage of this is that you can create modal tensions using 'guitaristic' bluesy licks.

Using this method the listener hears a familiar blues phrase, but because the lick is not played in its usual setting it takes on a whole new sound, creating very cool and well-phrased colour tone tensions.

When intervals span a distance greater than an octave they are said to be compound intervals. Colour tones are generally expressed as compound intervals rather than simple intervals (an octave or less) and there is a good reason for this.

Because colour tones are derived from additional thirds being stacked above the basic seventh triad, they technically only occur 'above' the chord, and even though they can be played in a lower octave they are still described as a compound interval. The difference between a compound interval and the simple interval it shares its name with is always 7.

$$9 - 7 = 2 \qquad 11 - 7 = 4 \qquad 13 - 7 = 6$$

So our previous three colour tones, the 2nd, 4th and 6th are now referred to as a 9th, 11th and 13th respectively.

In figure 1.12 a D minor pentatonic scale is superimposed over an Amin7 chord, the numbers beneath the scale indicate the intervals created in relation to A minor (the simple interval equivalents of the non-chord tones are in brackets).

Fig 1.12 Minor pentatonic 'up a fourth'

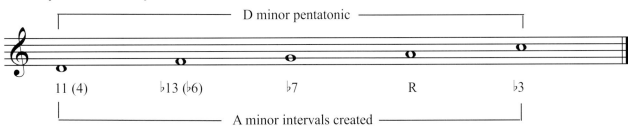

When a D minor pentatonic is superimposed over Amin7, the scale is being played a fourth above the parent chord. Playing a minor pentatonic a fourth above a min7 chord creates Aeolian modal tensions.

The minor pentatonic can also be superimposed a fifth above the parent min7 chord. In this instance Dorian tensions are created as in figure 1.13.

Fig 1.13 Minor pentatonic 'up a fifth'

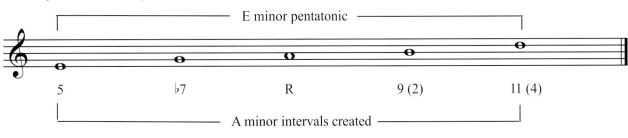

The Harmonic Minor

One of the major harmonic drawbacks of the Aeolian and Dorian modes is that both scales have a minor seventh as their diatonic V chord (see figures 1.5 and 1.9).

A Vmin7 chord creates no 'pull' back to the Imin chord and so does not set up the all-important V – Imin perfect cadence, essential for providing a satisfactory resolution back to the tonic. Figure 1.14 highlights the natural resolution tendencies in a V7 – Imin perfect cadence. The fifth intervals of both chords are unimportant and have little impact on the cadence; the real resolution is created by the third of the V7 (G♯) pulling up a half-step to the root of the Imin, and the minor seventh (D) pulling down a whole step to the minor third of Imin.

Fig 1.14 Minor perfect cadence

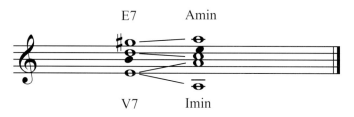

The harmonic minor scale is specifically designed to remedy the drawback highlighted above and thereby create the desired V7 – Imin cadence. As you can see in figure 1.15(a) the seventh step is major, a half-step below the octave root. In all other respects the scale is identical to the Aeolian mode.

Fig 1.15(a) The A harmonic minor scale

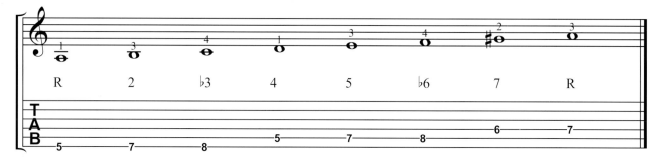

The harmonic minor is so-called because it was traditionally used in classical music to create harmony, and with good reason. A dominant seventh chord occurs diatonically on the fifth degree as illustrated in figure 1.15(b), creating the all-important perfect cadence in a minor key. Like the Aeolian mode, the harmonic minor is most frequently used when improvising over a tonic minor chord.

Fig 1.15(b) Diatonic harmonic minor chords

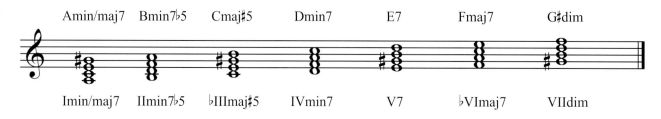

As we previously discovered with the Aeolian and Dorian modes, raising the third of each close-position voicing creates useable, 'guitar-friendly' shapes as illustrated in figure 1.16.

Fig 1.16 Diatonic harmonic minor chords – guitar voicings

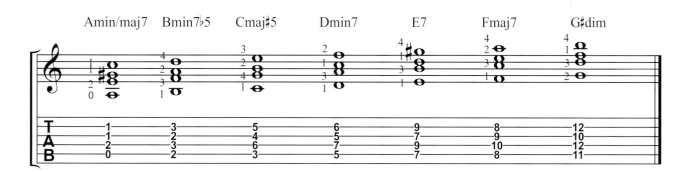

The major seventh of the harmonic minor scale also creates a diminished chord on the seventh degree (which we will be looking at later in the book), a major seventh with an augmented fifth on the third degree (ideal for creating major chord tensions but must be used with care), and a tonic minor chord with a major seventh.

The min/maj7 chord and arpeggio (figure 1.17) has a distinctive, angular sound that is often used as an ending chord when a dark, unsettling cadence is desired, conjuring up images of 1960s spy thrillers (electric guitars interestingly featured on many soundtracks in this genre – *The Ipcress File* is a classic example, and who could forget the wonderfully 'twangy' *James Bond* riff?).

Fig 1.17 Amin/maj7 arpeggio – shape one

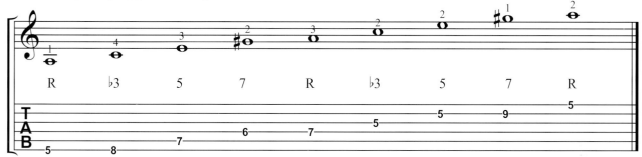

The harmonic minor is the only scale that contains the interval of a minor third (between the minor sixth and the major seventh) – all other scales are constructed from half- and whole steps only. As you will see this creates fingering issues in shape one of the scale (figure 1.18), which starts in fifth position

and switches to fourth position on the second octave. Shape one does not include the high minor third since this would involve playing two notes with the fourth finger, and spans a total of two octaves and a tone.

Fig 1.18 Harmonic minor – shape one

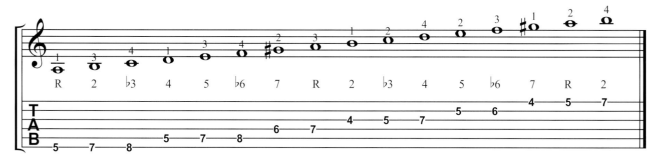

The remaining four EDCAG harmonic minor shapes (figure 1.19) either involve a mid-scale position shift or an out of position stretch at some point in the scale. Make sure you use the same fingering

both ascending and descending and don't forget to omit the colour tones to obtain the four additional min/maj7 arpeggio shapes.

Fig 1.19(a) **Harmonic minor – shape two**

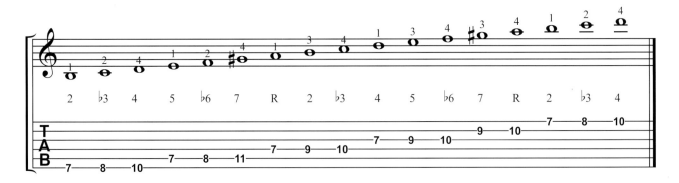

Fig 1.19(b) **Harmonic minor – shape three**

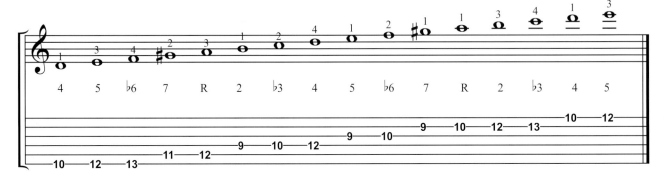

Fig 1.19(c) **Harmonic minor – shape four**

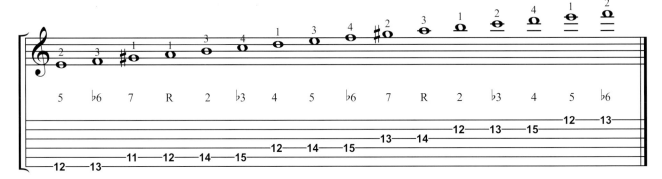

Fig 1.19(d) **Harmonic minor – shape five**

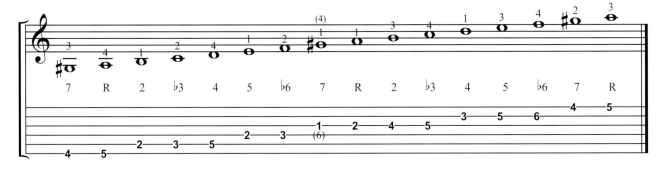

Like the harmonic minor scale, the jazz melodic minor also contains the major seventh interval; unlike the harmonic minor it also has a major sixth.

As we'll see, it is, in effect, the same as a major scale with a minor third; all of the intervals are major or perfect apart from the flattened third.

The Jazz Melodic Minor

The jazz melodic minor is so-called to distinguish it from the traditional melodic minor which, in the classical world, ascends with a major sixth and seventh but descends with a minor sixth and seventh. From a jazz musician's perspective this would render the scale unusable so it was decided to make the scale the same ascending or descending (with major 6th and 7th degrees) and it was duly renamed the jazz melodic minor. Note that the descending traditional version of the scale would actually be the same as the Aeolian mode.

Fig 1.20 The melodic minor

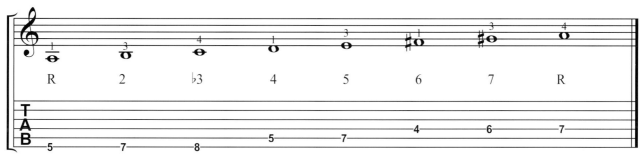

The diatonic melodic minor chords (figure 1.21(a)) also feature the all-important dominant seventh plus the hybrid minor/major seventh tonic chord. However the inclusion of the major sixth changes the II chord to a straight minor seventh, adds another dominant on the fourth degree, and most interestingly adds two min7♭5 chords on the sixth and seventh steps.

Fig 1.21(a) Diatonic melodic minor chords

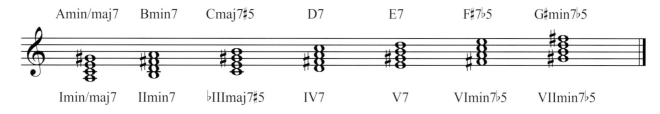

With two seventh chords and two, hopefully by now familiar, min7♭5 shapes, the diatonic melodic minor guitar voicings (figure 1.21(b)) should pose no problems apart from the slightly tricky Cmaj7♯5 shape that also occurred in the harmonic minor.

Fig 1.21(b) Diatonic melodic minor chords – guitar voicings

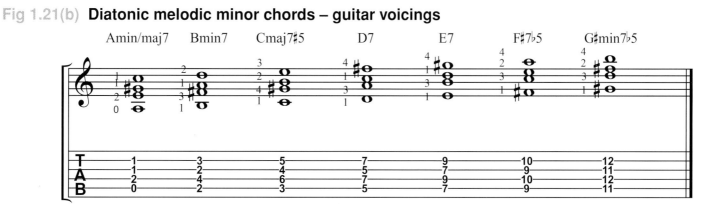

Shape one of the melodic minor scale (figure 1.22) involves an earlier shift to fourth position (only notes on the 6th and 5th strings are in fifth position) than in the harmonic minor, and consequently also has a span of two octaves and a tone.

Fig 1.22 Melodic minor – shape one

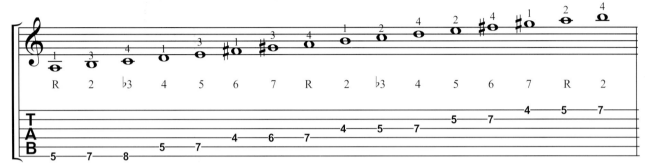

The remaining EDCAG shapes of the jazz melodic minor contain position shifts and numerous out of position stretches. When these involve the 4th finger, alternative 1st finger stretches are provided in brackets; whichever you decide to use, make sure you keep to the same fingering ascending and descending.

And don't forget the golden rule: **Always practise the min/maj7 arpeggio before the scale shape.**

Fig 1.23(a) Melodic minor – shape two

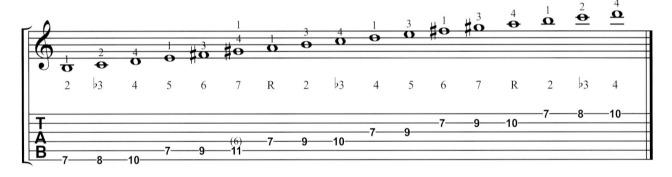

Fig 1.23(b) Melodic minor – shape three

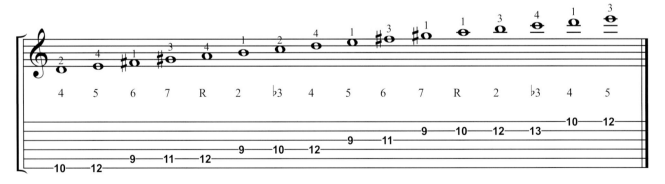

Fig 1.23(c) Melodic minor – shape four

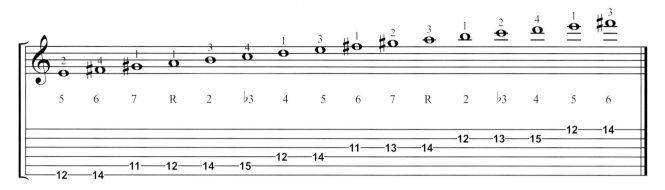

Fig 1.23(d) Melodic minor – shape five

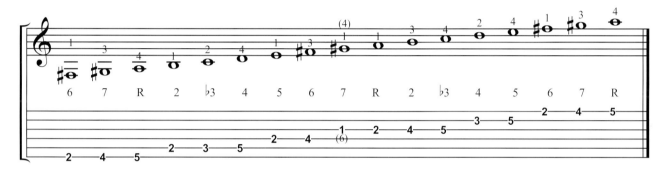

The following piece, 'Identity Crisis' is the second tune in this book. It's the perfect vehicle for you to practise improvising using not only the Dorian and Aeolian modes, but also the melodic and harmonic minor scales.

Remember that the jazz melodic minor is simply the Dorian mode with a raised (major) seventh step. Similarly the harmonic minor mode can be viewed as the Aeolian with a raised (major) seventh. Study the piece thoroughly before you try playing along with the backing track. The tune is played at a brisk tempo – practise with your metronome and slowly build up to the target of 150 b.p.m.

Phil Capone

♩ = 150   swing

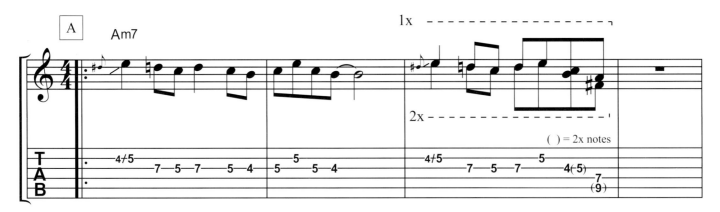

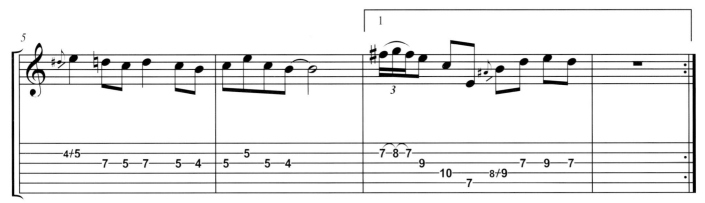

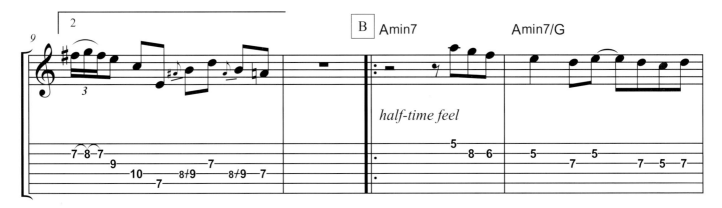

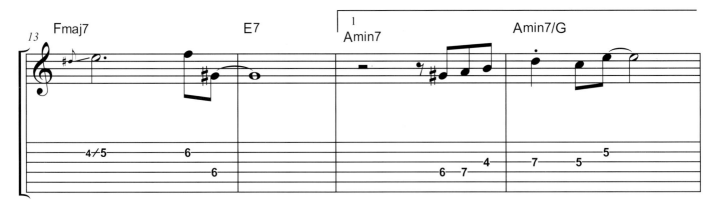

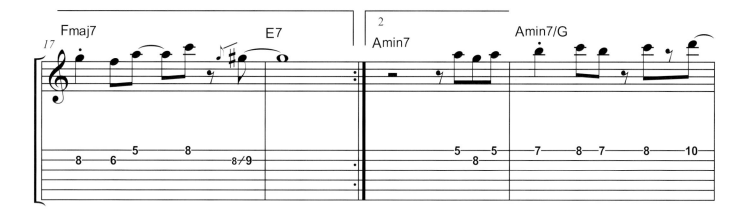

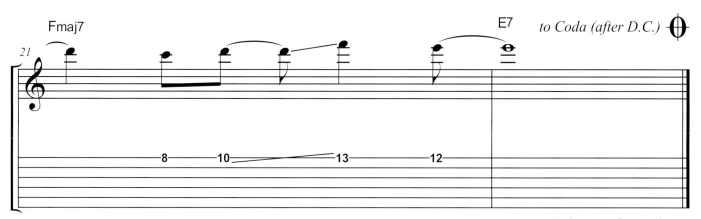

Solos on form then
D.C. al Coda

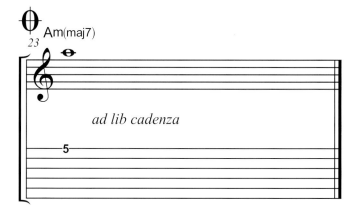

Checkpoint

Song Form

Just like 'Minor Jam' this tune has two contrasting sections, but in this arrangement each section repeats making it AABB form, 32 bars in total. Each section contains a 1st and 2nd time bar. (The A section also has a variation in the melody on the repeat, this is when the bracketed notes in bar three are substituted.) Play the 1st time bar the first time through to the repeat. On the repeat, jump the 1st time bar and play the 2nd, this takes you on to the

B section. The same 'route map' will apply in the B section. The solo chorus form is exactly the same but with straightforward repeats for each section; after your solo play the tune as before and end on the coda. The coda's cadenza is an improvised ending; remember to use the harmonic or melodic minor over the min/maj7 chord.

Identity Crisis – solo

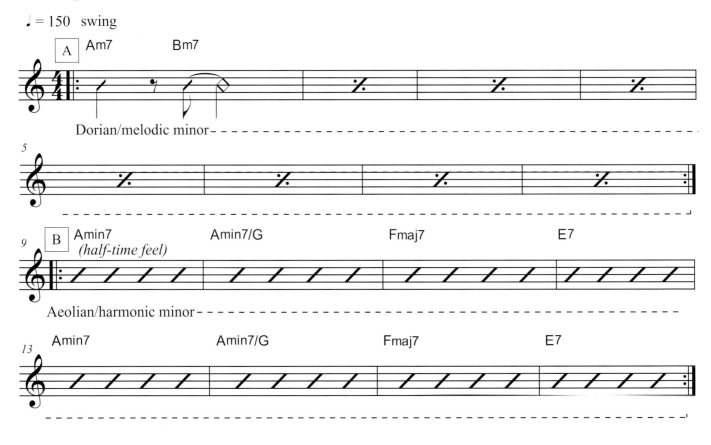

Grace Notes

Grace notes occur frequently in this tune; these are notes that don't have any time value of their own (hence they are written smaller than normal) and 'steal' time from the note that follows. Simply play the grace note and slide immediately to the main note. You may have noticed that these notes don't

start on scale notes, they are chromatic approach notes, pulling into the note from a half-step below.

Scale Choices

The A section of the tune and solo chorus is played over an Amin7 vamp (although the vamp is actually Amin7 to Bmin7, the overall tonality is Amin7), based on a Dorian/melodic minor note pool. If you include the major 7th interval from the melodic minor make sure it is used either as a chromatic approach note or a passing note as shown below. It will not sound good as a resolution note over a min7 chord!

Although the B section remains in the same key, the chord sequence shifts the tonality into darker, Aeolian/harmonic minor territory (this is intensified by the half-time rhythm section). Once again, the raised seventh of the harmonic minor should be treated with care except during E7 at the end of each four-bar sequence, this is where you should resolve to the G♯ just as the melody does.

a) as a chromatic approach note   b) as a passing note

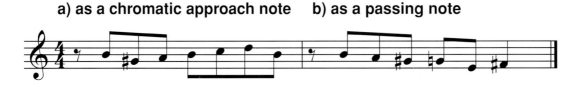

Assignments and Improvisation Tips

1. The example below summarises the similarities/differences between all four of the scales we have studied in this chapter. Ideally the scales should be practised in two groups: Aeolian/harmonic minor and Dorian/melodic minor (note that the second scale with the major seventh is darker than the first scale in each pair). If you apply the arpeggio-scale practice routine to every EDCAG pattern we have studied, you will not only be building a thorough knowledge of the fingerboard, but also ensuring that you have total control over the chord tone/colour tone palette, which is essential for effective improvisation.

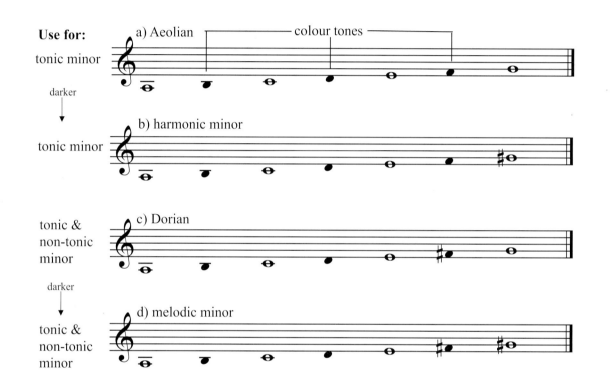

2. Ear-training is vitally important for the budding jazz musician. If you don't know what a note is going to sound like before you play it, you will not be creating a musical improvisation since you will only be playing random notes or memorised finger patterns. Each time you practise, set aside a little time for developing your ear. Play a minor seventh chord (anywhere on the neck, the more keys you practise in the better your ear will get) and practise singing colour tones and chord notes against it, checking your answers each time.

When you're practising scales, try singing the next note before you play it, this will really focus your attention and prevent you from 'switching off' once the fingering patterns are familiar.

33

Blue Note recording artist Pat Martino with the Gibson Pat Martino Signature Model guitar, built to Pat's specification by the Gibson Custom Shop. The guitar's features include twin '57 humbuckers, a flame maple archtop and ebony fingerboard.

2: Static Dominant 7th Chords

The Dominant 7th Chord & Arpeggio

The dominant seventh was traditionally used on the dominant step of the major or minor key to pull back to the tonic. When the chords are paired in this way they form an extremely powerful sequence called the perfect cadence or V – I. By deferring resolution to the tonic, or sidestepping to another chord as in an interrupted cadence, the listener's interest is maintained. Composers have manipulated this harmonic tension for hundreds of years and so it is a sound that our ears have become very familiar with.

The dominant seventh's harmonic instability is caused by the diminished fifth interval between the third and seventh. Musicians were actually banned from playing this interval in medieval times since it was feared the sound would summon the devil! The early blues musicians incorporated dominant sevenths freely into their compositions, hence the term 'the devil's music'.

It's difficult for us to appreciate how unorthodox the blues must have sounded. As time progressed, jazz composers stretched listeners' ears further by writing chord sequences scattered with non-diatonic dominant sevenths (called secondary dominants). In this chapter we will be exploring the different kinds of dominant sevenths that occur in jazz, and which modes can be used to apply the appropriate colour tones.

Fig 2.1 G7 arpeggio and chord

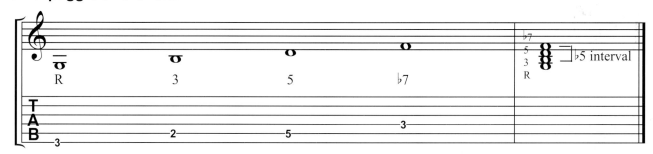

In figure 2.1 a G7 four-note arpeggio and close position chord voicing are illustrated. Notice the interval of a flattened fifth (often referred to as a tritone since a ♭5 = 3 tones/3 whole steps) between the 3rd and ♭7th intervals of the chord. It is this interval that gives the chord its dissonant quality.

By extending the basic G7 arpeggio to two octaves, the EDCAG shape one is achieved as shown in figure 2.2. The 4th finger stretch required to include the high major third in a dominant seventh arpeggio makes it an impractical inclusion so it extends to the root only, spanning exactly two octaves.

Fig 2.2 G7 arpeggio – shape one

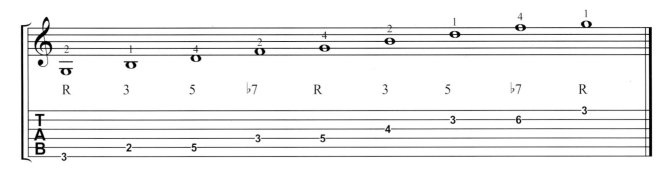

Like the minor seventh chords in the previous chapter, our five EDCAG dominant seventh shapes (figure 2.3) are four-note voicings. Remember that intervals are rarely doubled in jazz guitar voicings; that big six-string barre is a definite no-no! Chords are paired down to their simplest form to give a more concise sound and allow superfluous intervals (i.e. the root and fifth) to be easily omitted, allowing additional tensions to be added. Smaller shapes are also more mobile and easier to move around the neck when comping (accompanying).

Fig 2.3 Five four-note G7 voicings

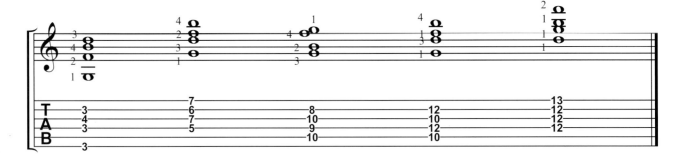

The Mixolydian Mode

While the blues was undeniably an important influence in the development of jazz, the blues approach to improvising on dominant sevenths is based on superimposing minor thirds over a dominant sound. Blues guitarists seldom stray far from the familiar pentatonic minor, skilfully wrestling with the scale and bending strings to create additional intervals as required.

String bending occurs less frequently in jazz since jazz guitarists have traditionally used heavy gauge, flat wound strings to achieve a fat, mellow sound. And although it's cool to occasionally use the minor pentatonic to inject a bluesy vibe over dominant sevenths, it would not be appropriate to use this scale exclusively.

The Mixolydian mode is an ideal choice for improvising over static or non-resolving dominant sevenths. This is the scale a jazz musician would use over the tonic chord in a twelve-bar blues. As you can see in figure 2.4, it contains the 4th, 5th and ♭7th of the minor pentatonic, but swaps the minor third for a major, and also includes the 2nd (9th) and 6th (13th) colour tones.

Fig 2.4 **The Mixolydian mode**

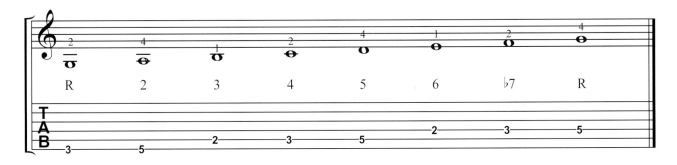

Since the Mixolydian mode is derived from the major scale just as the Aeolian and Dorian modes were, exactly the same chord types are produced (i.e. 3 x min7, 2 x maj7, 1 x dom7, 1 x min7♭5). However these chords occur on completely different steps of the scale as you can see in figure 2.5(a).

Fig 2.5(a) **Diatonic Mixolydian chords**

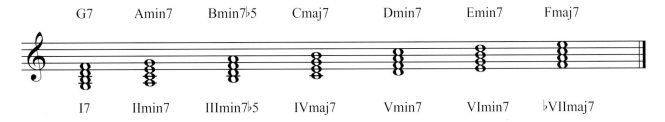

As before, the close position, stacked thirds voicings are useful for studying chord construction, but not very practical for guitarists due to the large stretches required to play them.

In the previous chapter we based each minor scale's diatonic chords on the fourth EDCAG shape (with a raised third). To remain in the related major key of C, all of the dominant chords and modes in this chapter will be analysed as G7. This places the lowest possible root at the third fret on the sixth string, therefore the diatonic Mixolydian guitar voicings (figure 2.5(b)) will now be based on the first EDCAG shape with a raised third and fifth (compare the G7 in figure 2.5(b) with the close position voicing in figure 2.5(a)).

Fig 2.5(b) **Diatonic Mixolydian chords – guitar voicings**

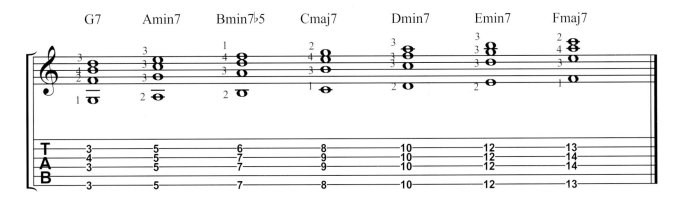

By extending the simple one octave scale across the fingerboard in second position, the full EDCAG shape one pattern is achieved (figure 2.6). As with the shape one arpeggio, the inclusion of the high third would involve an impractical stretch, hence our shape one finishes on the high 2nd (A) and spans a total of two octaves and a whole step.

Fig 2.6 Two octave Mixolydian mode – shape one

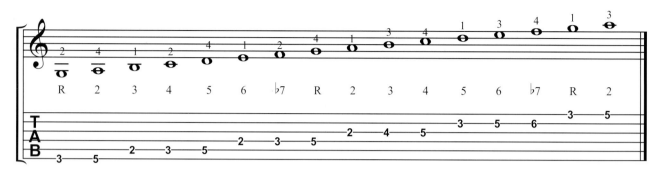

As before, applying this logic laterally along the fingerboard results in a total of five EDCAG scale shapes. Figure 2.7 annotates the remaining four shapes. Be aware that you have encountered all of these note patterns previously in the Aeolian and Dorian EDCAG shapes, i.e. shape two is the same as Aeolian shape one or Dorian shape four.

For this reason it is essential to ensure that you have the intervals under your fingertips and their relationship to the parent G7 chord (the intervallic names are more important than actual note names since these can be applied to other keys). The process of eliminating colour tones to achieve the remaining four G7 arpeggios will help to accelerate this process.

Fig 2.7(a) **Mixolydian mode – shape two**

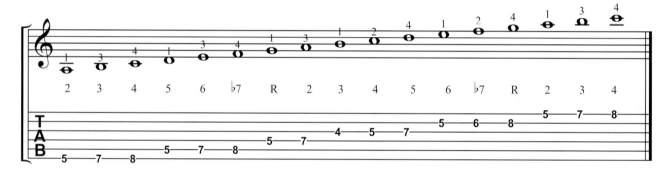

Fig 2.7(b) **Mixolydian mode – shape three**

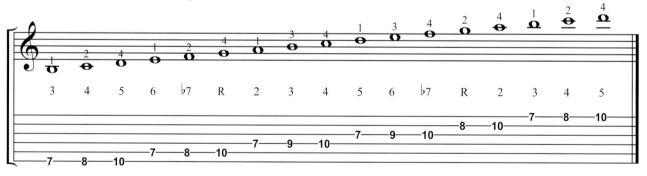

Fig 2.7(c) **Mixolydian mode – shape four**

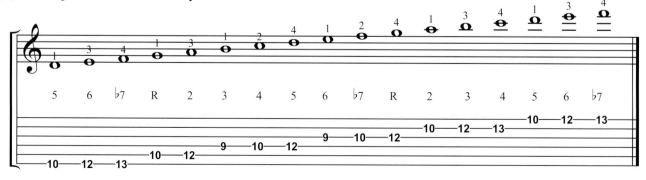

Fig 2.7(d) **Mixolydian mode – shape five**

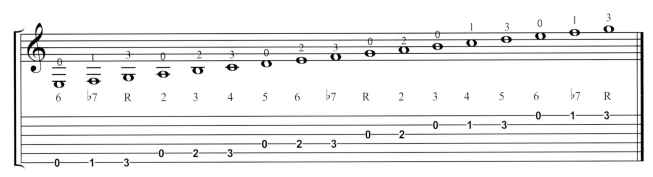

Dorian Superimposition

In Chapter 1 our exploration of jazz improvisation began from a minor perspective. The reasons for this are hinged around the minor pentatonic and its inherent 'guitar-friendliness', i.e. only two notes per string, familiarity to all players and playable with the 1st and 3rd fingers.

Although the Dorian mode adds two extra notes per octave, the pentatonic shape is still clearly 'visible' within the scale, and this makes the mode easier to play than the unfamiliar Mixolydian shape. Add to this fact that minor arpeggios sound super cool when superimposed over dominant sevenths, and

you have a good scale choice for dominant improvisation. In figure 2.8 the resulting intervals created from superimposing a Dorian a fifth above G7 are clearly defined. These intervals are identical to the notes in the Mixolydian mode, they are just approached from a different perspective when played as a Dorian a fifth above the chord. Remember that when directly relating colour tones to a chord type, they are always expressed as a compound interval i.e. greater than one octave. To convert a compound interval back to its simple counterpart, just subtract seven and retain the original quality e.g. maj 13 - 7 = maj 6.

Fig 2.8 **The Dorian-Mixolydian relationship**

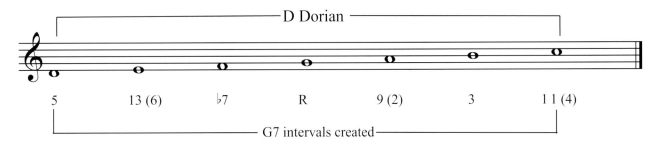

The following tune is a post-bop, modal-based exploration of static dominant seventh chords with a melody inspired by **Thelonius Monk**'s bluesy compositions. Each eight-bar section modulates up a half-step, enabling you to change key by simply moving whichever shape you are improvising on up a half-step with each chord change. Use all of the ideas we have explored in this chapter: G7 arpeggios, G Mixolydian and D Dorian modes.

3 | Seventh Heaven

Phil Capone

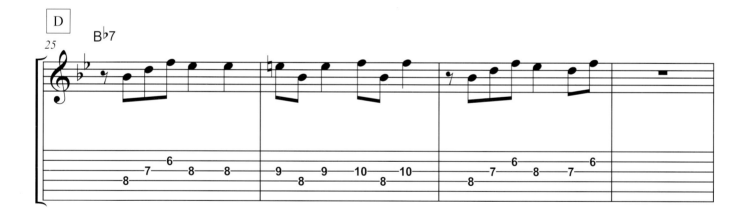

after solo D.C. al Fine

41

Seventh Heaven – solo

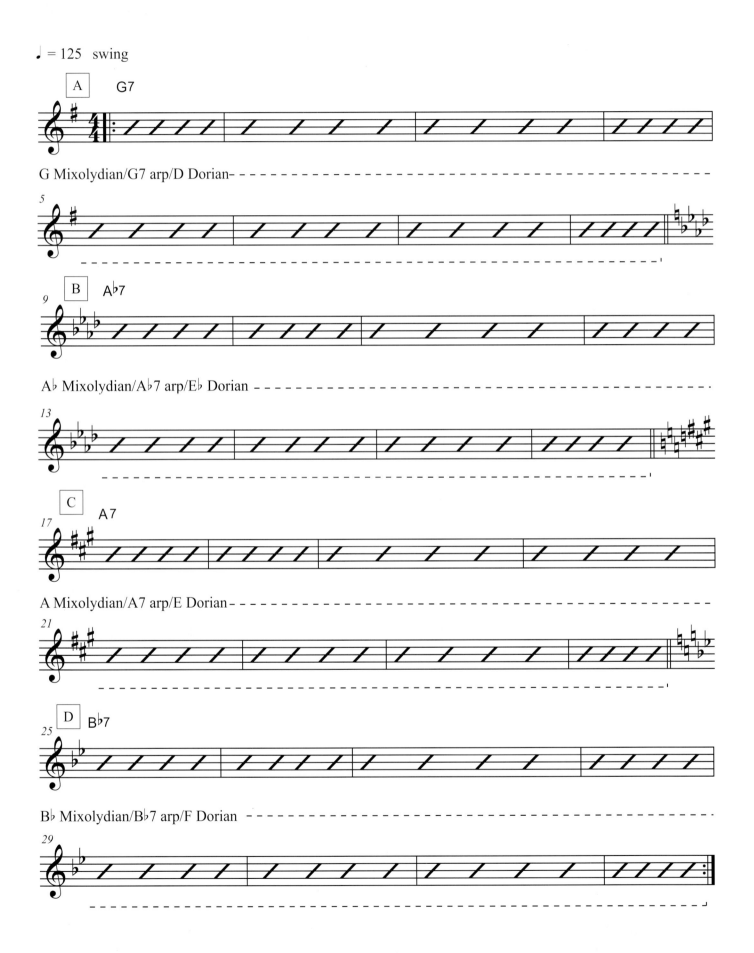

Checkpoint

Song Form

This tune uses ABCD form and is 32 bars long. Unusually, each eight-bar section modulates up a half-step and contains just one static dominant seventh chord. The A, B and D sections all use the same melody, albeit in different keys (so you simply shift the same fingering pattern up the neck). The C section is where the middle eight would normally occur in the more frequently used AABA song form, so the melodic content has been changed at this point.

Arpeggios

Arpeggios occur frequently in melodies – this is because they form an instant melodic fragment. The first bar of each phrase begins with a simple major triad, contrasted with the tension of a repeated 11th interval:

Analysing melodies and understanding how they work is a great way to improve your improvising skills. Improvising is, after all, the art of creating melodies 'on the fly'.

Playing Fourths

Playing fourths across the fingerboard can be tricky. In section C, notice that notes on adjacent frets are played with the same finger.

Don't barre all the notes at once but 'roll' your finger across the fingerboard starting with the tip of your finger on the lowest note. In this way you should be able to sound one note at a time (this technique was pioneered on the violin by the classical virtuoso Paganini).

Ending Phrases

...on a chord tone is less final than ending on a root note. Section A is made up of two four-bar phrases. The first phrase ends on the fifth and leaves the listener with the impression that there is more to come, while the second phrase ends on the root, providing a musical 'full stop' before the next section begins (see below). Once again, these melodic tools should be incorporated into your improvising vocabulary.

a) using a chord tone (bar 3)   b) using the root note (bar 7)

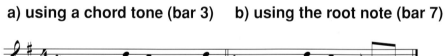

Assignments and Improvisation Tips

1. Modulation frequently occurs in jazz. Chromatic modulation (where the key or chord shifts up or down a half-step) should be easy on the guitar, just shift your shape up a fret, right? Yes, but it can actually be very confusing and disorienting at first, more tricky than shifting to a completely new shape or area of the neck because of overlapping patterns. So when you practise, make sure you familiarise yourself with the four keys in this piece: G, Ab, A and Bb. If you come up with a lick in one key, transfer it to the other three (and play it in different positions and octaves).

2. Harmonic time is not some weird new-age science, simply the ability to know which bar you are on when you are soloing. This is extremely important when soloing over a modal-based tune. When the chord change happens you should be

43

anticipating it in your solo, not simply being dragged along with the changes. This is much easier if you think in phrases when you solo, play four two-bar phrases and eight bars have gone by. Once again practising with your metronome (sounding on beats two and four) and thinking musically will help you to achieve this goal.

3. Ear training is crucial at every stage of this book to ensure you can really 'hear' what you've learnt. Play a G7 chord and try singing each of the chord tones against it. Start with the root, then the 3rd, 5th and ♭7th, checking your answer each time by playing the interval. Next, sing the three colour tones against the chord (9th, 11th, 13th). If you find this hard, don't worry, keep trying and your ear *will* improve.

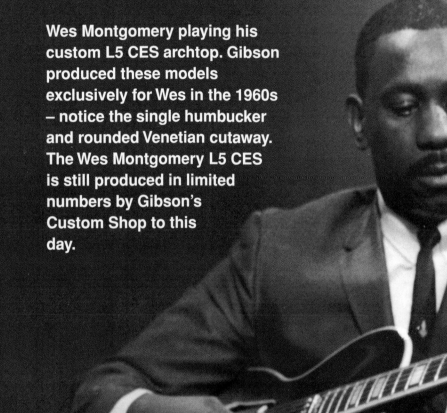

Wes Montgomery playing his custom L5 CES archtop. Gibson produced these models exclusively for Wes in the 1960s – notice the single humbucker and rounded Venetian cutaway. The Wes Montgomery L5 CES is still produced in limited numbers by Gibson's Custom Shop to this day.

The Phrygian Dominant Mode

The Aeolian, Dorian and Mixolydian are all modes derived from the major scale. However modes can also be formed from the harmonic and melodic minor scales. The minor modes are essentially a 20th-century phenomena, evolving from the pioneering work of the modal improvisers in the late 1950s and early 60s.

Unlike the major modes they don't have Greek names, in fact some of these modes have no names at all, while others may be known by more than one. When a name is given it is usually 'borrowed' from the major mode with the same colour tones.

One of the most useful harmonic minor modes is the Phrygian dominant. Built on the fifth step of the harmonic minor, it has a minor second (♭9) and minor sixth (♭13), colour tones also present in the Phrygian mode (built on the third of the major scale). Since it has a major third and a minor seventh (see figure 2.9) it provides an ideal note pool for improvising over dominant sevenths, especially a dominant seventh built on the V of a minor key. A dominant seventh occurring on the V of the scale (major or minor) is called the primary dominant. When built on any other step of the scale it is referred to as a secondary dominant.

Fig 2.9 **The Phrygian dominant mode**

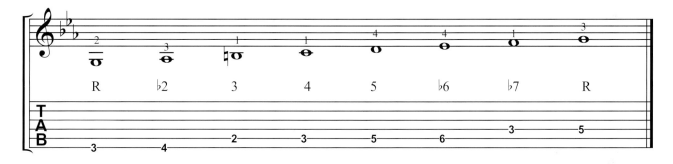

The diatonic chords derived from this scale will be identical to those created with the harmonic minor scale in Chapter 1 (figure 1.16), but they will of course occur on different scale steps when applied to the Phrygian dominant. The chords are notated in close position, stacked thirds in figure 2.10(a):

Fig 2.10(a) **Phrygian dominant diatonic chords**

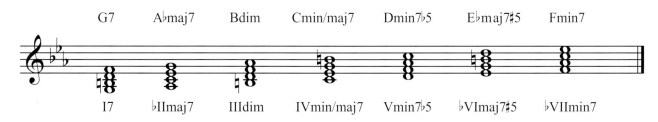

Since the lowest root note of the G Phrygian dominant is on the sixth string, just as it was in G Mixolydian, it makes sense to harmonise this mode with shape one type chords having a raised third and fifth (Chapter 1, figure 1.10). Don't worry about memorising every single shape, as we progress through the book each voicing will become more familiar as it is reintroduced in each chapter.

45

Fig 2.10(b) Phrygian dominant diatonic chords – guitar voicings

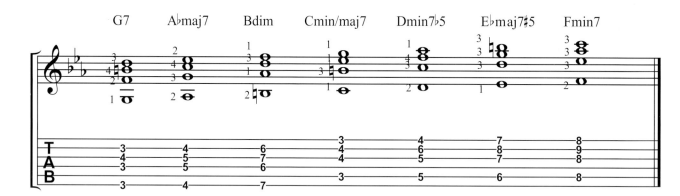

By grouping chords into one of three families: minor, major or dominant seventh (as in figure 2.11), you will see that we have encountered just seven different chords so far. It is the process of changing the closed voicings to open ones and then generating five EDCAG shapes from every possible variant that creates a plethora of chords.

Without understanding the intervals contained in each shape, and knowing how to change just one note to form a new chord, the process of learning all the possible different voicings becomes a Herculean task. If you know the intervals in a 9th chord, then you will also know how to raise or lower the 9th by a half-step to create a ♭9 or a ♯9 chord. *Voilà*, three chords for the price of one! Every scale and mode can also be categorised in this simple way, a concept used by many guitarists and frequently cited by the late, great jazz guitar virtuoso **Joe Pass**.

Fig 2.11 Organisation of chord types

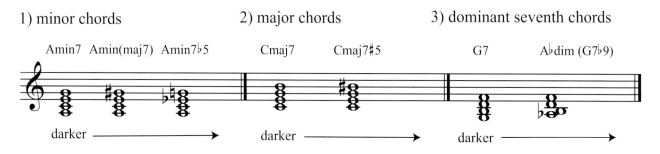

As before, the one octave mode is extended to produce a full shape one pattern (figure 2.12) that ex-

tends to the high minor second (♭9) and spans two octaves and a half-step.

Fig 2.12 Two octave Phrygian dominant mode – shape one

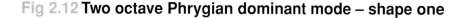
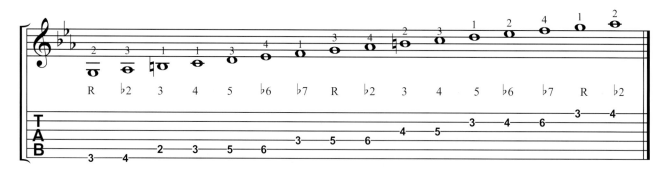

Figure 2.13 gives the remaining four EDCAG shapes. Notice that the patterns and fingerings are identical to the five harmonic minor shapes we looked at in Chapter 1. The Phrygian dominant starts with what would be shape four of the C harmonic minor scale, however it's important to remember that each note becomes a different interval when related to a V7 chord instead of a I chord. Notice that as in the Mixolydian mode earlier in the chapter, shape five is notated in open position. The shape should also be practised an octave higher at the twelfth fret, using the same fingering as shape three of the harmonic minor (Chapter 1, figure 1.19(b)).

Fig 2.13(a) Phrygian dominant mode – shape two

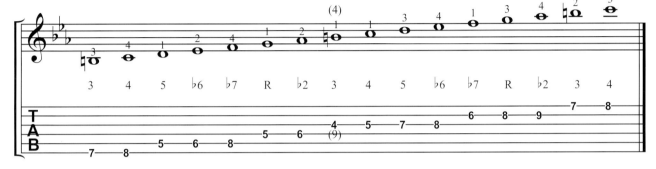

Fig 2.13(b) Phrygian dominant mode – shape three

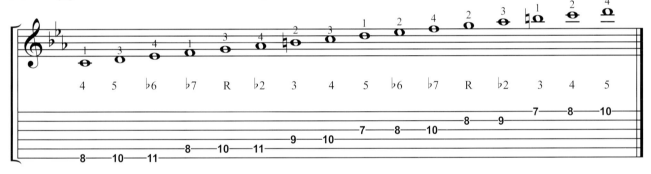

Fig 2.13(c) Phrygian dominant mode – shape four

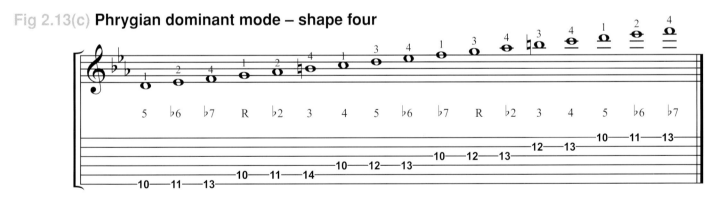

Fig 2.13(d) Phrygian dominant mode – shape five

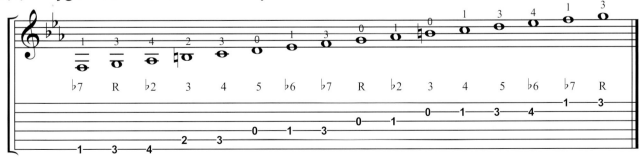

The Altered Scale

The altered scale is also known as the Superlocrian mode since it shares the same colour tones as the Locrian mode (from the seventh step of the major scale). This scale is built on the seventh note of the (jazz) melodic minor and can be used over a V chord (primary dominant) from either the major or minor key to highlight important resolution points.

Since it is the mode that contains the most tension-creating colour tones, it is described as being the darkest dominant seventh scale. Figure 2.14 has been notated in C major so that each accidental can be clearly observed; this key signature has no relevance to the scale's parent melodic minor key (which would actually be A♭ minor) and is simply the key of resolution (this could also be C minor).

Since the altered scale is generally used over unrelated primary dominants (unlike the Phrygian dominant) the parent key is irrelevant. You will notice from figure 2.14 that the fourth note has been changed from C♭ to B♮, this transforms it from a diminished 4th into a major 3rd, allowing the scale to 'fit' a G7 chord more logically. The B♮ is described as being the enharmonic equivalent of C♭ since it is technically the same note.

Fig 2.14 **The altered scale**

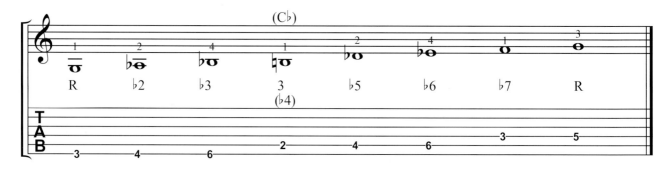

In order to achieve a tonic dominant seventh on the root of the altered scale, the tonic chord has also undergone a little harmonic tweaking. Ignoring the true third of the chord (B♭) and using the next note in the scale C♭ (enharmonic equivalent = B♮), changes it from a min7♭5 (the true diatonic chord on step VII of the melodic minor) to a dom7♭5. The remaining diatonic altered chords are exactly the same as would be derived from the parent melodic minor (figure 2.15(a)).

Fig 2.15(a) **Diatonic altered scale chords**

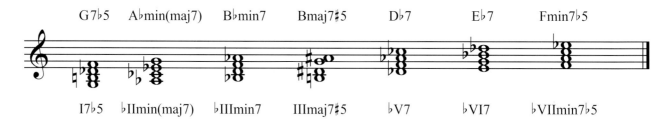

The diatonic guitar equivalents of these voicings are all shape one, raised third and fifth voicings as used in the Mixolydian and Phrygian dominant modes (figure 2.15(b)).

Fig 2.15(b) Diatonic altered scale chords – guitar voicings

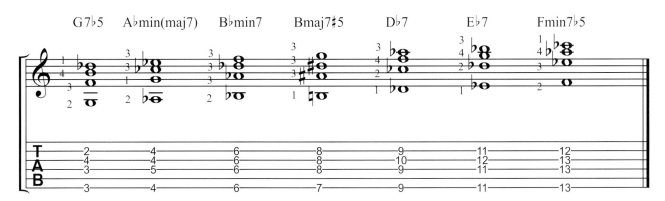

Altered chords are designed to create maximum tension before resolving back to a tonic major or minor. So any of the altered scale's colour tones can be added to a basic dominant seventh to spice things up: ♭5, ♯5 (♭13), ♯9 and ♭9. Piano players can add any or all of these colour tones to create dark, ominous clusters. We guitarists are not so fortunate and are forced to cherry-pick our colour tones (if the root is omitted it is possible to add a maximum

of two colour tones to a four-note voicing). Figure 2.15(c) demonstrates four dominant sevenths that are frequently used to create altered tensions. The ♭5/♯5 chords are the familiar shape one dominant seventh with the fifth raised or lowered a half-step. The two ninth chords are constructed from a R – 3 – ♭7 – ♭9/♯9 formula; this is essentially a close position ninth voicing with the fifth omitted.

Fig 2.15(c) Common altered chord voicings

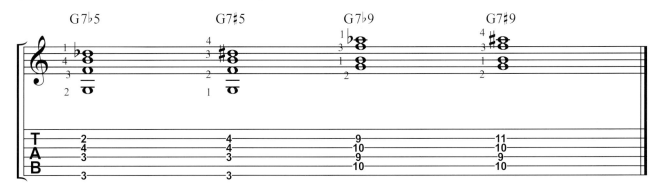

The inclusion of the ♭3 (♯9) interval in this scale allows the one octave shape to extend to a full two octave + 1½ steps as you can see in figure 2.16. Despite the enharmonic juggling necessary to transform this mode into a dominant scale, shape one of the altered scale is identical to shape one of the melodic minor apart from the starting note. The

scale starts on what would effectively be the seventh of the melodic minor; by playing both this and the second note with the 1st finger the familiar melodic minor fingering is retained. However, remember that each interval will change when related to a dominant chord a half-step below the minor scale's root.

Fig 2.16 Two octave altered scale – shape one

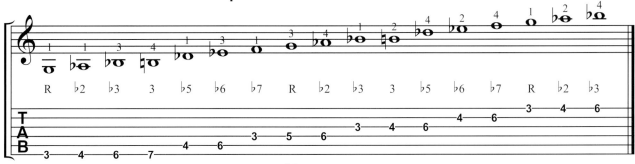

The remaining four altered scale shapes use the same fingering patterns as shapes two through four of the A melodic minor scale we learned back in Chapter 1, figure 1.23. The only difference is that all of these shapes are played a fret lower since this is effectively the A♭ melodic minor scale. However the content of each scale is very different, as you will notice from the intervallic spelling of each shape in figure 2.17.

It is vitally important that you consider each scale note in relation to a G7 chord. Play the corresponding dominant seventh chord for each shape first, i.e. before playing shape two of the altered scale play the second G7 voicing in figure 2.3 (p. 36). It is not necessary to play an altered chord before you practise the scale, in fact the tension notes are most effective when superimposed over a straight dominant seventh.

Fig 2.17(a) **Altered scale – shape two**

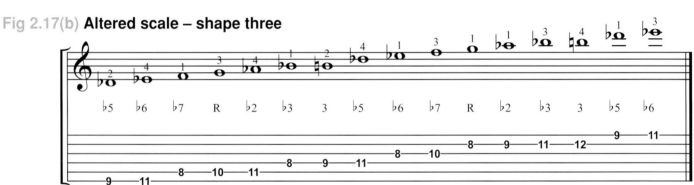

Fig 2.17(b) **Altered scale – shape three**

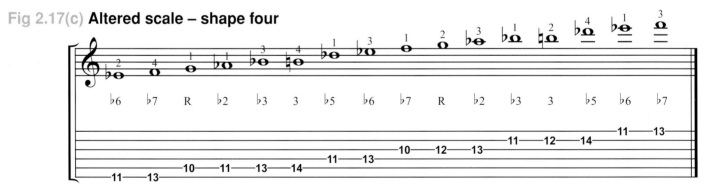

Fig 2.17(c) **Altered scale – shape four**

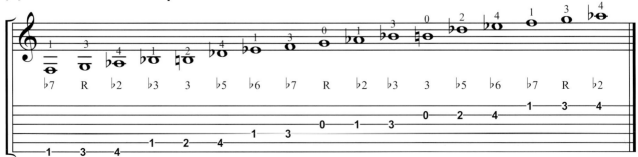

Fig 2.17(d) **Altered scale – shape five**

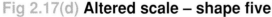

The following tune provides an ideal vehicle for you to practise the Phrygian dominant and altered scales. 'Secrets' was inspired by the ballad 'Yesterdays', a jazz standard that remains popular to this day and was penned by one of the most famous of all American songwriters, **Jerome Kern**. The dominant scales all occur in G with the exception of the C altered scale in bar six. Simply move the shape one altered G scale from the third fret up to the eighth to obtain the C altered scale.

4 | Secrets

Phil Capone

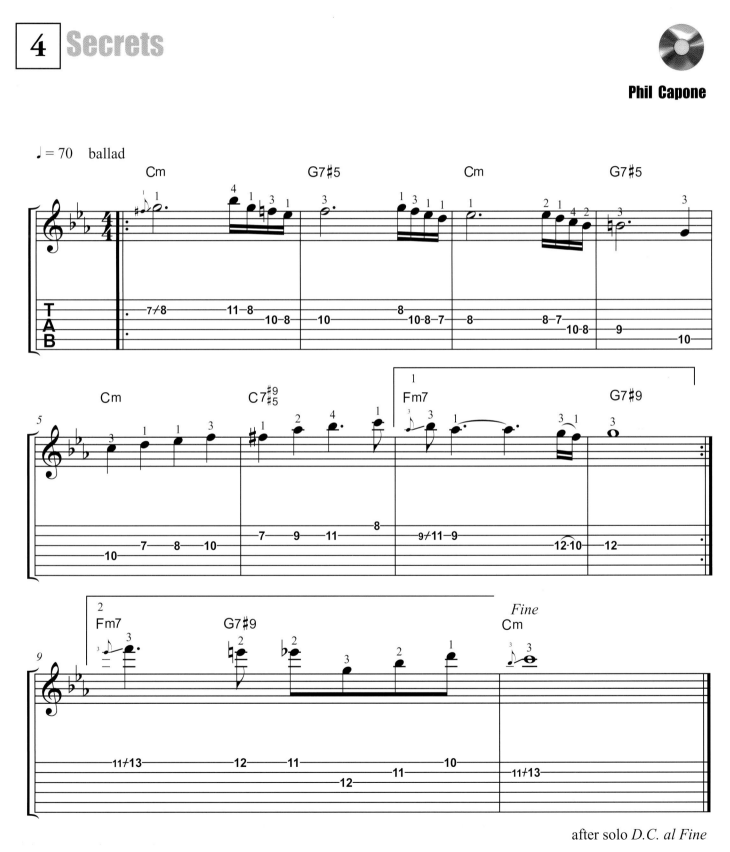

after solo *D.C. al Fine*

Secrets – solo

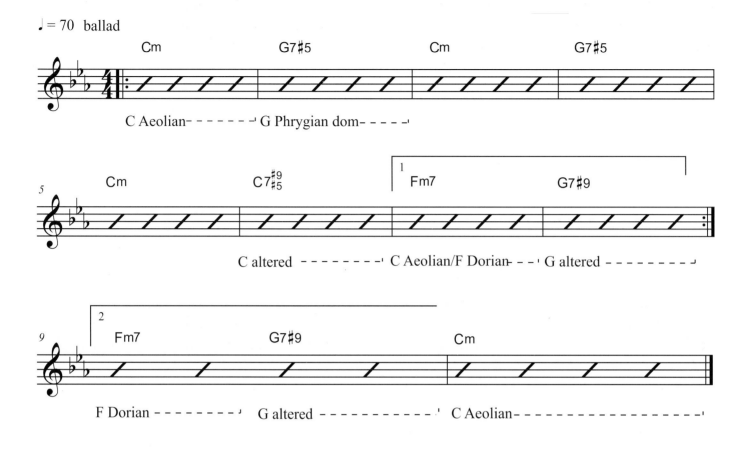

Checkpoint

Song Form

'Secrets' is a simple 16-bar form consisting of a repeated 8-bar section with a first and second time ending. This form would not produce a long enough sequence for an up-tempo swing tune, but works fine in the context of a ballad. As is the norm in jazz arrangements, this sequence is also used for the solo choruses.

Ballad Do's and Don'ts

Ballads are a hard call. Firstly, there is a lot of 'space' due to the slower tempo, which leaves the soloist exposed. Melodic creativity is consequently pushed to the limit since every note counts. Restraint and taste are paramount; if you let rip with all guns blazing it just won't suit the vibe of the song and you will be adding nothing musically.

Secondly, the rhythmic structure underpinning the ballad is complex. Melodies and solos are usually phrased with 'straight' eighth notes; swing eighths at slower tempos can sound too jaunty. Add to that the fact that the drummer will probably be playing a swing brushes pattern, and you begin to appreciate how difficult playing ballads can be.

Rhythm sections also often hint at an underlying double-time feel, and this may be capitalised on or ignored by the soloist at any time. Sometimes drummers will introduce a backbeat '2 & 4' hi-hat pattern which pushes the solo into a full blown double-time feel. When this happens the tempo doubles but the harmonic rhythm doesn't change, i.e. one bar of Cm becomes two bars of double-time Cm.

Swing Eighth Notes

Straight sixteenth notes feature throughout this tune. Playing them correctly is not easy, especially when superimposing them over a swing feel. Applying rhyth-

52

mic augmentation when you practise will help you to internalise the subdivision more quickly. In the example below, (a) is the first bar of the 'Secrets' melody written as is. Applying rhythmic augmentation results in (b) where the sixteenth-note phrase is expanded to an eighth-note phrase now spanning two bars. This process

is fantastic for assimilating complex or tricky rhythmic patterns quickly. Once you are comfortable with the concept you will be able to rhythmically augment phrases whenever you are faced with a tricky rhythm.

a) melody as written **b) applying rhythmic augmentation**

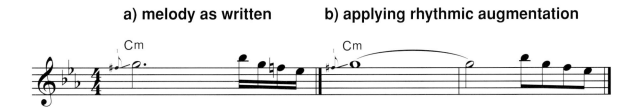

Assignments and Improvisation Tips

1. Metronome practice is vital when playing at slower tempos. Because there is so much space between each beat, it's very easy to inadvertently push the beat by speeding up or slowing down. Remember that in jazz, it is not the drummer's job to keep time for the other musicians; he/she is free to improvise simultaneously with the soloist. It is vitally important to develop a strong, rock-solid sense of time; this can only be achieved with consistent metronome practice.

2. Swing *and* straight eighths should be practised against a swing groove. This is a great tool for creating rhythmic tension and is something you should listen out for when playing your favourite CD's. You can practise this technique by setting your metronome at half the tempo you want to play at (disable any accents); count the pulse as '2 & 4' to replicate a drummer's hi-hat groove. The example below is a C minor lick that, like all phrases, will sound different when played straight or swing. The tempo is indicated as 140 b.p.m., so set your metronome to 70 b.p.m. Make sure you can count 1, 2, 3, 4 (with the 2 & 4 doubled on the metronome) comfortably before you try playing the lick.

3. Aural awareness is an essential skill that, like everything else, can only be perfected with repeated practice. The Mixolydian and Phrygian dominant modes create 'inside' sounds; they don't introduce dissonant tensions and should be easier to 'hear' than the 'outside' sounds created by the altered scale. The whole point of the altered scale is to create maximum tension during a tune's important resolution points, i.e. at the end of an 8- or 16-bar section or when temporary modulation occurs. Practise singing each of the altered colour tones (♭9, ♯9, ♭5, ♯5/♭13) against a basic four-note dominant seventh. Remember that these tension notes become more dissonant the closer they are to a chord's root note and will consequently be much harder to sing.

4. Listen! Listen to as much jazz as you can. Don't just listen to guitarists either, jazz is a language spoken by all instrumentalists and you need to be fluent if you want to join in the conversation! If you're listening to a CD and you hear a phrase you like, pause the player and try to work it out. Start with simple short phrases, you don't have to write anything down, just try to play what you hear.

5. Just as the four minor scales were summarised at the end of Chapter 1, this final example summarises the three dominant seventh scales we have explored during this chapter. There is no

fifth given in the altered scale: either the diminished (♭5) or augmented (♯5) fifth can be used to form an altered chord. Frequently the altered scale is simply superimposed over a basic four-note seventh chord having a natural fifth; in this scenario the scale provides four colour tones as illustrated.

Colour tone palette

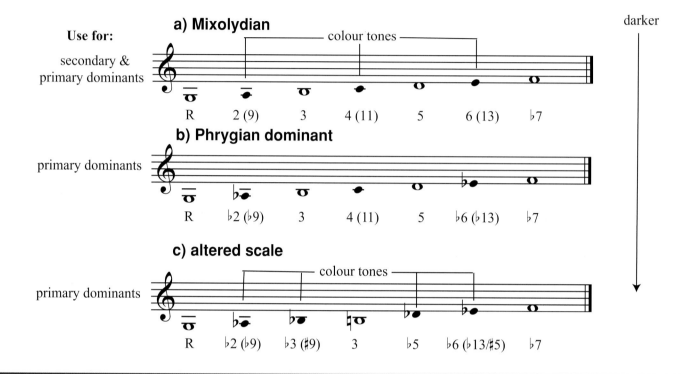

a) Mixolydian

Use for:

secondary & primary dominants

colour tones

darker

R   2 (9)   3   4 (11)   5   6 (13)   ♭7

b) Phrygian dominant

primary dominants

R   ♭2 (♭9)   3   4 (11)   5   ♭6 (♭13)   ♭7

c) altered scale

primary dominants

colour tones

R   ♭2 (♭9)   ♭3 (♯9)   3   ♭5   ♭6 (♭13/♯5)   ♭7

Martin Taylor demonstrating how to play a B7♯9 chord with feeling! Martin is playing a Yamaha AEX 1500 archtop — a model that can be heard on many of his later recordings.

3: Static Major 7th Chords

The Major 7th Chord & Arpeggio

The major seventh may be the sweetest sounding of all chords, but it contains a dissonant interval that is tempered by the other chord tones. In figure 3.1 below you can see how the outer notes of the chord form the interval of a major seventh. Played as a melodic interval (where the notes are sounded separately) these two notes just sound like a melodic leap. But when played as a harmonic interval (where the notes are sounded simultaneously) the major seventh's sound is jarring and dissonant. Our ears don't focus on this dissonant interval when we hear a maj7; we just hear a lush, full sounding chord. The major seventh's function is completely different to the dominant seventh we explored in Chapter 2. Relaxed and chilled out, this is a static chord that does not create a sense of impending harmonic movement like the dominant seventh.

Fig 3.1 **Cmaj7 arpeggio and chord**

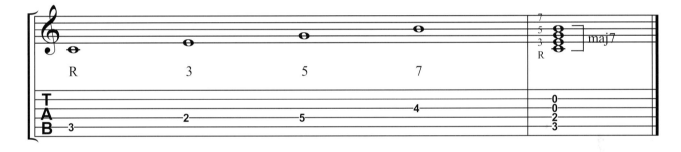

The EDCAG shape one, major seventh arpeggio (figure 3.2(a)) sits nicely under the fingers – played in seventh position, there are no 'out of position' stretches, and no awkward adjacent fret fingerings.

Fig 3.2(a) **Cmaj7 arpeggio – shape one**

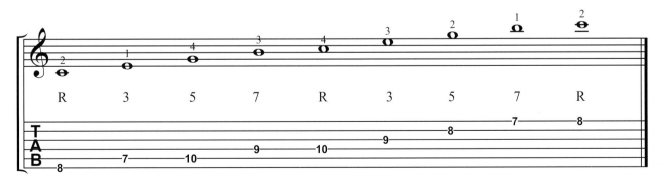

Because of the major 7th's 'guitar-friendly' shape, it can be played with sweep-picking to create lightening fast licks. This technique was used extensively by jazz guitar genius **Wes Montgomery**. Wes didn't play with a pick but used his thumb instead, a technique he stumbled on when trying to appease his neighbours with quieter practice sessions! By sweeping his thumb across the strings he was able to create fast flurries of notes and overcome the inherent limitations of using the thumb. The upper octave of the maj7 arpeggio (figure 3.2(b)) contains one note per string and is ideal for sweep-picked phrases. The technique can be used ascending, by playing a continuous down-pick from the low note, or descending by starting from the highest note and using a continuous up-pick. It is important not to hold the chord shape down, but to keep the fingers just above the strings and mirror the travel of the pick by quickly depressing and then releasing each finger.

Fig 3.2(b) Cmaj7 'sweep pick' arpeggio

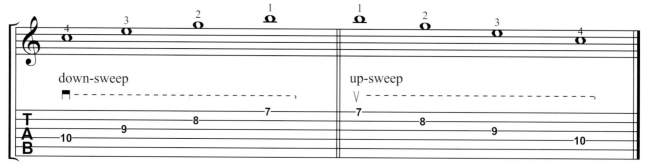

Figure 3.3 gives the five EDCAG major seventh chord shapes, which are all four-note voicings. If you compare these shapes with the five dominant seventh shapes in the previous chapter (figure 2.3), you will notice that the basic triad remains unchanged. Only the seventh interval is altered, by raising it a half-step the five Cmaj7 chords below are created. The only exception is the shape three chord – the Cmaj7 uses a true close position voicing (this is an open C shape with the first finger omitted). Cross referencing voicings in this way is very empowering, and demonstrates how a good voicing can be transformed into another chord type by simply changing a single note.

Fig 3.3 Five four-note Cmaj7 voicings

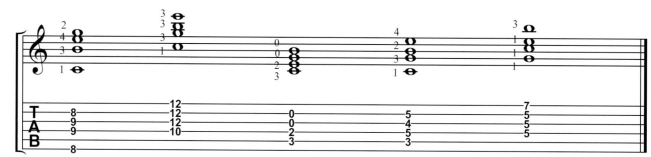

The Major Scale

The major scale is the most important sequence of notes in Western harmony. It is the 'pure' diatonic scale by which all other scales and intervals are measured. When the C major scale is played on the guitar its harmonic 'purity' is not visually apparent. Played on the keyboard it is clearly evident that this scale has no sharps or flats since it consists of white keys only. This means that the key signature for C major has no sharps or flats and so is the obvious key to use when analysing harmony. So when described in numeric terms none of the intervals are altered by ♭ or ♯ signs, hence the C major scale in figure 3.4(a) below contains only major or perfect intervals.

Fig 3.4(a) **The major scale**

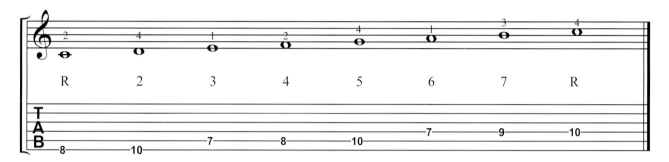

To summarise the quality of each major scale interval they are correctly identified as:

> **Root – major second – major third – perfect fourth – perfect fifth – major sixth – major seventh.**

N.B. A major interval becomes minor when lowered a half-step or augmented when raised a half-step. A perfect interval becomes diminished when lowered a half-step and augmented when raised a half-step.

Another extremely important feature of the major scale is the distinctive pattern of whole and half-steps that it creates:

> **W – W – H – W – W – W – H**
> **R – 2 – 3 – 4 – 5 – 6 – 7 – R**

To preserve this harmonic template when transposing the scale, sharps or flats (but not both) are added. This process is known as the cycle of fifths (see figure 3.4(b)), and it is a concept that is extremely relevant to the jazz musician. By starting the major scale a fifth higher on G the seventh step (F) has to be sharpened to retain the major scale pattern. Each time this process is repeated the previous sharp is carried forward and the new seventh step is sharpened. This sequence may also ascend in fourths through the flat keys where a flat is added on the fourth step of each new scale. So starting our scale in F requires the fourth step to be flattened (B♭) in order for the major scale pattern to be retained. Again, each time the process repeats, the previous key's flat is retained and a new one is added.

Fig 3.4(b) The circle of fifths

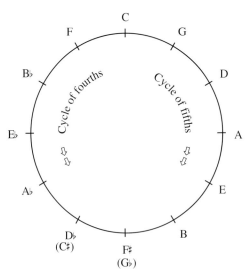

The overlapping sixth step can be F♯ or G♭. D♭ can also occur as the key of C♯. However due to the historical predominance of wind and reed instruments in jazz, flat keys are always more likely to be used than sharp ones. This presents a further problem for the guitarist since the guitar naturally leans towards sharp keys. Each open string is the root note of a sharp key and each 'dot' marking on the neck identifies a sharp key's root on the sixth string. So it is necessary for the aspiring jazz guitarist to become fluent in unfamiliar flat keys. The most frequently used jazz keys are F, B♭, E♭ and A♭. Saxophonists don't like playing in sharp keys and so the 'guitar-

friendly' keys of A, E and B are rarely used. 'Equal rights for jazz guitarists' ...yeah, I hear you man!

The Dorian, Aeolian and Mixolydian modes in the previous chapters are all derived from the major scale. Consequently the major scale produces the same diatonic chords (i.e. 2 x maj7, 3 x min7, 1 x dom7, 1 x min7♭5), they just occur on different scale steps (figure 3.5(a)). However only the major scales' harmonisation produces a dominant seventh on the fifth (dominant) step of the scale. It is this chord and its harmonic 'pull' back to the tonic that underpins all Western harmony.

Fig 3.5(a) Diatonic major chords

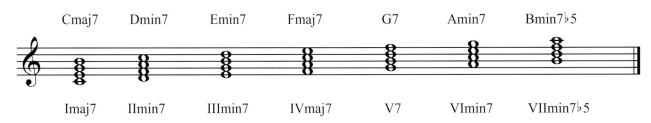

In the previous chapters you have learnt diatonic guitar chords with their roots on the fifth and sixth strings. The last string that can host a four-note, root position chord voicing is the 4th string, so the diatonic C major chords (figure 3.5(b)) have their root on this string. Once you have familiarised yourself with these shapes you will have mastered all of the possible root position, four-note, seventh chords. Cool! Any four-note, root position chord you encounter in the future will, in some way, be derived from one of these three types.

Fig 3.5(b) Diatonic major chords – guitar voicings

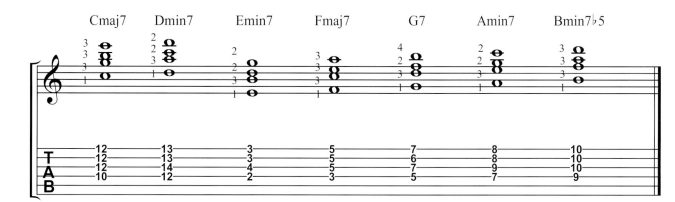

As with each of the previous scales and modes, by extending the basic one octave scale the EDCAG shape one is produced. In figure 3.6 you will notice that this ends on a high D (2nd), and so spans two octaves and a whole step.

Fig 3.6 Two octave major scale – shape one

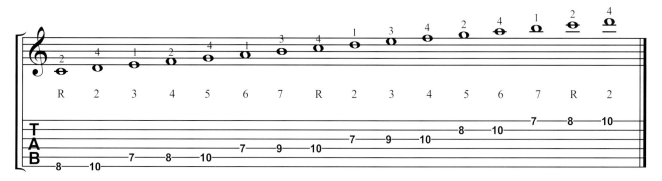

Expansion of the scale along the fretboard results in the remaining four EDCAG shapes (figure 3.7). Don't forget that you will recognise the following patterns from those previously encountered in the Aeolian, Dorian and Mixolydian modes, they will just be occuring on different scale steps. Once you are familiar with all five shapes, identify and exclude the non-chord tones to obtain five Cmaj7 arpeg-

gios. Don't forget that the essential shapes (and this applies to chords as well) to master are one and four, the remaining patterns can be gradually assimilated over a longer time-frame. Shapes one and four provide essential orientation points in any key and are based on the diatonic chords with their roots on the 6th and 5th strings respectively.

Fig 3.7(a) Major scale – shape two

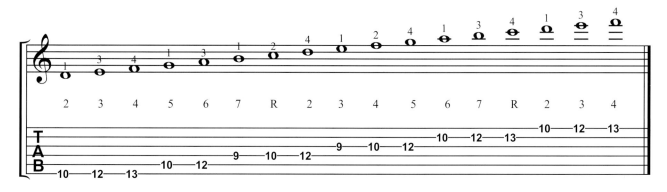

Fig 3.7(b) **Major scale – shape three**

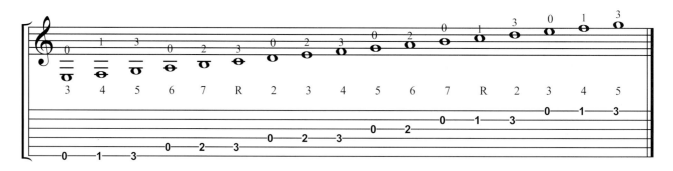

Fig 3.7(c) **Major scale – shape four**

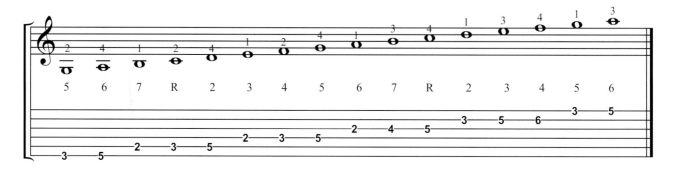

Fig 3.7(d) **Major scale – shape five**

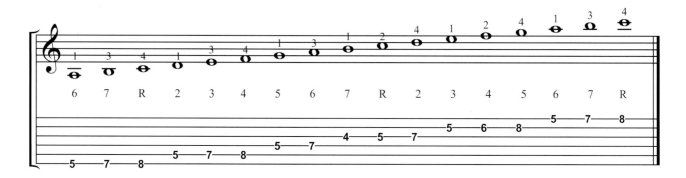

In the next section of this chapter, we will be looking at the major pentatonic scale. Try omitting the fourth and seventh intervals of the five major scale patterns above. This will not only produce the five major pentatonic EDCAG shapes, it will also help you to think about the notes you're playing when you're practising (as opposed to simply learning a meaningless fretboard pattern).

The Major Pentatonic

The main problem with the major scale is that it can appear uninspiring when you don't know how to use it. Firstly, it contains the fourth interval, which needs to be treated with caution, and secondly, it can sound as if it has had every last drop of the blues exorcised from it – and we guitarists love the blues!

The answer to this problem lies in the major pentatonic, and by re-examining the approach of blues guitarists who frequently use the scale, like the great **BB King**. Many post-fusion jazz guitarists superimpose bluesy licks over major chords, and their first scale choice would be the major pentatonic. The great Steely Dan sideman **Larry Carlton**, and ex-Morrissey-Mullen guitar virtuoso **Jim Mullen**, are just two examples of players who can effortlessly inject a shot of blues into the most unlikely and 'un-bluesy' chord sequences.

In Chapter 1 we studied the Aeolian mode and discussed its relative minor relationship to C major. This minor-major relationship is the key to understanding how to use the major pentatonic. Once you've played the C major pentatonic (figure 3.8) the shape will probably seem familiar – it is also shape two of the A minor pentatonic. This effectively means that you can play your favourite minor pentatonic licks over the relative major chord. One thing you will need to bear in mind of course is that the root notes, or more importantly the resolution notes, will have changed (e.g. the root of the A minor scale becomes the 6th when played against a C major chord).

Fig 3.8 C major pentatonic arpeggio – shape one

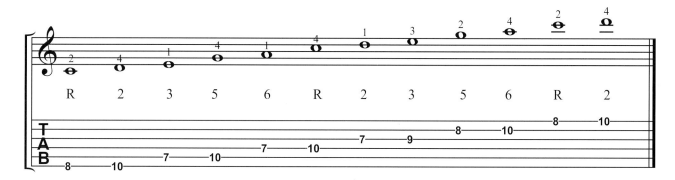

Once you've experimented with this idea it will soon become apparent that you can sneak in the ♭5 interval from the relative minor blues scale when 'thinking' in the relative minor key. This extra note becomes a chromatic passing note between the 2nd and 3rd of the major pentatonic as illustrated in figure 3.9. This scale is known as the major blues scale.

Fig 3.9 The major blues scale

The extended shape one major blues scale spans two octaves and two whole steps in order to include three chromatic passing notes (figure 3.10).

Fig 3.10 **C major blues scale – shape one**

Pentatonic Superimposition

If you want to outline specific maj7 chord tones in your solo, then the major pentatonic scale is not a good choice since it contains no 7th. Another way to achieve major tonality is by using pentatonic superimposition. By playing the minor pentatonic a major 3rd above a maj7 chord (i.e. starting on the 3rd of the major scale) then all of the major seventh's chord tones can be produced (apart from the root).

The chord tones and chord extensions produced from this marriage are illustrated in figure 3.11. The intervals are expressed in relation to a Cmaj7 chord, hence the use of compound intervals in the description (scale steps are given in parenthesis).

When superimposing it is no longer necessary to concentrate on the notes of the host chord, but simply to play familiar pentatonic licks. Because the licks have a melodic integrity of their own the superimposition works – as long as you know where to start! This results in a very different sound palette to the major pentatonic approach, and can be used to create some very cool and hip sounds.

Fig 3.11 **Minor pentatonic 'up a third'**

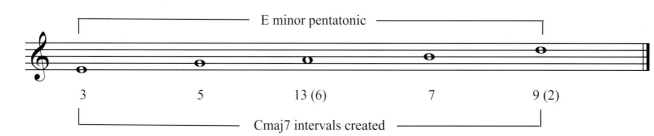

The following tune, 'Happy To Be Blue', is an ideal opportunity for you to experiment with all of the improvising techniques we have looked at in this chapter. Although the A sections also contain the chords of Dmin7 and Emin7, the underlying tonality is C major, so you can apply C major ideas to the entire sequence. In the B section you will need to transpose your C major ideas to the keys of F major and A♭ major. The A♭ major is used over the D♭ major chord to create Lydian sounds – more on this later in the chapter!

5 Happy To Be Blue

Phil Capone

♩ = 125   swing

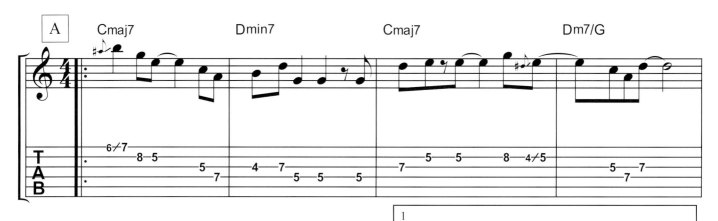

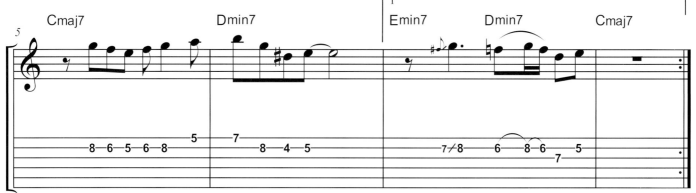

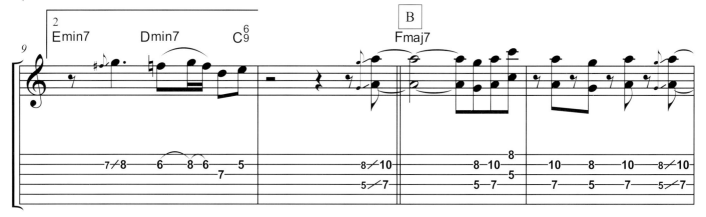

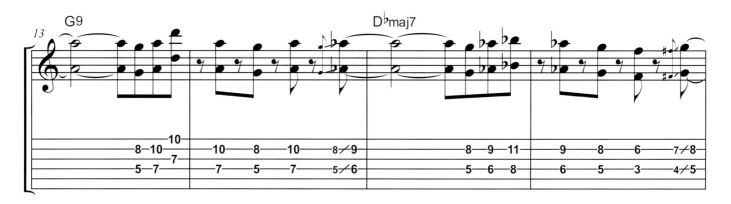

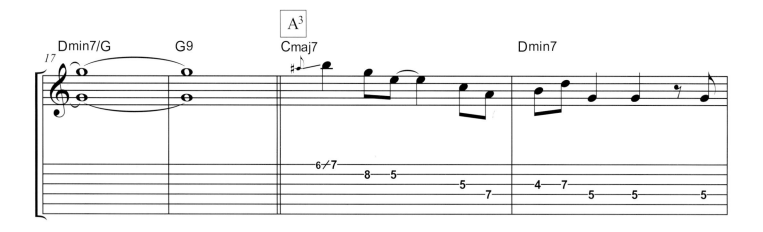

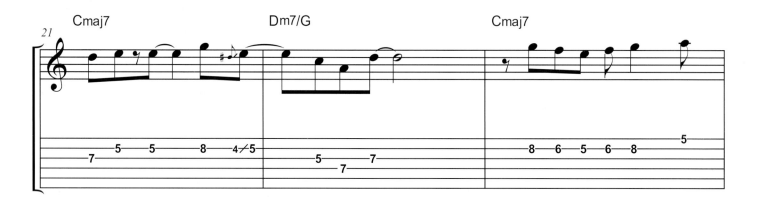

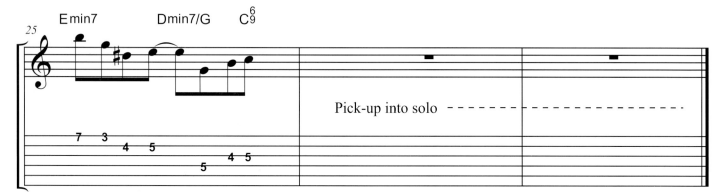

After last solo *D.C. al Fine*

Happy To Be Blue – solo

♩ = 125   swing

Checkpoint

Song Form

'Happy To Be Blue' employs one of the most commonly used song structures in jazz, the AABA song form. AABA sequences are usually 32 bars long and basically consist of two contrasting eight-bar sections, 'A' and 'B'. As its name suggests, the 'A' section is played twice, and is then followed by the middle section, 'B' (sometimes referred to as 'the bridge'), and finally concluding with a restatement of the 'A' section. 1st and 2nd time endings are often used for the first two 'A' sections (A1 and A2); this allows the '2nd time' ending to conclude the tune before entering the middle eight. As in 'Happy To Be Blue', the last two bars of the final 'A' (A3) are often used as a pick-up into the solo section.

Slash Chords

One of the first things you'll notice when looking at this chart is the Dm7/G chord in the fourth bar. This isn't some strange polytonal chord voicing, merely the slash chord equivalent of G11. Slash chords are frequently used in all genres of popular music. However in jazz they are generally used to indicate a modal voicing. In the previous chapter we studied the effects of superimposing D Dorian over a G7 chord when improvising. Dm7/G is the chordal equivalent of this superimposition and generates the same compound intervals as you can see below:

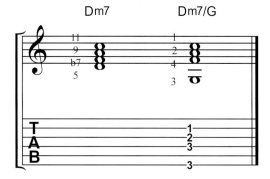

The point of using this chord instead of a straight G7 is to keep the tonality firmly within C major. Dm7/G is a 'mild-mannered' dominant chord; the absence of the 3rd (B) allows the improviser to more or less ignore it and continue 'thinking' in C major.

C6/9

When the melody of a tune ends on the tonic, a maj7 chord is not an appropriate chord to use – the presence of the major 7th interval in the chord will clash with the melody. If you're working with a singer, you run the risk of not being booked again! A straight major chord is rarely used in jazz because of its rather plain sound. So traditionally the maj6 chord was used in jazz cadences. However this too now sounds plain, and so the 9th is also added to create a little more colour.

It's important to know the difference between a 6/9 chord and a maj9 chord – the latter would also include the major 7th interval (all ninth chords include the seventh since they are constructed by stacking a further third on top of the four-note seventh chord, thus creating a five-note chord). The example below demonstrates a basic C6 voicing (notice the absence of the 5th and the doubled root), and a C6/9 voicing. By raising the fifth an octave, the intervals rise in 4ths from the 3rd (E) creating a cool, contemporary voicing.

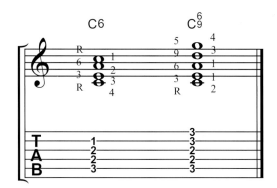

Assignments and Improvisation Tips

1. Octaves, where the melody note is doubled an octave lower to thicken the sound, are another technique pioneered by the late **Wes Montgomery**. Remember, Wes didn't use a pick but played with his thumb – this made his octaves sound characteristically deep and mellow. However octaves also sound great when played with a pick, and are pretty much *de rigeur* for today's jazz guitarist, so it's a technique well worth mastering.

In the example below, the upper octave of the C major pentatonic has been harmonised in octaves. Notice that when the high note is on the 3rd or 4th string, the octave shape spans two frets and should be played with the 1st and 3rd fingers. When the high note is on the 1st or 2nd string you should play the octave shape (now spanning three frets) with your 1st and 4th fingers. Practise octaves with down-picks first, laying your first finger gently across the strings to damp the unwanted open notes.

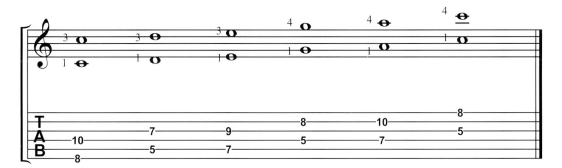

2. Comping is a technique that needs practising just like any other. For harmony players like guitarists and piano players, accompanying skills are paramount. If you play a weak solo then (as long as you've managed to remain in key!) you only have your own demons to face. But playing a bad accompaniment can ruin another musician's solo, and so you run the risk of being shouted at, or worse, not being re-booked!

Now that we have learnt four-note chords with their roots on each of the lowest three strings, you have a good repertoire of voicings to start creating 'comping licks' with. The example below illustrates a typical comp for the first four bars of this tune. Notice how the phrase mixes staccato (short) and legato (long) notes with syncopated rhythms to create an interesting comp. It is essential to approach your accompaniment from a rhythmic perspective otherwise it can sound flat and uninspiring. The Emin7 chord in the penultimate bar has been used to create a Cmaj9 voicing. The relationship between Em7 and Cmaj7 is the same when applied to chords or scales – just as we superimposed Emin pentatonic over Cmaj7 to create cool major sounds, the same principle can be applied to chord voicings.

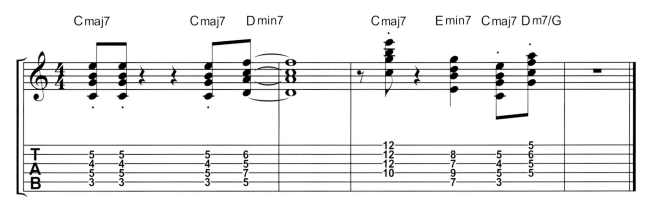

3. Diatonic arpeggios should be incorporated into your daily scale practice. They are an invaluable tool for improvising and will help to take your fingerboard knowledge to the next level. The example below illustrates how to practise shape one of the major scale by playing an arpeggio on each scale step. This exercise can be played entirely in seventh position using normal shape one fingering, the notes are just much harder when played in this way. However, all jazz musicians practise their scales using this method. It not only builds a more effective technique than just practising scales in a linear fashion, but also ensures that every possible four-note arpeggio can be recalled and played instantly. Arpeggios are fundamental to effective improvisation, period. Once you have mastered shape one of the major scale, apply the techniques to the other four shapes and, ultimately, to every scale and mode you practise.

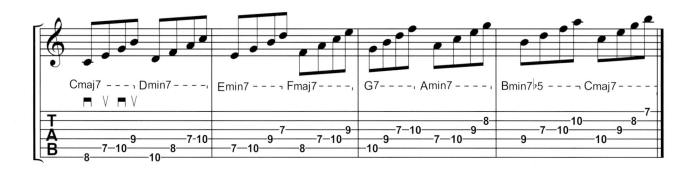

4. Aural skills are essential for the jazz musician. This music is played spontaneously; the notes you play should be heard in your head first, and you need to be able to immediately recognise, by ear, what the musicians around you are playing. This is impossible without an advanced aural awareness. The major scale produces a familiar pattern of whole and half-steps that you should be able to 'hear' more easily than some of the previous modes we have studied. So practise singing the scale regularly; when you are confident, sing the numbers of the intervals as you progress through the scale. Try jotting down a short sequence of numbers, (e.g. 1, 4, 6, 2, 5) and try singing them. This will be easier if you start on the root. Check your results by playing the sequence on the guitar. The more you do this, the more confident and efficient you will become at 'pre-hearing' root movements, melodies and licks.

The Lydian Mode

The Lydian mode is essentially a major scale with an augmented fourth, which is a half-step higher than the major scale's fourth. This single difference produces a distinctive sounding scale that has a more contemporary, angular feel to it.

The augmented fourth can be used as a colour tone and will sit quite happily on top of a maj7th chord – unlike the perfect fourth of the major scale. Figure 3.12 below shows the C Lydian mode (derived from the fourth step of the G major scale). This allows easy comparison with the C major scale.

Fig 3.12 **C Lydian mode**

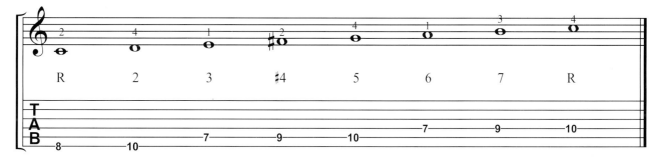

Because of the Lydian mode's greater harmonic stability (every non-chord note is a colour tone), many argue that this scale is the true 'parent' major scale. In 1953 the famous jazz pianist and composer George Russell published his hugely influential harmonic 'bible' the *Lydian Chromatic Concept Of Tonal Organization*. The book turned the whole concept of major scale-derived tonality on its head, and pioneered the modal jazz movement that would follow later in the decade.

Since the Lydian mode is derived from the major scale, harmonising the mode with diatonic seventh chords (figure 3.13(a)) creates the same quantity and quality of chords as all the other major modes. However you will notice that when compared to the C major scale, the harmonised Lydian mode produces some unusual differences (e.g. the dominant chord on the second degree and the min7♭5 chord on the raised fourth).

Fig 3.13(a) **Diatonic Lydian chords**

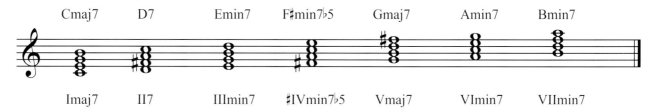

We have now used all of the possible four-note, root position seventh chords in our diatonic harmonisations. But we're not done yet! The 'guitar-friendly' versions of the close position diatonic Lydian chords have been converted to inversions with their lowest note (the 5th) on the fourth string (see figure 3.13(b)). Every chord voicing in figure 3.13(b) is simply a close position voicing with the fifth

dropped an octave. The first five shapes are also an octave higher than the voicings in figure 3.13(a).

Fig 3.13(b) Diatonic Lydian chords – guitar voicings

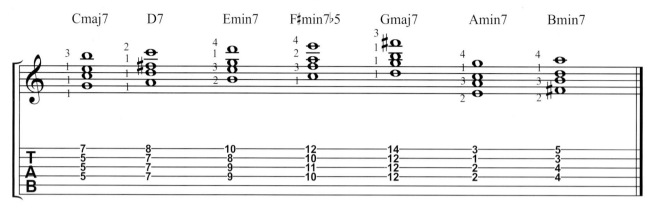

An inversion is created when a chord has a note other than its root note as the lowest voice. The 5 – R – 3 – 7 voicings used throughout the Lydian harmonisation in figure 3.13(b) are known as second inversion chords, since they have the fifth as their lowest note.

Because seventh chords are constructed from four notes, it follows that there are four possible inversions (including root position) for each type of seventh chord. The maj7 inversions are summarised in figure 3.13(c) below.

Fig 3.13(c) Cmaj7 inversions

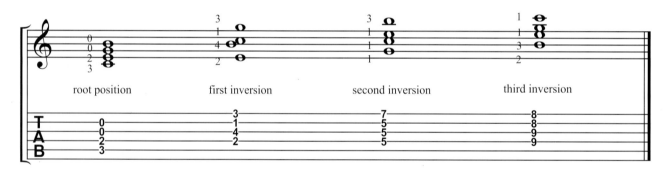

First inversion = 3rd as lowest note
Second inversion = 5th as lowest note
Third inversion = 7th as lowest note

The skilled accompanist can spontaneously mix root position chords and inversions to create smooth voice leading. Voice leading occurs when the notes of a chord move to the next nearest available chord tone (with common tones remaining stationary). The opposite of this harmonic movement is parallel voicing – best thought of as a barre chord shifting along the guitar neck – where the new chord retains the same voicing as the previous chord (figure 3.13(d)).

Fig 3.13(d) Voice leading vs. parallel motion

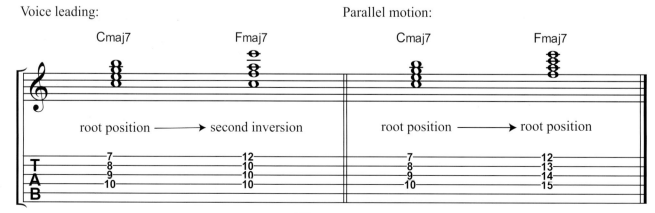

By now the expansion of the one octave scale to create a full EDCAG shape one pattern should be a familiar routine. Figure 3.14 annotates the shape one Lydian which, like the major scale, spans two octaves + one whole step. Unlike the major scale this pattern sits nicely under the fingers due to the repeated string patterns occurring across the scale. The eagle-eyed amongst you will also have spotted that this pattern could be Aeolian shape four, Dorian shape two or the major scale shape three. Some players like to relate each pattern to every possible scale that it could be used for. Others prefer to treat each shape as an individual pattern with its own particular set of chord and colour tones. A mixture of both approaches tends to work best.

Don't forget that we are not just dealing with patterns here; you need to know what a note is going to sound like before you play it. Each scale provides its own distinct set of colour tones and, just like a painter, you need to know how each 'colour' will effect the whole picture before you apply it.

Fig 3.14 Two octave Lydian mode – shape one

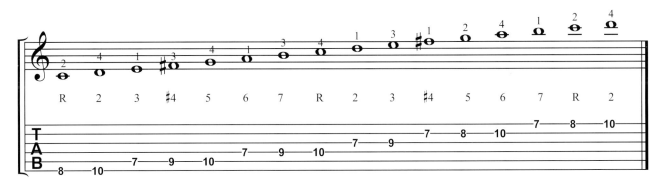

The remaining four Lydian shapes are presented below in figure 3.15. Remember that it is shapes one and four that you should be concentrating on, ultimately working outwards from these two shapes until you have learnt the entire fingerboard as one big pattern for each scale or mode. Since both the maj7 chord and arpeggio shape remain unchanged from the major scale, playing each pattern in the strict sequence of chord, arpeggio and scale in each pattern should seem less of a chore!

Fig 3.15(a) Lydian mode – shape two

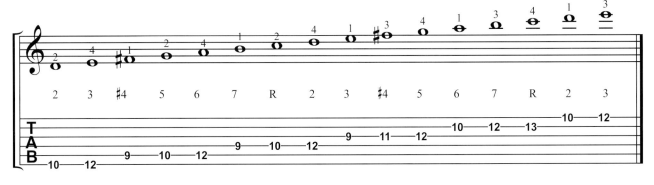

Fig 3.15(b) Lydian mode – shape three

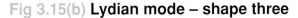

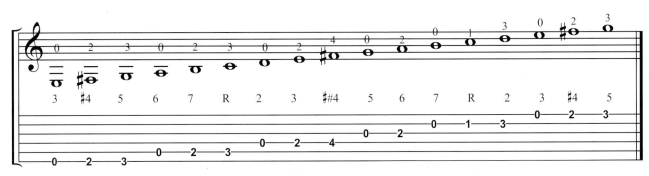

Fig 3.15(c) Lydian mode – shape four

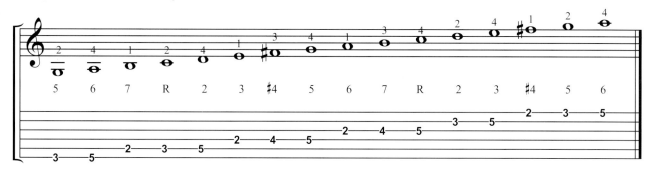

Fig 3.15(d) Lydian mode – shape five

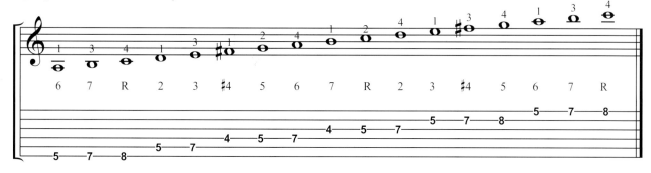

Pat Metheny is famous for his striped shirts and his beloved Gibson ES-175 guitar. In this shot the latter is missing – depicted instead is the prototype Archtop PM series guitar built exclusively for him by Ibanez guitars.

Using Pentatonic Superimposition To Create Lydian Sounds

In the same way that the minor pentatonic was used to create maj7 sounds earlier in this chapter, so it can also be used to create Lydian textures. To create Lydian colour tones the minor pentatonic should be played a half-step below, i.e. starting on the major 7th of the chord. Figure 3.16 demonstrates the chord tones and colour tones that result from this superimposition. Remember that colour tones are usually expressed as compound intervals when related to a chord type.

Fig 3.16 **Minor pentatonic 'down a half-step'**

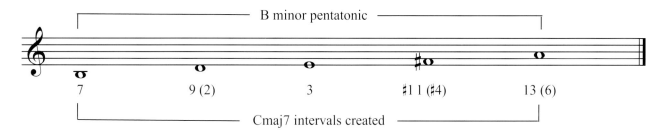

Only two chord tones are generated from this superimposition: the 3rd and the 7th. These two notes are the most important in any chord because they describe the chord's quality. The 3rd and 7th are often referred to as the guide tones and many players frequently use guide tones when comping – these notes perfectly outline the basic harmony and leave the soloist free to add whatever colour tones they choose.

Remember that for the superimposition to sound good you should play licks that work well within the minor pentatonic framework, i.e. bluesy! This injects phrasing that the listener will be familiar with, whilst the unusual root-scale relationship ensures the licks never sound clichéd.

The next tune, 'Winter Sun', is inspired by the chord sequence of 'Phase Dance' – a **Pat Metheny** composition that featured on his 1978 album *The Pat Metheny Group*. There is no tonic maj7 chord in this tune (Dmaj7), so you will need to use the Lydian mode for both the B♭ maj7 and the Gmaj7 chords. Until you're familiar with all the Lydian shapes, start your improvising with the shape one pattern. This is in fifth position for B♭ and second position for G.

6 Winter Sun

Phil Capone

♩ = 155 Latin rock

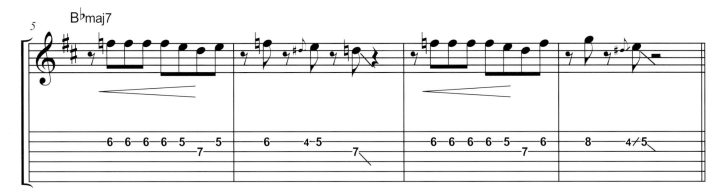

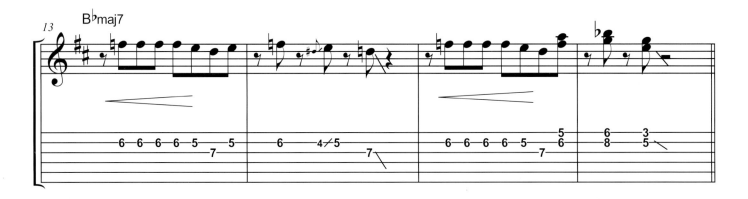

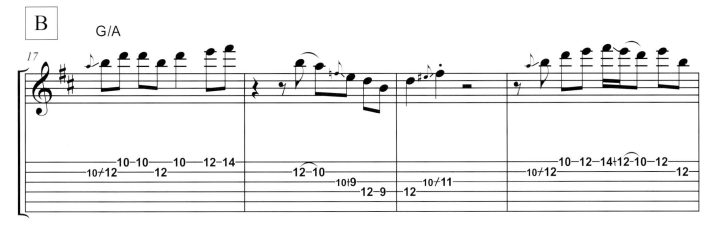

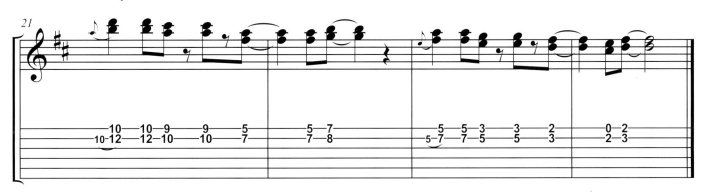

After last solo *D.C.*
(fade out on A section)

Winter Sun – solo

♩ = 155   Latin rock

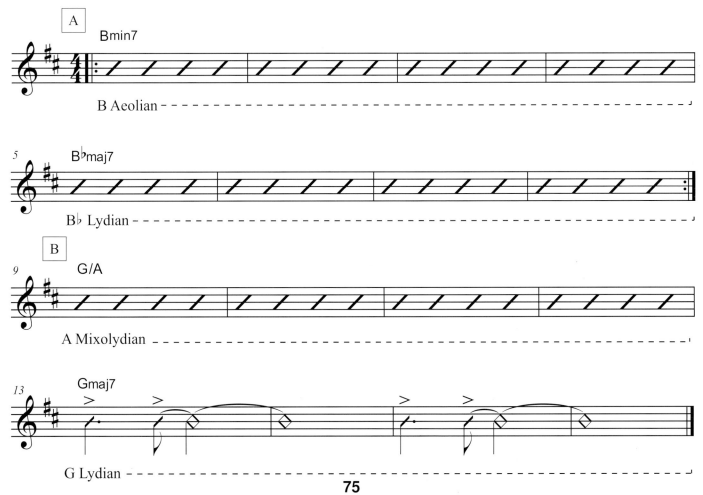

Checkpoint

Chord Sequence

The chord sequence of this tune is quite unusual because of the chromatic shift on the second chord. The tune is written in the key of B minor with a contrasting 'B' section that modulates to the relative major without resolving to the tonic chord (D):

'A' section: Imin7 (Bmin7) VIImaj7 (B♭maj7)
'B' Section: IV/V (G/A) IVmaj7 (Gmaj7)

All of the modes are diatonic to Bminor/D major with the exception of the B♭ Lydian. Theoretically it would be possible to improvise entirely in D major, diverting to F major for the B♭maj7 chord. However this would not produce very musical results; even with modal chord sequences it's essential to reference chord tones in your improvisation.

Double Stops

Playing two notes simultaneously is referred to as a double stop, and these most commonly occur on the guitar as thirds, fourths or fifths. This is because these intervals occur on adjacent strings and are easy to play with a single down- or up-pick.

Thirds provide a very 'sweet' sounding harmonisation and are used in this tune to add interest during the 'A' sections' restatement. To facilitate the legato, 'Metheny-esque' phrasing (frequently copied in fusion styles), the double stops should

Slash Chords

In the previous chapter, Dmin7/G was used to describe a modal voicing. F/G would also have produced the same voicing due to the minor-major relationship between Dmin7 and F. So the G/A that occurs in this tune could also have been written as Emin7/A, but the former is used because it better describes the chord's function as a suspended dominant seventh. As you can see below, this results in an identical chord shape, but the spelling suggests A Mixolydian as opposed to E Dorian.

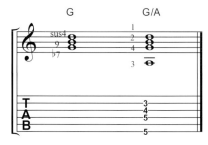

be played on the same string. The example below demonstrates how the D major scale (G Lydian) can be played ascending on the 1st and 2nd strings. Notice that major thirds are played with the 1st and 2nd fingers, while minor thirds are played with the 1st and 3rd fingers. It is important to maintain this fingering throughout.

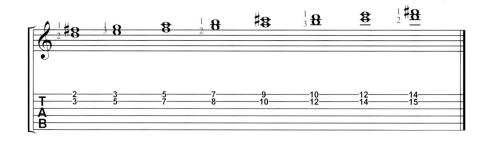

Double Stop Hammer-ons

Pat Metheny has always acknowledged his American Midwest upbringing for providing a strong country influence, and he celebrates this in his playing style and compositions. Playing double stops with hammer-ons (as in the 'B' section) effectively emulates the sound of a pedal steel guitar, and this technique is now widely used by contem-

porary jazz guitarists. Below is an example of a commonly used country-style lick applied to a Dmaj7 chord (this also sounds cool over the relative minor – Bmin7).

Assignments and Improvisation Tips

1. Straight eighths should be played throughout this tune. This is our first 'non-swing' tune since it is based on a Latin-rock fusion groove (there will be more on Latin styles in Chapter 7).

2. Playing 'across the changes' is essential when you are improvising over 'blocks' of harmony. In order to make your improvising sound interesting, practise phrases that start at the end of a four-bar section and continue into the next chord. This approach is especially effective when playing across unrelated chords as in the 'A' section of this tune.

Here's an arpeggio-based lick that plays right through the chord change, starting on Bmin7:

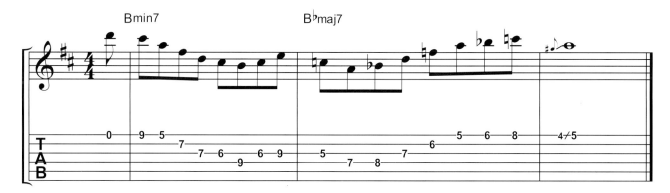

Another approach is to play an ascending or de-scending scale pattern that changes on the first beat of the new chord, or on the last note of the previous bar as shown below.

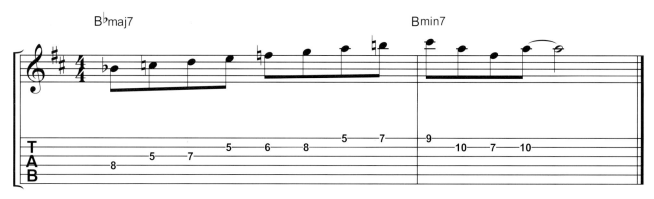

3. Comping in Latin styles normally involves fairly strict adherence to traditional rhythmic patterns. But since this is essentially Latin-rock fusion, a more relaxed approach can be adopted. The first example overleaf is a comping idea that works well over Bmin7. Notice the use of staccato, legato and syncopation – all of these techniques are essential for creating interesting comping ideas. The second voicing is Bmin9 – this chord shape was encountered earlier in this chapter as a Cmaj7, second inversion voicing. Don't forget that you can always substitute relative major/ minor ideas when comping (or soloing for that matter!).

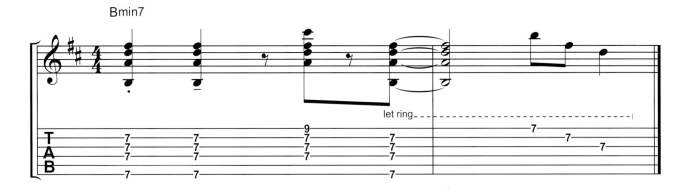

In this next example, the rhythmic idea of the Bmin7 comp has been retained and applied to a B♭maj7 chord. By retaining the rhythmic pattern in this way, a sense of continuity is established.

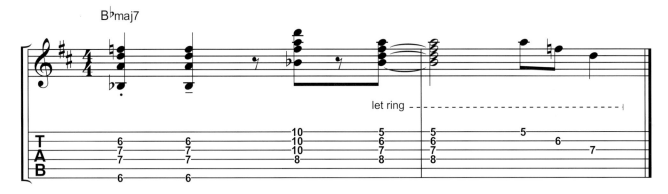

4. Learn the chord sequence! You will not improvise on a tune effectively if you are reading the chord sequence, period. This is a great song to establish a learning system with since it only contains four chords. Think of the chords in numerical terms (as in 'Checkpoint' above), and sing the root movement, as shown below:

You will notice that each four-bar section has been compressed into one bar – it's not the precise duration of each chord we are concerned with for this exercise, it's more important to be able to 'hear' the relationship between the roots correctly. When you can sing this confidently, try singing the basic seventh chord for each root note as shown below (notice that G/A is abbreviated to A7sus4).

4: The II – V – I

The Major II – V – I

The II – V – I is the most important chord progression in jazz, no question. It's a harmonic movement that can be found in all of the great jazz standards in the *Great American Songbook*. Some tunes such as **Clifford Brown**'s 'Joy Spring', or **Jerome Kern**'s 'All The Things You Are', are based entirely on modulating II – V – I sequences, and have long been considered essential 'workouts' for the aspiring jazz musician.

Even the groundbreaking chord sequence of **John Coltrane**'s seminal 'Giant Steps' contains four II – V – I progressions, each one set in a different key. So whatever kind of jazz you are into, the key to fluent improvisation lies in understanding and mastering the II – V – I. Figure 4.1 illustrates the sequence in C major using standard shape one and four guitar voicings.

Fig 4.1 **The major II – V – I**

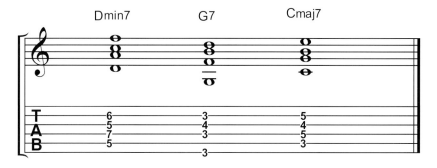

By applying the modal knowledge we have learned in previous chapters, the sequence can easily be divided into three modal centres: 1) Dorian (IImin7), 2) Mixolydian (V7) and 3) Ionian/major (Imaj7), as illustrated in figure 4.2.

Fig 4.2 **II – V – I modal implications**

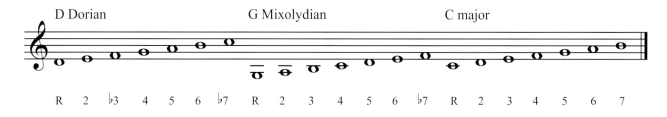

These modes provide a useful note pool for improvising over slower II – V – I sequences, but at faster tempos or where the chord changes occur 'two in the bar', they do not provide a practical solution; the chords will be moving too quickly to allow a 'mode per chord' approach. Also, since all of the notes are derived from the same tonal centre (with both the Dorian and Mixolydian being derived from the same major scale), simply whizzing up and down the modes will neither describe the underlying harmonic movement nor result in a convincing improvisation.

79

Major II – V – I Guide Tones

By removing superfluous intervals, such as the fifth and the root, the II – V – I progression can be stripped down to its key components (i.e. the guide tones) as illustrated in figure 4.3. (Notice how one note remains constant in each chord change.)

Fig 4.3 II – V – I guide tones

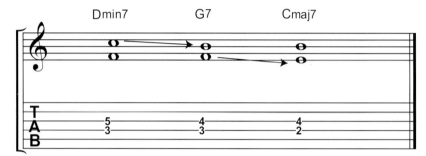

These two-note chords (diads) not only provide excellent comping voicings, but also provide an alternative solution to improvising over the II – V – I sequence. By approaching your solo from a guide tone perspective, even a string of fast-moving chord changes becomes more manageable.

Figure 4.4 demonstrates how this approach not only produces melodic lines, but also perfectly outlines

the underlying harmony. This typical be-bop chord sequence occurs in the 'B' section of 'Joy Spring', but can also be found in many other tunes such as **Charlie Parker**'s 'Ornithology'. Arpeggio notes and scale tones have been added to flesh out the melody (these intervals are in parenthesis), and occur on the unimportant beats of each bar (i.e. when the chord is static).

Fig 4.4 The guide tone approach

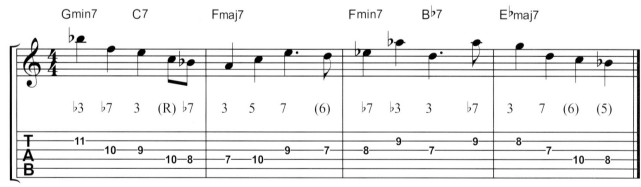

Reintroducing the bass notes G and C to the guide tone sequence (figure 4.5) allows the progression to be reinterpreted as V7sus – V7 – I. This simplification can be applied 'on the fly' when improvising and is extremely useful when confronted with 'two to the bar' chord changes at fast tempos.

Fig 4.5 V7sus – V7 – I

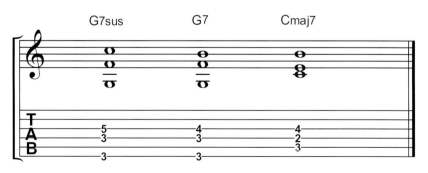

Major II – V – I Arpeggios

The arpeggio approach to II – V – I improvisation simply expands on the guide tone principle by adding the remaining notes of the arpeggio (i.e. the root and fifth). Arpeggios provide the most effective approach for negotiating a II – V sequence. Figure 4.6 shows how easy it is to transform a simple arpeggio pattern into a cool lick by applying tried and tested jazz techniques.

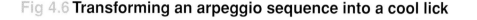 **Fig 4.6 Transforming an arpeggio sequence into a cool lick**

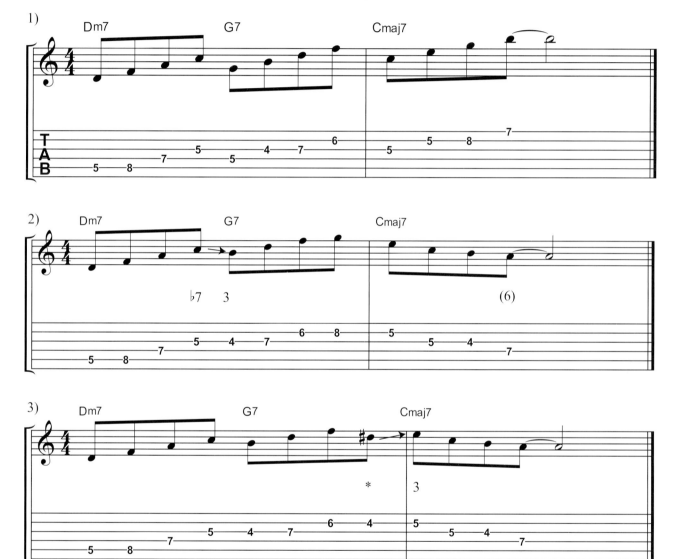

Ex 1: A basic eighth-note pattern that ascends from the root of each arpeggio. Although this perfectly maps out the changes, it's too much like a practice sequence to sound hip.

Ex 2: The last note of the Dmin7 arpeggio (C) is resolved to the nearest available chord tone of the new chord (B). Notice that the Cmaj7 arpeggio now descends and ends on the sixth (A). The sixth interval is frequently used as a resolution note in bop-style licks.

Ex 3: Finally a chromatic approach note (indicated by *) is added at the end of the second bar, creating a greater 'pull' to the third of the Cmaj7 chord (D♯ – E). *Voilà,* a basic arpeggio pattern has been reborn as a hip and cool bop lick!

In figure 4.5 we discovered that the II chord could be dispensed with completely. Consequently a bar of II – V could be perceived as one bar of chord V as in figure 4.7 below. The extra notes are colour tones generated by the Mixolydian mode.

Fig 4.7 V – I lick

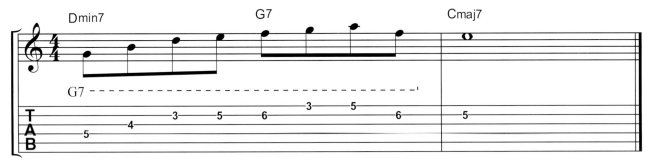

Wes Montgomery would frequently turn this idea onto its head and treat a bar of II – V simply as one bar of IImin7. This is exactly the same as the Dorian 'up a fifth' superimposition (D Dorian over G7) that we explored earlier in Chapter 2. By mixing Dmin7 chord tones with colour tones from the Dorian mode, super cool licks can be created. Figure 4.8 illustrates this technique.

Fig 4.8 II – I lick

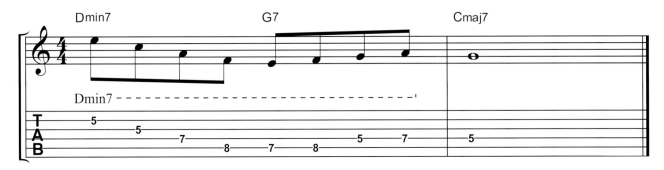

When a II – V progression spans two bars (i.e. one chord per bar), you can simply treat the sequence 'as is' or superimpose two one-bar II – V licks as shown in figure 4.9 below.

Fig 4.9 II – V – II – V lick

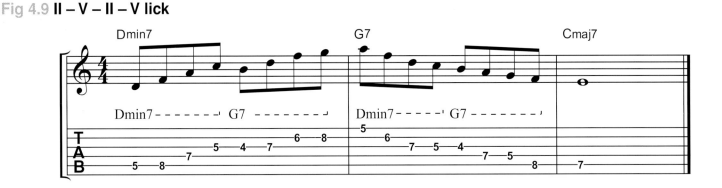

All of the techniques we have explored for improvising over a major II – V – I sequence can be put into practice in the following tune, appropriately titled, 'Hitting The Changes'. Since the tune modulates twice you will need to transpose your ideas into E♭ and F major – this can initially be overcome by simply shifting your ideas up the guitar neck. However by practising every lick you learn in all five EDCAG positions you will be able to change keys more fluently without leaping around the guitar neck.

7 Hitting The Changes

Phil Capone

♩ = 150 swing

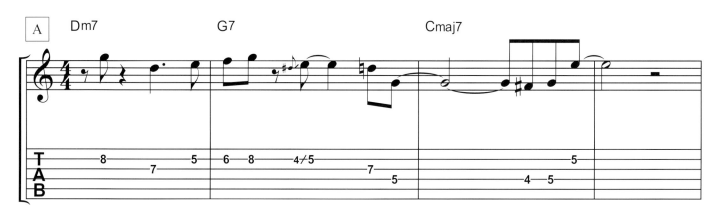

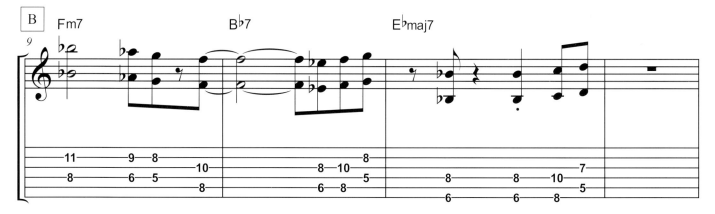

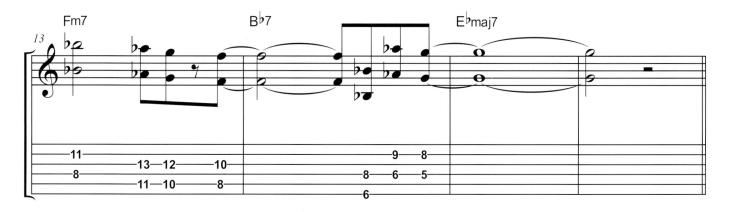

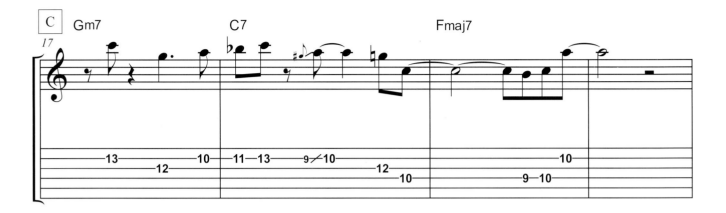

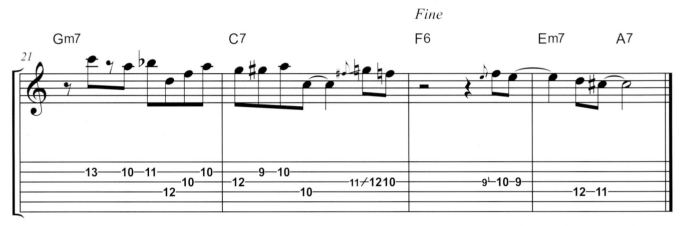

After last solo D.C. al Fine

Checkpoint

Song Form

This 'ABC' structure comprises three eight-bar sections; each section modulates to a new key, encouraging you to practise transposing your licks. The 'B' section has a contrasting melody while the 'C' section restates the original tune a fourth higher.

Shifting Tonal Centres

Each II – V – I progression is repeated to provide maximum familiarity in each key. At the end of each chorus a one-bar II – V provides modulation back to the original key of Dmin. This is a major II – V (in D) that provides an unexpected harmonic twist when it resolves to a minor chord (Dmin7). Major II – V's that resolve to a minor chord are generally only effective when leaving a major key as in this instance; unless it is written into the tune, it is not advisable to substitute a major II – V for a minor II – V.

Comping 'Four In A Bar'

A 'fours' comp has been used in this piece to provide a more traditional-sounding accompaniment. This style of comping adheres to a strict quarter note rhythm and is useful in many different musical situations, e.g. when sharing accompaniment duties with a pianist, or providing a solid harmonic backdrop for a vocalist. Check out **Freddie Green**'s impeccable rhythm work on any of the many **Count Basie Band**'s recordings – he was **Basie**'s guitarist for nearly 50 years. The best voicings for this type of comping are essentially guide tones with an added root note as shown below:

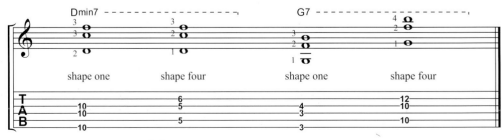

84

Hitting The Changes – solo

♩ = 150 swing

A Dm7 G7 Cmaj7

D Dorian - - - - - - - ⌐ G Mixolydian - - - - - - ⌐ C major - ⌐

5 Dmin7 G7 Cmaj7

B
9 Fmin7 B♭7 E♭maj7

F Dorian - - - - - - - - ⌐ B♭ Mixolydian - - - - - ⌐ E♭ major - ⌐

13 Fmin7 B♭7 E♭maj7

C
17 Gmin7 C7 Fmaj7

G Dorian - - - - - - - - ⌐ C Mixolydian - - - - - - ⌐ F major - ⌐

21 Gmin7 C7 F6 Emin7 A7

Guide tones/arpeggios - - - - - - - ⌐

The use of inversions and passing chords creates a smooth, **Freddie Green**-style comp. By keeping your quarter notes even and introducing a slight emphasis (pick slightly harder) on beats 2 and 4 your 'fours' comp should start to swing:

Inversions and substitutions (note the use of the II chord's dominant D7 in bar one) are frequently used to create subtle voice leading, and there are several good books available devoted entirely to this subject.

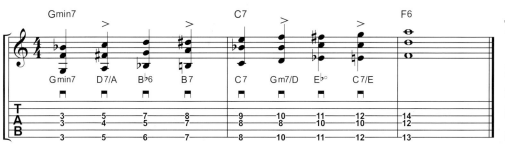

The F6 chord

Since this tune has a more traditional feel, the F6 chord is the chord of choice for resolution in bar 23.

Assignments and Improvisation Tips

1. Octaves were first encountered in the middle section of 'Happy To Be Blue' in Chapter 3. However, it's worth reviewing the correct fingering otherwise those smooth legato octave phrases will remain out of reach. When the high note is on the 3rd or 4th string, the octave shape should be played with the 1st and 3rd fingers. When the high note is on the 1st or 2nd string you should play the octave shape with the 1st and 4th fingers. Octaves also sound better played with down-picks, but if you want to get closer to the 'Wes sound' then don't be afraid to go the whole hog and just use your thumb. Many great players do this, including the great fusion guitarist **Lee Ritenour**. Simply hold the pick between your 1st and 2nd fingers to free up that thumb!

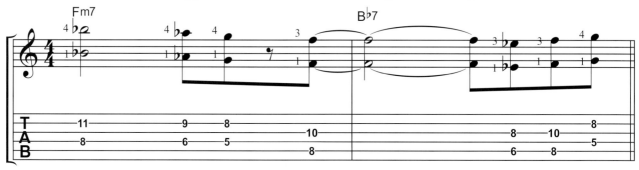

2. Encirclement is a technique that sounds cool when used in conjunction with guide tones. It involves playing the note above and then below the target guide tone with resolution usually occurring on the chord change. The lower note sounds best when occurring as a chromatic approach note. The higher note can be diatonic (taken from the parent mode of the chord), or chromatic (i.e. a half-step above the target guide tone). This technique is applied to the 'A' section of the tune below:

3. Sing, sing, sing! It is crucial to keep developing your 'ear'. As your technique and harmonic knowledge expand, your aural skills will need to be continuously honed in order to keep them at the same level. Remember that jazz is a spontaneous art form that demands a good ear. The II – V – I progression is such a ubiquitous progression in jazz that you must be able to recognise it instantly. You will also need to recognise any II – V that is modulating away from the tonal centre. See if you can sing the root movement for a full chorus of 'Hitting The Changes'. Once you can do that try singing the various modulations after singing a C root note:

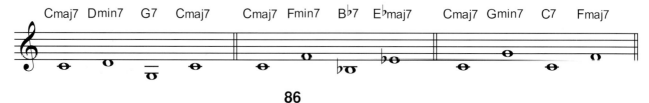

The Minor II – V – I

The minor II – V – I uses diatonic chords from two different scales, the harmonic minor scale and the Aeolian mode. This may sound complicated, but in reality these two scales are very similar, being separated by just one note: the seventh.

When we first examined the harmonic minor scale in Chapter 1, we discovered that the raised (major) seventh provided a dominant seventh chord on the fifth step – enabling a perfect cadence to occur naturally in the minor key. Therefore the harmonic minor is an essential ingredient of the minor II – V – I since it creates the all-important V7 chord on the fifth step:

Fig 4.10(a) **The minor II – V – I**

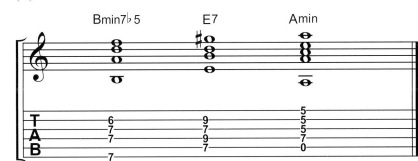

The min7♭5 (frequently written as Bᵒ) is often described as a 'half-diminished chord'. This is because it shares the diminished chord's minor third and diminished fifth, but not its diminished seventh (figure 4.10(b)). Hence the term 'half-' diminished. This is a sketchy description at best and doesn't really describe the chord's true harmonic function – it belongs to the minor chord family whereas the diminished is essentially a dominant seventh chord. Unfortunately it's a lot easier to shout out the changes on a gig using the term 'half-diminished' as opposed to 'minor seventh, flat five'. So be prepared to encounter this description frequently!

Fig 4.10(b) **min7♭5 vs. diminished**

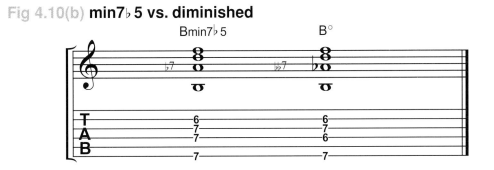

Using our familiar EDCAG system, five indispensable Bmin7♭5 shapes can be created (see figure 4.11). All of the EDCAG shapes you have been presented with in this book should be transposed to as many keys as possible, starting with shape one and shifting the order of shapes as necessary to ensure that the lowest frets are included.

Fig 4.11 **Five EDCAG Bmin7♭5 voicings**

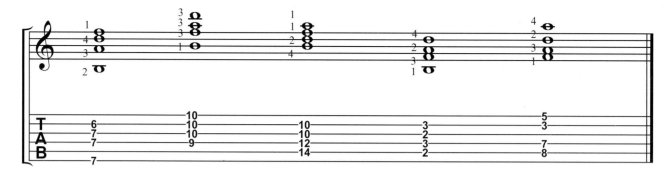

A full, shape one, Bmin7♭5 arpeggio is illustrated below in figure 4.12. Notice that when compared to a regular min7 arpeggio there is only one difference: the fifth is flattened (diminished). The pattern bears more than a passing resemblance to the minor pentatonic/blues scale, so it should sit under your fingers quite naturally.

Fig 4.12 **Bmin7♭5 arpeggio – shape one**

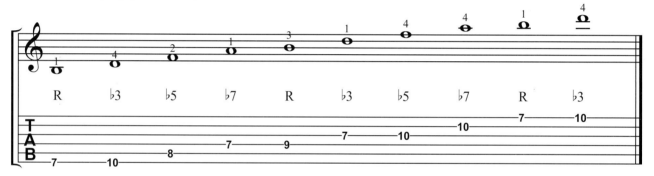

The obvious scale choice for a min7♭5 chord is the Locrian mode, which is constructed from the seventh step of the major scale. This is because the diatonic chord on the seventh step of the major scale is a min7♭5 chord (Chapter 3, figure 3.5). Due to the familiar relative major-minor relationship, this is exactly the same note pool as the related Aeolian mode with just a sideways shift in chord tones: by starting the Aeolian mode on the second step, the Locrian mode is created, as illustrated in figure 4.13 (notice how every step, apart from the fourth, is flat).

Fig 4.13 **The Locrian mode**

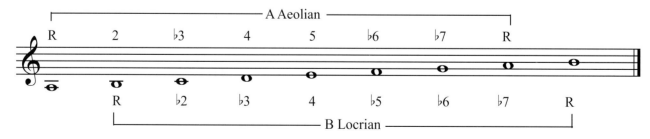

By starting the B Locrian mode in seventh position and extending it so that it spans two octaves plus a minor third, the full shape one EDCAG pattern is achieved (figure 4.14). Notice that this shape is exactly the same as the shape one C major scale (Chapter 3, figure 3.6).

Due to its similarity to the major scale, you can simply use the remaining four C major shapes (Chapter 3, figure 3.7) to achieve the remaining four EDCAG Locrian shapes. However don't forget that the chord tones will be in different locations, so it is well worth taking your time to assimilate each pattern (while simultaneously learning the corresponding arpeggio shape – remember these are simply the min7 with a flattened fifth).

Fig 4.14 Two octave Locrian mode – shape one

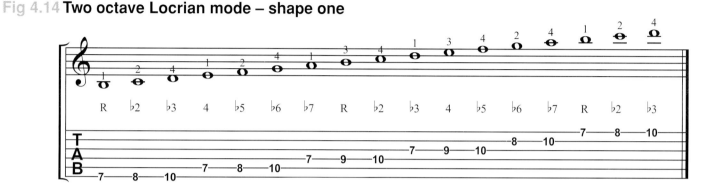

The tonic chord of the harmonic minor is Amin/maj7 (Chapter 1, figure 1.16). However although the min/maj7 is a great chord to end a tune on, it is just too 'dark' to use in non-final perfect cadences. So by changing the I chord to a min7, the minor II – V – I progression starts and finishes with the Aeolian mode, diverting to the harmonic minor only on the V7 chord. Notice that it's the fifth mode of the harmonic minor, the Phrygian dominant (Chapter 2, figure 2.9), that is the correct scale for this chord and not the harmonic minor in root position:

Fig 4.15 Minor II – V – I modal implications

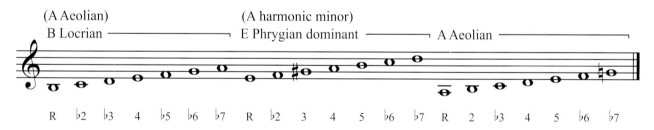

Minor II – V – I Licks

We explored various methods for creating major II – V – I licks earlier in the chapter. All of the techniques that were used (i.e. guide tones, chromatic approach notes etc.) can be applied just as effectively in the minor key. The following examples (figure 4.16) are based on a two-bar II – V – I with the resolution occurring in the second bar. Once you have conquered the two-bar progression you should find it quite easy to extend your ideas over longer sequences.

Fig 4.16(a) **Using guide tones**

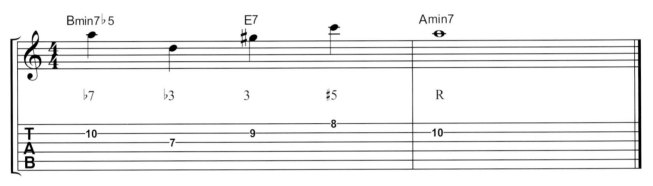

Figure 4.16(a): This lick illustrates the simple, yet effective use of guide tones to negotiate the minor II – V – I. Notice that the second note used over E7 is not strictly a guide tone since it is a ♯5. However, altered tensions such as the ♭9, ♯9, ♭5 and ♯5 can be used to replace either the 3rd or the 7th. The ♯5 sounds particularly good when used over a V7 chord because it is the minor 3rd of the resolution chord and so adds a cool bluesy vibe to your improvisation.

Fig 4.16(b) **Arpeggio based**

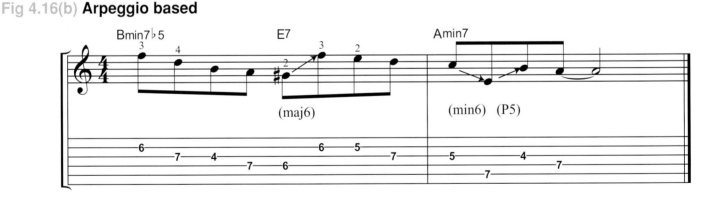

Figure 4.16(b): An arpeggio-based lick that also uses a couple of intervallic leaps to create interest. Sixths are 'wide' intervals and will always sound cool when you incorporate them into your licks. Notice that the leaps do not occur between the all-important chord changes – keep these harmonic shifts as smooth as possible by always moving to the nearest available chord tone.

Fig 4.16(c) Chromatic chord tone connection

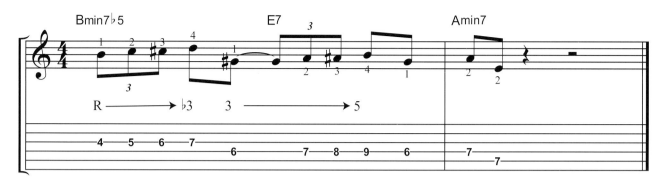

Figure 4.16(c): The last example illustrates how chord tones can be connected chromatically using triplets, and works best when the chord tones to be 'connected' are a minor third apart (e.g. R – ♭3, 3 – 5, ♭7 – ♭9).

As we learned in the major II – V – I sequence, you are free to ignore the II chord and treat the progression as simply V – I. This is a useful approach when 'blowing' over an up-tempo tune, or when confronted with a string of non-resolving II – Vs. In figure 4.17 the min7♭5 chord is ignored and the improviser 'thinks' in E7 only. Notice the use of the double chromatic approach to the 3rd of E7 (G♯) – this technique is also encountered in blues and country music; it's not exclusive to jazz.

Fig 4.17 V – I lick

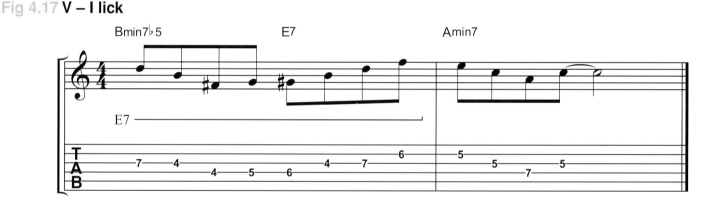

Creating Tension

When extra tension is required e.g. at the end of an 'A' section, or at the end of a tune, then the altered scale (see Chapter 2) can be used instead of the harmonic minor.

When using this scale over a two-bar progression then simply treat the II – V as one bar of the V7 chord as in figure 4.18 below.

Fig 4.18 Altered scale V – I lick

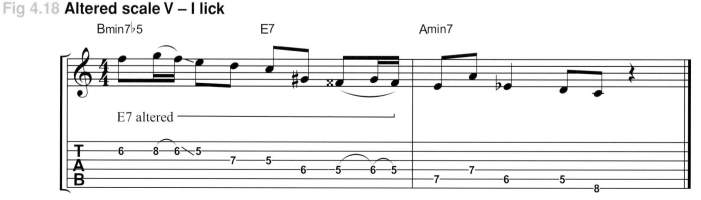

Because the minor II – V has a stronger pull back to its resolution chord than the major equivalent, ignoring the V chord and treating the progression as II – I is not so effective in the minor key.

Back in Chapter 2, we discovered how the altered scale was built on the seventh step of the melodic minor scale. Therefore minor arpeggios can be su-perimposed a half-step above a dominant seventh chord to create altered tensions. The instantly recognisable melodic integrity of the arpeggio ensures that, although the tensions applied are quite dark, your altered licks will always sound melodic and sound super cool. Figure 4.19 illustrates an effective use of this superimposition:

Fig 4.19 **Using minor arpeggio up a half-step**

Notice that the resolution chord is Amaj7 in the above example. The minor II – V is frequently used to resolve to the major key, and this is when the use of the altered scale is most effective. Resolving to a major chord in the minor key has a long history in classical music, and is called the *tierce de Picardie*. Because the major II – V uses a min7 as its II chord (and the frequently added ninth would create a major third in the minor key), the theory doesn't work so well in reverse (unless the major II – V occurs as a modulation in a major key or uses an altered dominant as the V chord).

The following tune is a perfect opportunity for you to explore all of the techniques we have studied in this chapter. Although it contains entirely minor II – V progressions, these also resolve to a maj7 chord in two different instances and so provide ample opportunity for you to also explore altered tensions.

Phil Capone

♩ = 130 swing

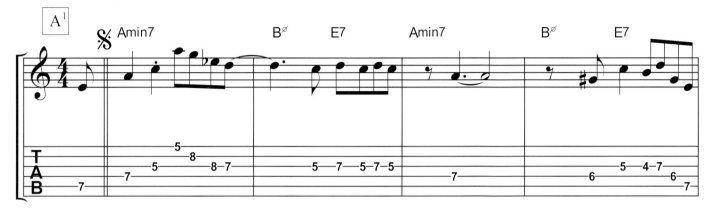

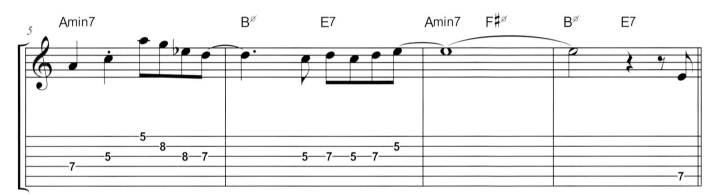

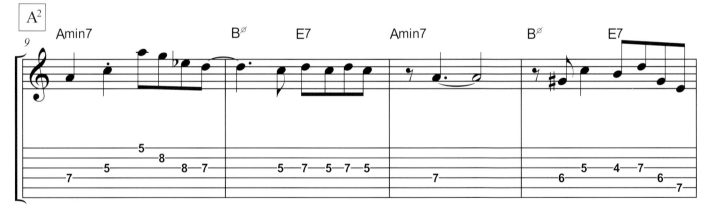

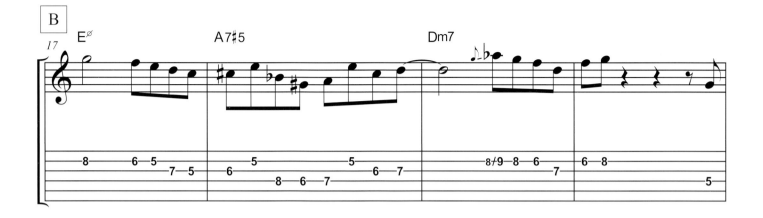

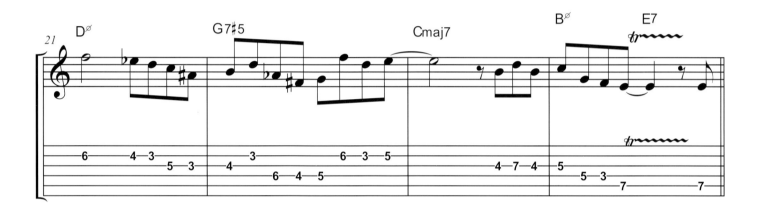

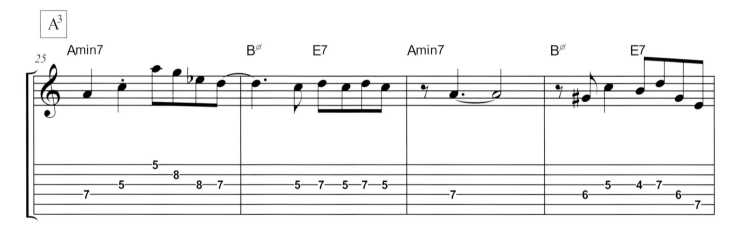

After last solo D.S. al Fine

Three Way Freeway – solo

♩ = 130 swing

N.B. Although B Locrian and E Phrygian dominant are indicated over the recurring tonic II – V – I, the short time spent on each chord will make the arpeggio/guide tone approach preferable. The modes can then be used to provide passing notes, colour tones etc. as required.

Checkpoint

Song Form

'Three Way Freeway' uses the well-used 'AABA' song form that we first encountered in the previous chapter with 'Happy To Be Blue'. Songs constructed in this format often use similar sequences, so you will sometimes hear musicians describing the changes to a tune by relating them to other standards e.g. 'a *rhythm changes* bridge' or 'a Honeysuckle Rose A-section'. 'Three Way Freeway' could be described as having an 'A' section similar to 'Softly As In A Morning Sunrise' (with the last 8 resolving to A major); the 'B' section would be referred to as the bridge of 'Alone Together' or 'Night In Tunisia'. This is a quick and easy way to describe a song's chord sequence at a gig – the key would also be given and any slight differences would be picked up 'by ear' as the song is played.

Minor To Major

Don't forget that you can also achieve a minor to major II – V – I by simply adapting your existing licks to 'fit the changes'. By re-examining figure 4.16(b), you will see that

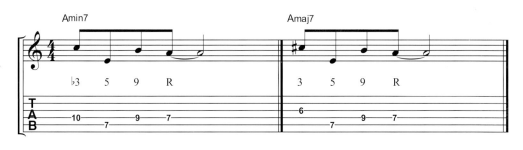

only one note in the last bar needs to be changed to enable the lick to resolve to Amaj7, as shown in the example above. Some licks are harmonically ambiguous (such as figure 4.16(c)) because the third of the resolution chord is not stated, and can therefore be used in a wide range of harmonic situations e.g. when the II – V resolves to a dominant seventh.

Dominant 7th Replaces Tonic Minor?

You will no doubt have noticed that the final chord of this piece is D9. This is a frequently encountered substitution, particularly at the end of a minor key tune when the written tonic minor is replaced 'on the fly' by the rhythm section. The substitution adds a bluesy twist to what would otherwise be a rather dull minor perfect cadence, without straying too far from the key centre. The example to the right illustrates the similarity between Amin6 (the min6 frequently replaces the darker min/maj7 as a tonic minor) and D9 – notice that only the root changes.

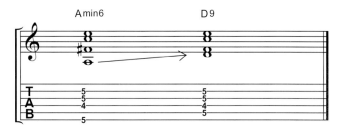

In Chapter 2, we learned how the Dorian mode can be superimposed a fifth above a dominant chord, making seventh chords more 'guitar-friendly'. So there is no need to stray from the tonic minor when the rhythm section is playing D9, in fact your licks will sound cooler if you 'think' in A minor. To heighten the bluesy vibe you can use the A blues scale:

Assignments and Improvisation Tips

1. Learn the changes! If you don't know the changes of a tune off by heart you can't expect to create a convincing solo; worrying about what chord comes next or, worse still, reading the chords from a chart is not the way to approach the art of improvisation.

Musicians think in terms of numbers (written as roman numerals) when analysing sequences and this is an incredibly effective approach to memorisation. It is also something that can easily be practised in short bursts away from your instrument e.g. when travelling or watching TV.

The sections of 'Three Way Freeway' would be summarised in numeric terms as:

A section

Imin7 / / / IImin7♭5 / V7 / x3
1x ending: Imin7 / VImin7♭5 / IImin7♭5 / V7 /
2x ending: Imaj7 (2 bars)
3x ending: IVdom7 (2 bars)

B section

Minor II – V – I modulating up a fourth (4 bars)
Minor II – V – I resolving to relative major (4th bar
     minor II – V back to original key)

Thinking through the changes in this way will enable you to learn more tunes in less time. It will also help you to assimilate songs in a 'keyless' way – essential when on the spot transpositions are demanded by singers!

2. Anticipating the changes. Once you have learnt the changes to a tune you will be able to approach soloing from a more authoritative perspective – no longer will you be 'chasing' the changes i.e. being dragged by the rhythm section from one chord to the next. When an important modulation occurs, e.g. as in the 'B' section of this tune, try to lead into it by starting your phrase at the end of the previous bar. In the example below you can see how anticipation of the Emin7♭5 (which would occur over Amaj7) creates an effective improvisation over the first 4 bars of the 'B' section. It is not uncommon to anticipate a chord even earlier in the bar – this creates 'outside' tensions that resolve perfectly when the rhythm section 'catches up'.

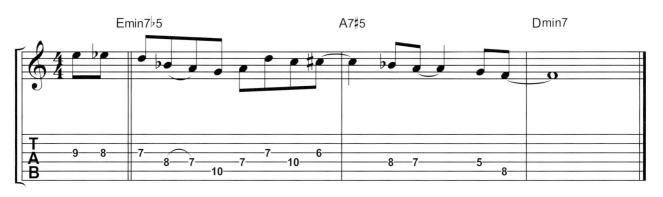

3. Sing the root movement. When learning a new tune using the numeric approach described above, try to sing the root movement of each separate sequence. For instance, you could start by just singing a II – V – I movement over two bars. Don't worry about the actual pitches you are singing – greater accuracy in this area will develop over time – but instead concentrate on getting the relative pitch correct. So to sing a II – V with correct relative pitching, you would ascend a perfect fourth (or descend a perfect fifth) from any starting note. The same interval relationship (i.e. up a 4th/down a 5th) exists between the V and I chords.

4. Compile your own 'lick library'. Being a good jazz musician is 99% perspiration and 1% inspiration! There is no magic involved and, although it may seem as if a soloist is plucking notes out of the air, he or she will have spent many years constantly practising in order to become a convincing (and entertaining) improviser. So don't make the mistake of thinking it is in some way 'unmusical' or 'unartistic' to learn licks and write them down. Start transcribing your favourite players, and keep the licks in a 'lick library'. Practise your licks every day, and make sure you can play them in different keys, EDCAG shapes, different octaves, etc.

Jim Mullen sporting cool shades and playing his Aria FA-65 archtop with pick guard removed. Jim plays with his thumb in the Wes Montgomery tradition – note how he 'anchors' his right hand by grabbing the bottom of the guitar with his fingers, also his left hand technique, with thumb creeping over the top of the neck.

5: The Jazz Blues Progression

The Basic Blues Progression

The blues evolved from early Afro-American plantation and prison songs in the late 19th century. Around the same time a heavily syncopated music called ragtime was also developing. This new music drew on wider influences than the blues, and incorporated elements of folk and brass band music. So it is widely believed that jazz was born from a fusion of ragtime and blues. Whereas ragtime's popularity was short-lived, the blues has never been 'out of fashion' and has contin-

ued to evolve; consequently it remains an influential force in jazz to this day. Blues musicians often accompanied themselves on piano or guitar and would often play choruses of different lengths, sometimes eleven or even thirteen bars long. Ironically it is the early jazz musicians who standardised the blues into the twelve-bar sequence we know and love today. Below you can see the standard twelve-bar blues sequence in C major, with numeric annotation added above to allow easy transposition:

Fig 5.1 **Basic 12-bar blues**

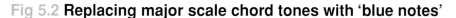

The importance of the blues in jazz has always been understood, and cross-pollination between the two genres continues to this day. It is no coincidence that each new jazz movement has incorporated an element of blues influence; the greatest jazz musicians understand that if you don't include the blues in your playing, then you're not really playing jazz at all.

The term 'blue note' is used to describe the minor third and minor seventh, and their use over chords that do not normally contain these intervals. Blue notes are generally played as an approximation rather than a precise pitch (i.e. as a quarter tone bend on the guitar). Jazz musicians frequently superimpose these notes over 'straight' major chords (like the major seventh). When applied to a major scale the 'blue notes' are generally used to replace the original scale tones (figure 5.2).

Fig 5.2 **Replacing major scale chord tones with 'blue notes'**

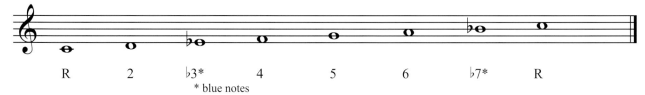

Before **Charlie Christian** turned the jazz world on its head with his amplified solos, the guitar's role in jazz was strictly limited to accompaniment. Since the early guitar players did not improvise, they had no influence on the evolution of the popular jazz

keys. Consequently the jazz guitarist has little choice but to become fluent in unfamiliar keys that would not occur in other genres such as rock or country. Gone are the 'guitar-friendly' keys of E and A major (sax players find these awkward to play in);

and in their place are the keys of F, B♭, E♭ and A♭ major. It is also 'expected' that the jazz guitarist will acknowledge the major tonality of the tonic (I7) chord in their improvisation. So the blues-rock 'minor pentatonic fits all' approach is a definite no-no! Many of the great blues guitarists such as

BB King and **Freddie King** also incorporate major tonality into their solos, juggling major and minor pentatonics to great effect. Using the major pentatonic scale is the easiest way to begin 'majorising' the blues sequence.

The Major Pentatonic

Figure 5.3 illustrates the major pentatonic and minor pentatonic side by side for easy comparison. Notice that the major pentatonic has no seventh at all, and the 'blue' notes are only

contained in the minor pentatonic (hence the frequent superimposition of the minor pentatonic over major chords to create 'blue note' phrases).

Fig 5.3 **Major vs. minor pentatonic**

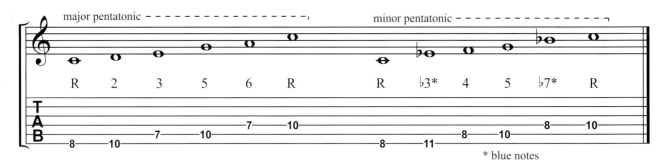

* blue notes

By expanding the one octave C major pentatonic scale across the fingerboard, the full shape one EDCAG shape is achieved (figure 5.4).

Fig 5.4 **C major pentatonic – shape one**

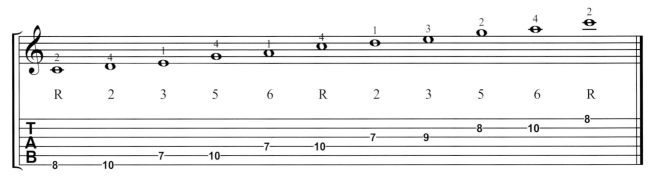

Remember that special 'major = minor down a ♭3' relationship (i.e. the relative minor key) back in Chapter 1? If you take another look at the major pentatonic above you'll notice it's the same pattern as shape two of the minor pentatonic. This means that you can play minor pentatonic licks a minor third below any major chord to achieve major pen-

tatonic tonality. However although this is an effective short-term fix, it's not the best way to achieve musical results. Check out figure 5.5 opposite to see how the chord tones change, and be aware that if you keep 'thinking' in the relative minor you'll be hitting the sixth of the major key when you play a relative minor's root note.

Fig 5.5 Major vs. superimposed minor chord tones

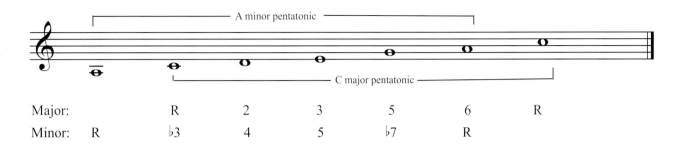

Major:		R	2	3	5	6	R
Minor:	R	♭3	4	5	♭7	R	

To find the remaining major pentatonic shapes simply adapt the remaining four EDCAG minor pentatonic shapes by referring to the conversion chart below. Remember that the chord tones will change as indicated in figure 5.5.

Minor pentatonic (down ♭3) ←	→ Major pentatonic (up ♭3)
Shape one	Shape five
Shape two	Shape one
Shape three	Shape two
Shape four	Shape three
Shape five	Shape four

This relationship can be reduced to the formula: **minor = major up ♭3 (-1)**. So to convert a minor pentatonic shape to major, rename the scale using the letter name a minor third (♭3) higher. Remember that '-1' means that once converted the shape number will be one pattern lower in the five pattern EDCAG system, e.g. A minor pentatonic shape one = C major pentatonic shape five.

Reversing the formula gives: **major = minor down ♭3 (+1)**. The major pentatonic can then be converted by renaming the scale with the letter name a minor third lower. Once converted the '+1' means you apply the shape number one step lower in the EDCAG system, e.g. C major pentatonic shape five = A minor pentatonic shape one.

The Mixolydian Mode

We first encountered the Mixolydian mode back in Chapter 2, where it was used to improvise over static dominant sevenths in 'Seventh Heaven'. The Mixolydian is the true parent scale of a tonic dominant chord, and is simply the major pentatonic with an added perfect 4th and minor 7th as illustrated in figure 5.6. These extra notes provide the missing ♭7 chord tone and the perfect 4th passing note – the 4th should only be played as part of a sequence (i.e. stepwise or as part of an arpeggio pattern) since it will clash with the major third of the underlying harmony if sustained.

Fig 5.6 The major pentatonic/Mixolydian mode

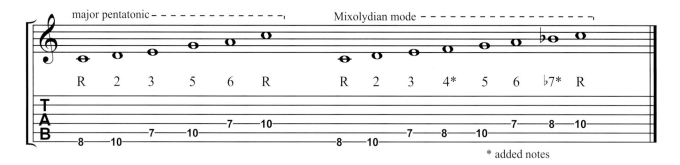

If it is possible to use the Mixolydian mode for improvising over chord I of the blues, then it follows that you can also use it over chord IV (starting on the same note as the chord). Figure 5.7 below illustrates which Mixolydian modes would be used in a C blues sequence (we'll deal with the G7 chord in the next section).

Fig 5.7 Use of the Mixolydian mode

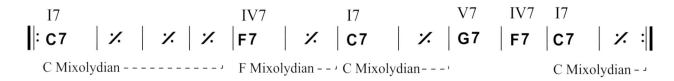

In Chapter 2 we discovered that by playing the Dorian a fifth above a dominant seventh, we could create the Mixolydian sound from a 'guitar-friendly', minor perspective. This theory can also be applied to the blues, and it's a great way to 'jazz up' your blues playing.

All the great players use this technique over blues changes – listen to the recordings of **Pat Martino**, **Wes Montgomery**, and the late **Emily Remler** (who produced some wonderful albums in her tragically short career) for some great examples.

To create Mixolydian colour tones over chord I of a blues, simply play the Dorian mode up a fifth (i.e. starting on G for C7). And, just as the tonic (C) blues scale can be used to create cool bluesy sounds over chord IV (F7), so the tonic (C) Dorian can be used to create cool Mixolydian colour tones over chord IV (i.e. starting on C for F7).

In figure 5.8, the G Dorian is superimposed over

C7 to create a hip bop-style lick. Notice that two diatonic (i.e. using only notes from the parent scale) arpeggios are used in this lick. Remember that arpeggios are 'secure' melodic fragments – melodic-sounding licks are invariably arpeggio based. By ensuring that you learn new licks in all five EDCAG shapes, you will find it easy to transpose them to new keys.

The second lick in figure 5.8 demonstrates how, by transferring the lick to shape one (you will find it easier to do this in the same key at first), it can also be used over chord IV (F7). A good tip for transposing licks and melodies is to remember the starting note – in this case the lick begins on the root (R).

Fig 5.8 **Using the Dorian over chord I and IV**

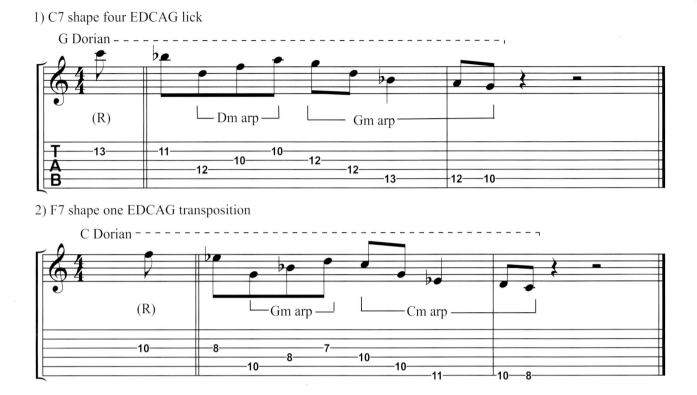

1) C7 shape four EDCAG lick

2) F7 shape one EDCAG transposition

The Basic Jazz 12-bar

The first change that jazz musicians made to the simple 12-bar blues sequence was to replace the simple V – IV movement in bars 9 and 10 with a more sophisticated II – V – I progression. This change allowed the improviser to create melodic lines and introduce traditional V – I perfect cadence tensions. The key to understanding the jazz blues sequence lies in understanding the various points at which the II – V chords can be in-troduced. These can be either resolving or simply moving to yet another II – V as in the most com-plex of all jazz blues chord progressions, 'Blues For Alice' written by **Charlie Parker**. In figure 5.9 you can clearly see the differences between a standard blues and a jazz 12-bar blues progression. Notice the addition of the extra IV chord in the 2nd bar, and the II – V in bar 12 preceded by the dominant of the II chord (A7).

Fig 5.9 **12-bar blues vs. basic jazz blues**

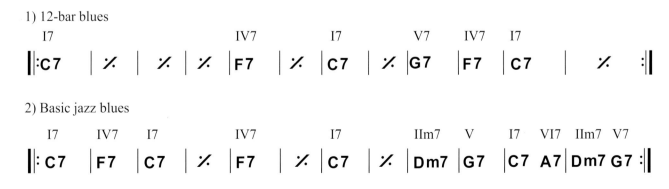

1) 12-bar blues

2) Basic jazz blues

The following tune 'Sunnyside Up' is loosely based on **Sonny Rollins'** 'Sunnymoon For Two' and is a great example of a medium tempo swinging blues.

The chord sequence is identical to the 'basic jazz blues' outlined above but occurs in the popular tenor (sax) player's key of B♭.

Phil Capone

♩ = 135 swing

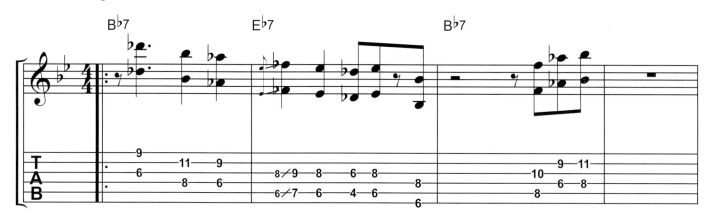

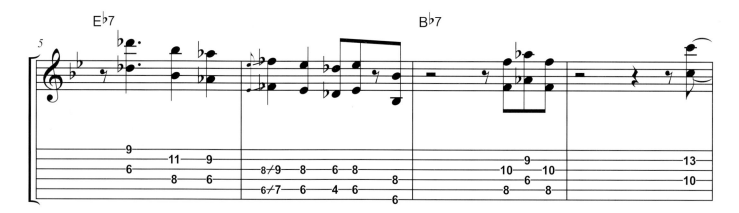

Fine

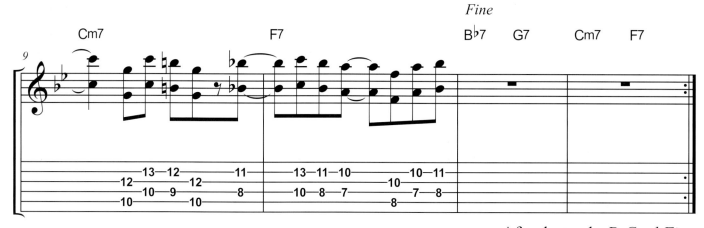

After last solo *D.C. al Fine*
(play head 2x)

Sunnyside Up – solo

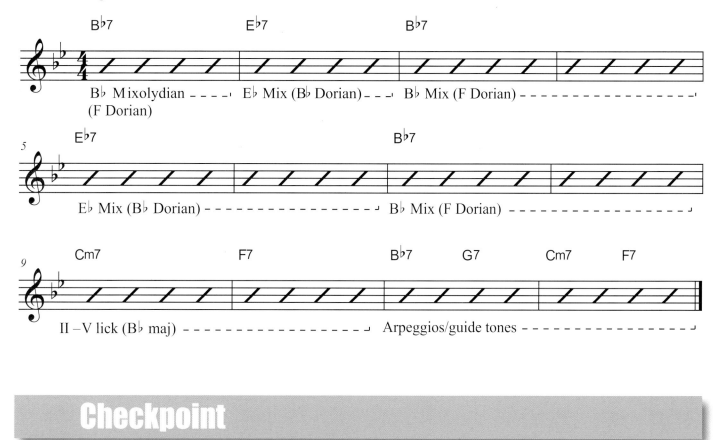

♩ = 135 swing

Bb7   Eb7   Bb7

Bb Mixolydian _ _ _ _ ⌐ Eb Mix (Bb Dorian) _ _ _ ⌐ Bb Mix (F Dorian) - - - - - - - - - - - - - - - ⌐
(F Dorian)

Eb7   Bb7

Eb Mix (Bb Dorian) - - - - - - - - - - - - - - ⌐ Bb Mix (F Dorian) - - - - - - - - - - - - - - - ⌐

Cm7   F7   Bb7   G7   Cm7   F7

II – V lick (Bb maj) - - - - - - - - - - - - - ⌐ Arpeggios/guide tones - - - - - - - - - - - - - - ⌐

Checkpoint

Song Form

'Sunnyside Up' is based on a regular jazz 12-bar blues form. Because the sequence is quite short, it is common practice for the tune to be repeated before and after solos, so play the repeats on the 'head' both times when playing along to the backing track.

Occasionally a middle eight will be added, transforming the jazz blues into a long AABA form. In this scenario 'A' would be the same as a regular 12-bar jazz blues and 'B' a middle eight (which usually modulates).

Examples of this include the standards 'Black Coffee' and 'One Mint Julep'. Check out Blue Note guitarist **Kenny Burrell**'s instrumental version of 'One Mint Julep' recorded with organist **Jack McDuff** in 1963; although not released at the time, this has subsequently featured on several compilations.

II – V – I

As we discovered earlier in the chapter, the familiar V – IV movement that occurs in bars nine and ten of a regular blues is replaced with a II – V – I sequence in jazz. To create a convincing improvisation it is essential that you 'follow the changes' at this point with an appropriate II – V – I lick.

We explored various ways of negotiating this progression in Chapter 4, but you should also back up this harmonic analysis with plenty of listening and transcribing. Some of the finest examples of jazz blues soloing can be heard on the numerous recordings by **Kenny Burrell**, **George Benson**, **Wes Montgomery**, or for a more contemporary slant check out ex-**Miles Davis** guitarist **John Scofield** or the wonderfully bluesy **Jim Mullen**.

The Turnaround

A turnaround occurs at the end of most jazz sequences (usually in the last two bars of a progression), and its principle function is to simply 'turn the song around' back to the start. Turnarounds will be explored in greater depth in Chapter 8; in the meantime here are a couple of ideas to start you off:

a) Motivic tranposition

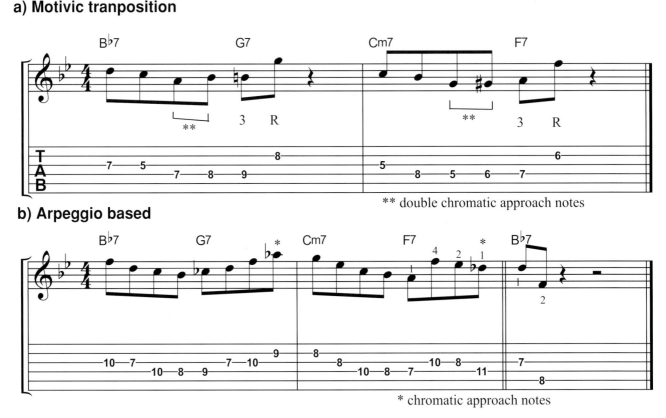

** double chromatic approach notes

b) Arpeggio based

* chromatic approach notes

The first example of a turnaround lick above uses a very common improvising tool: motivic transposition. This approach involves taking an idea created 'on the fly' when improvising, and adapting it 'to fit' subsequent chord changes.

Obviously it takes a long time to become proficient at such a spontaneous technique, but once mastered, it guarantees any improviser that elusive quality: melodic cohesion. In other words, your solos will no longer be unconnected phrases; they will have continuity that will make your soloing more appealing to the listener.

Notice the use of the double chromatic approach notes that precedes the 3rd of each dominant seventh chord.

The second turnaround lick is constructed using the arpeggio approach explored in Chapter 4. Notice the use of non-diatonic chromatic approach notes (in this instance approaching the chord tones from above), and the final resolution that occurs on what would be bar 1 of the new chorus.

The final option for approaching a turnaround is to simply do nothing! Overplaying is a 'crime' that many improvisers are guilty of – don't feel that you have to solo constantly; be brave enough to let a couple of bars pass by (without losing track of the changes). The old maxim 'it's not what you play, but what you leave out' is worth remembering at all times...

Assignments and Improvisation Tips

1. Remember that guide tones are not just for constructing solos – you can use them to create extremely effective comping voicings. As you have already discovered, the 5th can be omitted from any chord without compromising the chord type. Similarly, the root note can also be omitted in ensemble situations, allowing the bass player greater freedom to create contrapuntal lines. By playing each of the three pairs of examples below, you will notice how your ear still recognises the chord's qualities even with the root and fifth omitted.

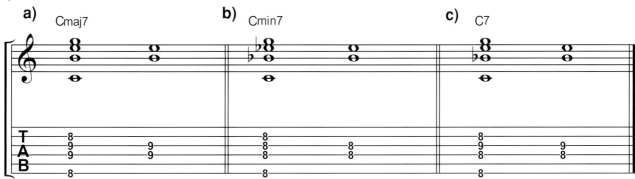

The entire blues progression can therefore be harmonised with guide tone voicings as demonstrated below. By using guide tone comping you will not be 'treading on the toes' of the soloist – a solid harmonic backdrop is provided. The improviser is free to add whatever tensions they choose without being 'bullied' by an overbearing accompaniment.

2. Melody and changes should always be memorised. You can't inject feeling and subtlety into your playing if you haven't learnt the tune. Similarly, if you're having to read the changes when you're soloing you won't produce a great solo – all of your conscious thoughts need to be focused on playing melodically within the harmonic structure.

3. Don't forget that for maximum benefit, you should practise all of the tunes in this book with a metronome in addition to using the backing track. Using a metronome will allow you to build your tempo gradually, and help you develop a strong rhythmic awareness. So the tune, comping and improvising should all be practised independently of the backing track, using a metronome as discussed in the very first tune in this book, 'Minor Jam'. Practising improvising with a metronome may seem a strange concept, but if you can imagine the changes in your head while you are playing you will play much stronger ideas, with or without accompaniment.

4. If you find your creativity drying up then try singing! Isolate a short section, no longer than four bars, play the chords (just sound them on the first beat and let them ring), and sing whatever comes into your head. You may want to practise singing the root notes and guide tones of each chord before you start, but there are no rules! Singing is the purest and most natural way to create music – don't be afraid to sing ideas when you practise.

Kenny Burrell with his Gibson Byrdland archtop with Florentine cutaway. Unusually these guitars have the pickup selector mounted below the pick guard as standard.

Modulating To Chord IV

So far we have examined the jazz blues in its basic form. To make the sequence more challenging from an improvising perspective, further II – Vs are added at strategic modulation points. The first of these II – Vs precedes the IV7 chord in bar five:

Fig 5.10 Adding a II – V in bar 4

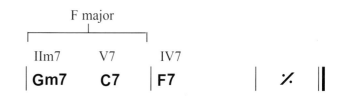

I7	IV7	I7	IIm7	V7	IV7		
C7	F7	C7	Gm7	C7	F7	∕	

Technically this is a major II – V despite the fact that it resolves to a dominant seventh. However dominant sevenths, just like major chords, can be preceded by major or minor II – Vs. Many players add altered tensions over the dominant of IV7 to heighten the sense of modulation. Figure 5.11 illustrates how the altered scale (see Chapter 2) can be used to create cool licks over this sequence. Both phrases start in the third bar, allowing the altered tensions to be introduced as the lick builds.

Fig 5.11(a) Modulation to chord IV7 – treating II – V as one bar of V7

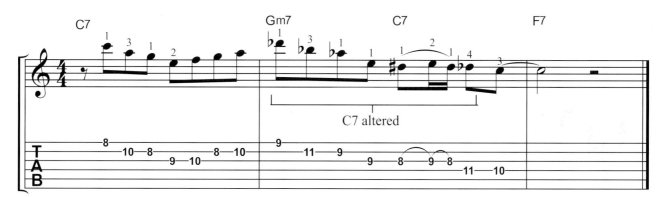

Figure 5.11(a) demonstrates how the IIm7 chord can be ignored completely – an altered C7 lick is played for the full bar. This would be much less effective if it wasn't 'set up' by the preceding motif – the listener hears the lick as an idea shifted up a half-step. In figure 5.11(b) an arpeggio approach is used, with each chord change anticipated a beat early to create a greater sense of motion. Note the use of the tonic blues scale – this always sounds cool when applied to the IV7 chord since it heightens the major to minor effect (F7 shares many common tones with Cm6).

Fig 5.11(b) Modulation to chord IV7 – resolving to tonic blues scale

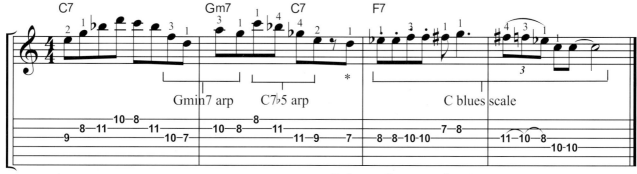

* chromatic approach note

The VI7 Chord

In 'Sunnyside Up', you will remember that the dominant of the IIm7 chord (VI7) was added to the eleventh bar, creating a turnaround to drive the sequence back to the start of the chorus. The VI7 secondary dominant can also be added to the eighth bar (figure 5.12(a)) where it again functions as the dominant of IIm7, allowing the addition of dominant tensions. Because the VI7 resolves to a minor chord, your scale choice here should be the Phrygian dominant mode (see Chapter 2):

Fig 5.12(a) **Adding VI7 to bar 8**

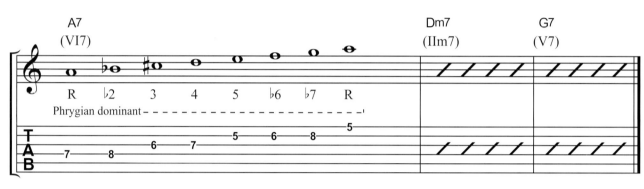

The VI7 chord has long been used as a 'functioning' secondary dominant (i.e. non-diatonic but resolving up a fifth to a minor or another dominant seventh) in jazz. However during the be-bop era, the min7♭5 was added in front of the VI7 chord to transform it into a fully fledged minor II – V. Adding a minor II – V to bar eight is another common harmonic 'tweak' that jazz musicians will (almost instinctively) add to a jazz blues. Figure 5.12(b) illustrates how bars seven through twelve appear with this minor modulation included:

Fig 5.12(b) **Adding minor II – V to bar 8**

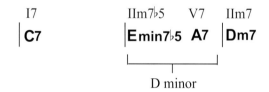

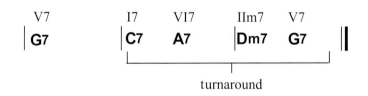

Since each chord only lasts two beats, the best way to play over this short minor II – V is to apply the techniques explored in Chapter 4. Guide tones, arpeggios and chromatic approach notes are all extremely effective methods of not just 'hitting the changes' but also creating the tension and release that will keep your solo moving forward.

Don't forget that you can also ignore the IIm7♭5 altogether and play a dominant seventh lick for the full bar, incorporating Phrygian dominant or even altered scale colour tones (see Chapter 4, figures 4.17–4.19). However be aware that Phrygian colour tones are more 'inside' (i.e. diatonic) and altered tensions 'outside' (i.e. non-diatonic), the latter working best on a true modulation (i.e. preceding chord IV7, or in bar 10 over the final V7 before the turnaround) where the tension can be completely resolved.

The Diminished Chord

The diminished chord is frequently added to bar 6 of the blues. It's a harmonic enhancement that is also found in traditional blues tunes. Many guitarists don't like to see diminished chords in a chart because they simply don't know how to deal with them.

The late, great **Joe Pass** created complex improvisations and dense accompaniments that belied his simple harmonic philosophy. Joe categorised chords into three families: major, minor and dominant seventh. Major and minor chords are static;

dominant sevenths create tension and are therefore motion chords (i.e. the tension is resolved only by moving to a static chord). Since the diminished chord also creates tension, it belongs to the dominant seventh family. The diminished chord's instability is created by the presence of the dissonant tritone ($\flat$5) interval – an interval that also occurs in dominant sevenths. In figure 5.13(a) you can clearly see the similarity between F7 and F♯ diminished. In fact, F♯ diminished could simply be viewed as F7$\flat$9 with the $\flat$9 as the chord's lowest note:

Fig 5.13(a) The diminished chord

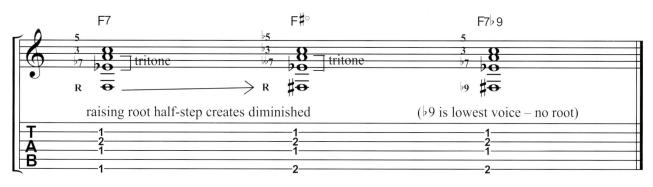

raising root half-step creates diminished ($\flat$9 is lowest voice – no root)

When written in a chord chart, the diminished symbol is generally used (e.g. F♯°). It is also sometimes written as F♯°7 (the '7' affirming the presence of the diminished seventh). However jazz musicians

automatically include the seventh when playing a diminished chord, so this detail is really superfluous. The three most commonly used diminished voicings are illustrated below in figure 5.13(b).

Fig 5.13(b) Three diminished voicings

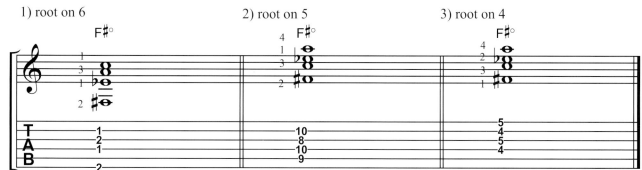

Diminished chords defy the EDCAG system because the chord repeats itself as an inversion when played a minor 3rd (three frets) higher. F♯ diminished contains exactly the same notes as A°, C° and E$\flat$°. Rise another minor 3rd and you're back to F♯ – clever eh?

Now fasten your safety belts, cos' I'm gonna fly us a little closer to the sun! Since there are only two notes (G and A$\flat$) between F♯ and A, it follows that there can only be a total of three diminished chords as you will see from the table overleaf:

111

Fig 5.13(c) The three diminished groups

Group 1: C – E♭ – G♭ – A
Group 2: D♭ – E – G – B♭
Group 3: D – F – A♭ – B
N.B. Enharmonic equivalents should be applied as necessary; e.g. D♭ = C♯

Musical mathematics aside, all this information has extremely practical applications. Take the group 1 diminished chords above, the four notes in the group spell out the notes contained within any of the component diminished chords (e.g. C diminished = C – E♭ – G♭ – A, A diminished = A – C – E♭ – G♭). So that means you can use any chord within the same group as an alternative voicing. Need an E♭ diminished? Play C°, G♭° or A° and you'll still be playing E♭°.

The diminished arpeggio is an essential tool for improvising over diminished chords. The two octave shape (figure 5.14(a)) can be shifted up or down the neck in minor thirds just like the chord. By using the diminished grouping theory above, it is easy to apply a 'one shape fits all' philosophy for applying this arpeggio over any diminished chord.

Fig 5.14(a) Two octave diminished scale

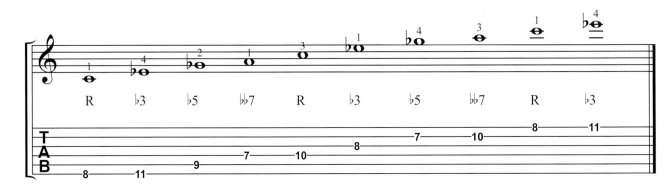

Remember the close relationship between F7 and F♯°? If we think of these two chords as IV and ♯IV° in a C major blues then, since the tonic blues scale sounds cool over chord IV, then it stands to reason it will also sound cool over ♯IV° since the chords share three common notes. However the natural fifth contained in the blues scale can sound a little 'off' so this note is best avoided. By omitting this note from the blues scale, we end up with a minor pentatonic (♭5) scale:

Fig 5.14(b) Minor pentatonic with ♭5

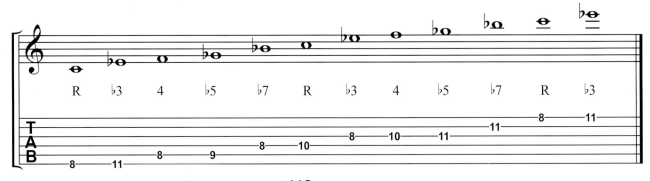

With two extra II – Vs and the ♯IV diminished
chord added, our jazz 12-bar blues is transformed
into the following progression:

Fig 5.15 Complete 12-bar jazz blues

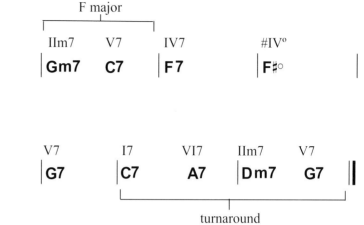
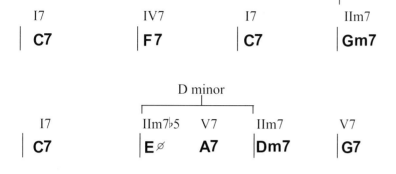

The last tune in this chapter 'Mr Smith Called' incorporates all of these extra changes. The famous
recordings of organ virtuoso **Jimmy Smith** (who
collaborated with many fine guitarists including
Kenny Burrell, **George Benson**, and **Wes
Montgomery**) were the inspiration for this tune.
Although this chord sequence incorporates many
harmonic twists and turns, it's not essential to play
over all of them. Don't be afraid to let some changes
go by – sometimes less really is more.

Phil Capone

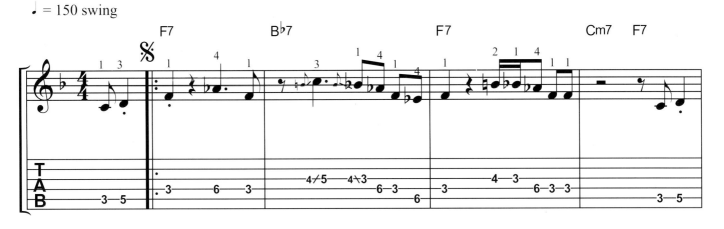

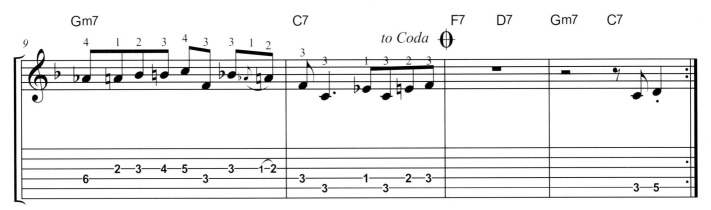

After last solo D.S. al Coda

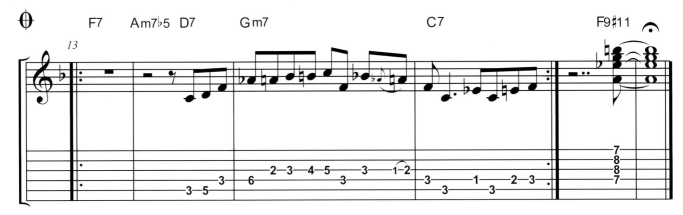

Mr Smith Called – solo

♩ = 150 swing

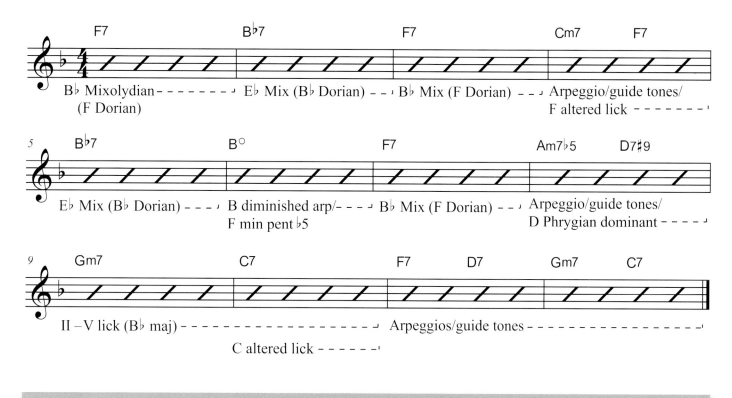

Checkpoint

The 'Three Time' Ending

Commonly used in many jazz standards, the 'three time' ending involves repeating the closing phrase of a tune three times as its name suggests. When a turnaround occurs after the phrase, this is usually 'tweaked' to push the sequence back to the first bar of the three time ending, as in this tune. The second bar of the coda employs a minor II – V to steer the harmony back to Gm7 for further repetitions of the closing melody. The example below highlights the differences between the two turnarounds used in this tune:

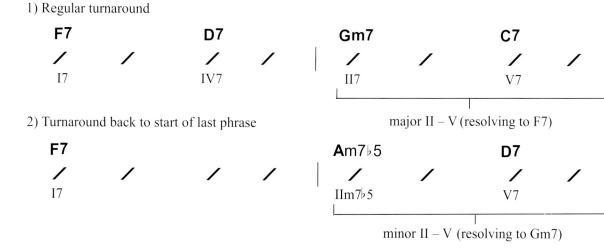

Timbre vs. Position Shifts

The problem with TAB and fingering detail is that it suggests you can only play the music in one position. Unlike, say the piano, there are many different ways to play the same note on the guitar. Frequently when I'm learning a tune I'll experiment with various fingerings until I find one that works for me. It's not just about finding the easiest fingering either. Take the tricky chromatic phrase that starts in bar eight of this tune. It could also be played as

shown below – however, this involves playing the D in the pick-up as an open string, which would make it sound different to previous pick-up phrases. Ideally all the phrases in a tune should have the same timbre and texture in order to achieve melodic cohesion. In 'Mr Smith Called' the chromatic phrase in bar nine is played entirely on one string. This results in a thicker, horn-like quality that is lost when using the fingering indicated below.

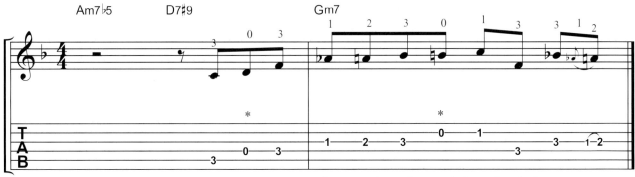

* open strings change timbre of melody notes

The 9♯11 Dominant Seventh

You have probably already spotted the exotic chord that concludes this piece, a favourite ending chord with jazz musicians. It's particularly useful for concluding the jazz blues since it adds spice without straying too far from the tonic dominant seventh. The F9♯11 is created by stacking two further thirds above F7, adding the 9th and ♯11 (♭5) tensions as shown here. Notice that the top four notes of this new chord are the same as Cmin/maj7.

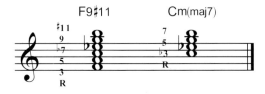

The notes that the F9♯11 shares with a Cmin/maj7 are more than just an interesting coincidence. Remember how we have previously used the Dorian

up a fifth from a dominant seventh to create hip, jazzy licks? Substitute the jazz melodic minor scale for the Dorian and you will instantly be creating even cooler and hipper licks, trust me! The major seventh interval in the melodic minor creates the hot n' spicy ♯11 when played a fifth above a dominant seventh:

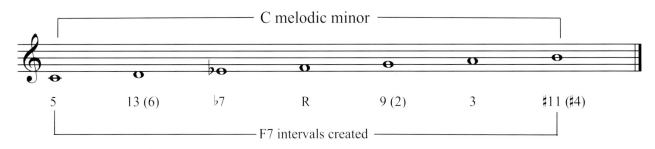

As with all superimpositions, you need to be aware of the underlying chord tones (i.e. F7 not Cm) in order to hit 'secure' resolution notes at the end of your phrases.

Assignments and Improvisation Tips

1. Remember that whole chorus of the blues that we mapped out with guide tone voicings for 'Sunnyside Up' (p.107)? All you need to do is transpose these voicings from the key of B♭ to F and then add all the extra II – Vs. Aim to keep the notes on the middle (3rd and 4th) strings as before. For the ♯IV diminished chord, remember that the ♭3rd and ♭♭7th are the true guide tones which are used to create the all-important tritone interval. Once you have isolated the tritone you can move it up or down the fretboard in minor thirds (three frets) to generate inversions as shown below:

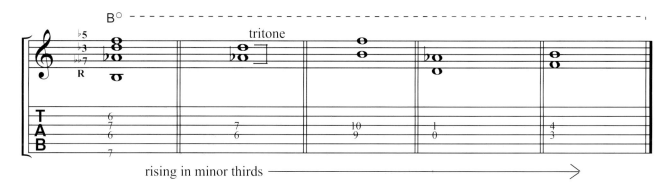

2. One of the best ways to build your improvising skills is to practise linking arpeggios through the chord changes using constant eighth notes. Identify the trickiest section of the tune, in this case the last four bars, and use your metronome to ensure you don't slow down when the going gets tough! The legendary **Pat Martino** is a master at creating impossibly long eighth-note phrases at breakneck tempos, sometimes spanning several modulations.

3. Keep varying your ideas. Use as many different approaches as possible when you are practising. When using arpeggio-based ideas as above, practise your lines ascending and descending, and make sure you are just as comfortable starting on chord tones other than the root. Don't forget to try playing eighth-note lines with 'straight' as well as swing eighths.

4. Use your voice. If you run out of ideas, use the most melodic tool you own for inspiration: your voice. If you find it difficult to pitch at first, pick a starting note, play it and then copy it. Then try singing a short phrase beginning on this note (while playing the chords on the guitar).

George Benson playing his Signature Series Ibanez GB 200 model archtop guitar. Something has definitely caught George's eye – he's not paying attention to his sixth-position lick at all!

6: Adding Colour

The Minor 9th

Any seventh chord (major, minor or dominant) can be 'spiced up' by adding chord extensions to the basic voicing. Just as the seventh chord is created by stacking a third above a basic triad, so extensions are created by stacking further thirds above a seventh chord. This system is used to create five-note (ninth) and six-note (eleventh) chords.

Using extensions will add harmonic depth to your comping, and open up a whole new world of expression when improvising. In this chapter we will be learning the theory behind the chords, how they can be voiced effectively on the guitar, and how to improvise over them by using four-note seventh arpeggios.

We started our exploration of jazz guitar with the minor seventh chord, so appropriately, our first extended chord will be the minor ninth. It is important to remember that a ninth chord includes the previous seventh extension in the voicing – it is not to be confused with 'add9' or 'sus2' voicings that simply bolt a ninth onto the basic triad, or replace (suspend) the third with a major second. Figure 6.1 illustrates a Dmin9 chord – both the arpeggio and the chord can be thought of as Fmaj7 (the relative major chord) superimposed over a D bass note. Every type of ninth chord (major, minor or dominant) can be viewed as a superimposed seventh (but of a different quality, i.e. major7 creates minor9) over a root note – a useful theory for creating ninth sounds when improvising.

Fig 6.1 **Dm9 arpeggio and chord**

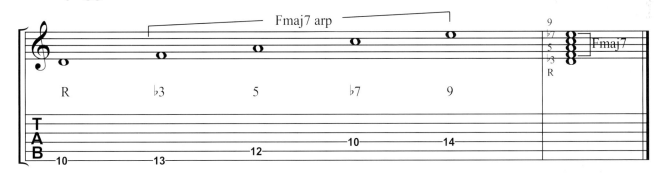

The full shape one Dmin9 arpeggio is annotated in figure 6.2 below. Notice that just as the Dmin9 chord can be viewed as Fmaj7/A, so the Dmin9

arpeggio can be considered as two Fmaj7 arpeggios 'stacked' above a D bass note.

Fig 6.2 **Dm9 arpeggio – shape one**

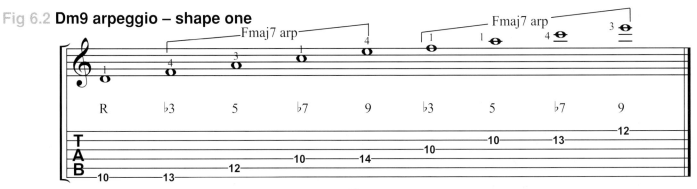

Although it is important to practise the full five-note arpeggio (in order to understand the relationship of the ninth to other chord tones visually and aurally), in reality jazz guitarists rarely improvise with anything bigger than a four-note shape. So to create ninth colour tones over a minor 9th (or minor 7th) chord simply play the relative major seventh arpeggio a minor third above the chord:

min9 arpeggio = maj7 arpeggio up a minor 3rd

The same philosophy is generally applied when voicing a min9 chord. In figure 6.3 you can clearly see that three out of the five EDCAG Dmin9 voicings are actually Fmaj7 chord shapes.

Fig 6.3 **Five four-note Dm9 voicings using the 'EDCAG' system**

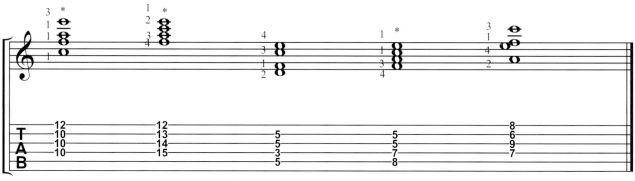

* Fmaj7 voicings

Even when a 'true' min9 voicing is used the root and/or fifth are generally omitted to maintain a manageable four-note shape (notice shape three has no 5th, while shape five omits the root). Notice also that the shape five voicing places the ninth in the same octave as the minor 3rd. Although the ninth is technically a compound interval (i.e. greater than an octave), and naturally occurs a major 7th above the minor 3rd in a 'stacked thirds' voicing, it is often voiced an octave lower and voiced next to the minor 3rd to create a more interesting voicing.

The Dominant 9th

The dominant ninth chord is popular in blues, country and funk music, so it is a sound you are probably already familiar with. **James Brown**'s guitarist **Jimmy Nolen** used the ninth chord so regularly ('Sex Machine', 'I Feel Good') that it is now *de rigueur* to use the dominant ninth (instead of a dominant seventh) in funk and related fusion styles. Figure 6.4 illustrates a G9 arpeggio and close position, stacked thirds voicing. As with the minor ninth chord, adding a third to a four-note dominant seventh chord creates the dominant ninth. Notice that the dominant ninth can also be viewed as a Bmin7b5 superimposed above a G root.

Fig 6.4 **G9 arpeggio and chord**

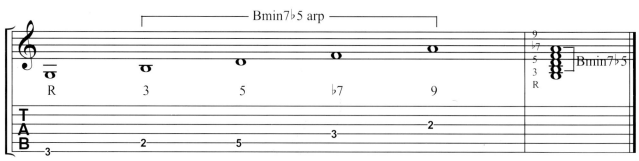

In jazz, the ninth is a relatively 'safe' colour tone to add to a dominant seventh: the ♭9 and ♯9 create far more tension and these will be analysed later in the chapter. In our exploration of dominant seventh chords (Chapter 2) we examined the role of secondary dominants, i.e. dominant sevenths that are not built on the fifth degree of the scale and so do not occur diatonically. The secondary dominant may be described as functioning (resolving up a fourth/ down a fifth) or non-functioning (non-resolving). Non-functioning secondary dominants can safely be changed from sevenths to ninths:

Fig 6.5 The dominant ninth as a non-functioning secondary dominant

1) 'A' section of 'Take The 'A' Train'

I		IIdom9*		II	V	I	VI7	II	V
Cmaj7	⁄.	D9	⁄.	Dm7	G7	Cmaj7 A7		Dm7	G7

2) Bars 9–16 of 'There Will Never Be Another You'

IV	IVm	♭VIIdom9* I	VI	IIdom9*		II	V
A♭maj7	A♭m7	D♭9 E♭maj7	Cm7	F9	⁄.	Fm7	B♭7

The two octave EDCAG shape one, dominant ninth arpeggio can also be considered as two min7♭5 arpeggios starting a major 3rd above the chord's root. Once again, you should practise the arpeggio as written, but be aware that in an improvising situation, the four-note min7♭5 arpeggio is a more useful tool for effectively describing a dominant ninth.

Fig 6.6 G9 arpeggio – shape one

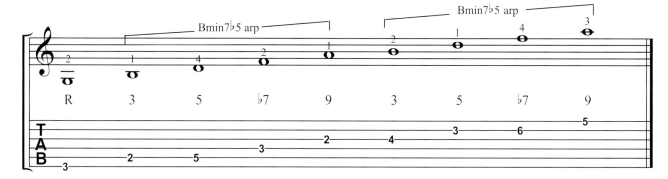

As with every chord type that we have studied, you should familiarise yourself with all five EDCAG shapes for G9 (figure 6.7). Notice that the two rootless voicings, shapes one and three, are actually Bm7♭5 voicings. Harmonic context (with or without root notes) is the single most important factor in deciding whether our ear hears a dominant or a minor chord.

Fig 6.7 Five four-note G9 'EDCAG' voicings

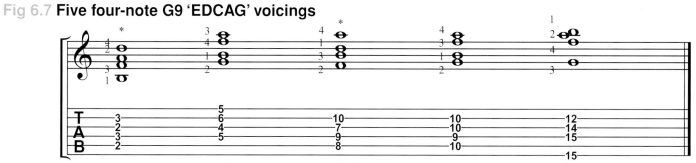

* Bmin7♭5 voicings

The Major 9th

The major ninth chord is not to be confused with the major(add9) chord. As illustrated in figure 6.8 below, the major ninth is a four-note major seventh chord with the additional stacked third creating the ninth. As with all types of 9th chords, it is generally understood that the term describes a chord that also includes the seventh.

Major(add9) chords, as their name suggests, are simply a major chord with a ninth 'bolted on' to the basic triad. This is also occasionally seen in minor chords, e.g. min(add9), but never in the dominant since the seventh is crucial to create that all-important tritone between the 3rd and ♭7th.

Fig 6.8 **Cmaj9 arpeggio and chord**

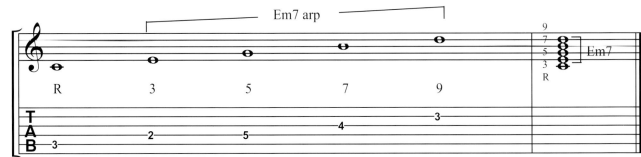

Earlier in Chapter 3 we discovered that an E minor pentatonic scale could be used to create cool licks over a Cmaj7 chord. The close relationship between E minor and C major becomes even more apparent when studying the Cmaj9 chord and arpeggio since

a Cmaj9 chord could also be viewed as Emin7 over a C bass note. In figure 6.9 the full shape one Cmaj9 arpeggio can clearly be seen to contain two Emin7 arpeggios built above a C root note.

Fig 6.9 **Cmaj9 arpeggio – shape one**

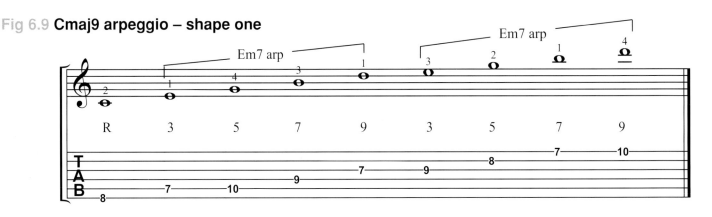

Five EDCAG major ninth shapes (figure 6.10) can be derived from the close position model illustrated in figure 6.8. Notice that the first three voicings contain no 3rd and are actually a G major triad superimposed over a C bass note. It is not possible to include the 3rd, 7th and 9th in every maj9 guitar voicing, and so the 3rd is frequently omitted. The major tonality of the triad (G), when superimposed over the C bass note, effectively describes the major tonality of the chord despite the absence of the 3rd.

Fig 6.10 Five 'EDCAG' Cmaj9 voicings

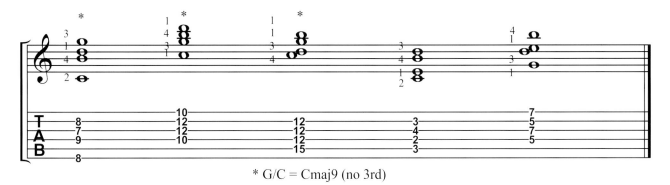

* G/C = Cmaj9 (no 3rd)

Using 7th Chords To Create 9th Chords

All of the ninth chords in this chapter (major, dominant and minor) can be created by substituting a specific seventh chord (i.e. maj7, min7♭5, min7) a third higher. This creates instant ninth voicings for comping or cool licks for improvising – the choice is yours!

So to summarise, any ninth chord/arpeggio can be created by superimposing a seventh chord/arpeggio a 3rd above the root (major 3rd above for major and dominant chords and a minor 3rd above for minor chords):

min9 chord/arpeggio ⟶	maj7 chord/arpeggio starting on ♭3rd (up min 3rd)
dom9 chord/arpeggio ⟶	min7♭5 chord/arpeggio starting on 3rd (up maj 3rd)
maj9 chord/arpeggio ⟶	min7 chord/arpeggio starting on 3rd (up maj 3rd)

The Dominant 11th Chord

By stacking a third above a ninth chord the eleventh chord is created. As with ninths, it is understood that an eleventh chord will also contain the 7th and 9th intervals. The most

frequently encountered eleventh chord is the dominant variety and, as you will see from figure 6.11, the best voicing is achieved by using a 'slash' chord, i.e a triad superimposed onto a bass note.

Fig 6.11 G11 (F/G) arpeggio and chord

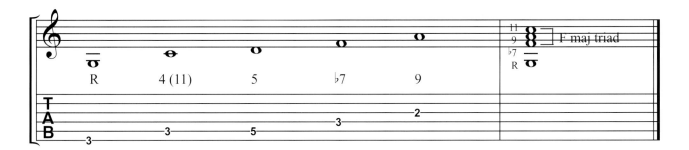

Slash chords are so-called because their chord symbol is written as two letters separated by a 'slash' (as in F/G). The left-hand symbol indicates a triad while the right-hand symbol indicates a bass note. So our G11 chord is frequently described as F/G, which as you can see above, is essentially G9sus4 since there is no third present in the voicing. There are no hard and fast rules regarding the correct symbol to use for this frequently used chord, you are just as likely to see it written as G11, F/G, G9sus4 or even Dmin/G. Just remember that you will achieve the best voicing by superimposing a triad with its root a tone below the dominant chord e.g. for G11 play an F triad over the G root = F/G.

Because the eleventh chord contains no third, it is a benign dominant that exerts far less pull to the tonic than a regular dominant; the absence of the third means that the unsettling tritone interval is no longer present, making the chord more stable.

In Chapter 2 we explored the potential of using the 'Dorian up a fifth' when improvising over dominant chords. This Dorian mode and related minor seventh arpeggio are perfect for creating cool licks over a dominant eleventh when played a fifth higher. By applying this technique you are effectively treating the V11 chord as IIm7 – we explored the special relationship between the II and V chords in Chapter 4 (figure 4.5).

Frequently, eleventh chords are used in a dominant pedal 'vamp' sequence in the major key, often alternating between the dominant eleventh (V11) and the tonic major seventh played over the dominant pedal bass note:

Fig 6.12 **Dominant eleventh vamp**

In this situation you can create cool melodic licks by ignoring the V11 chord altogether and just playing tonic major scale phrases as demonstrated in figure 6.13. Notice how the lick is constructed by essentially ignoring the fact that the sequence is based on G9sus; the lines are created by 'thinking' in C major and focusing on C major chord tones. Bass players seldom 'walk' through sequences such

Fig 6.13 **C major lick over F/G vamp**

as this and will usually stick to a G pedal note (so-called because the bass note remains constant as the chords above change).

The first tune in this chapter, 'Wake-Up Call', will enable you to fully explore 9th and 11th tensions when soloing and comping along with the backing track.

11 Wake-Up Call

Phil Capone

♩ = 160 swing

Half-time feel

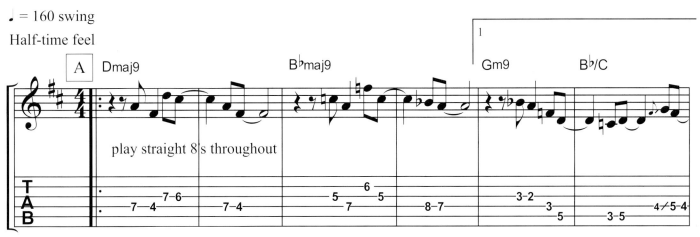

play straight 8s throughout

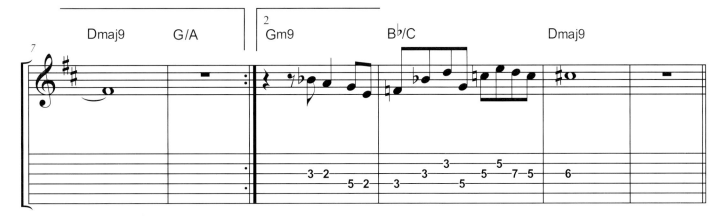

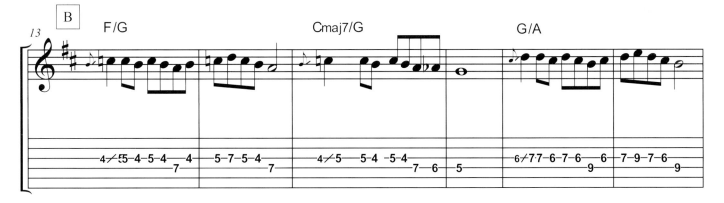

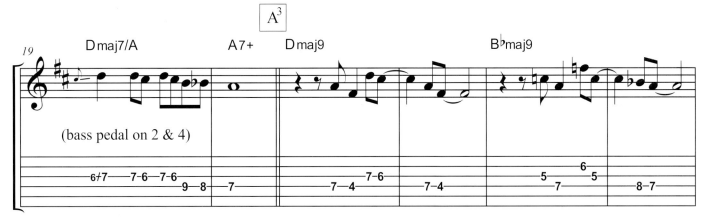

(bass pedal on 2 & 4)

© 2007 Schott Music Ltd, London

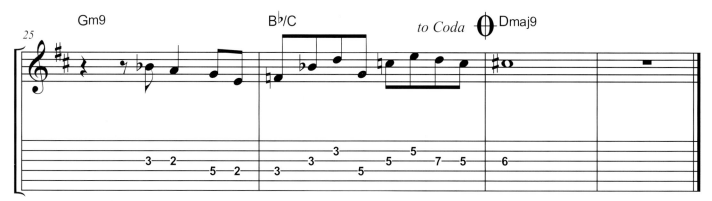

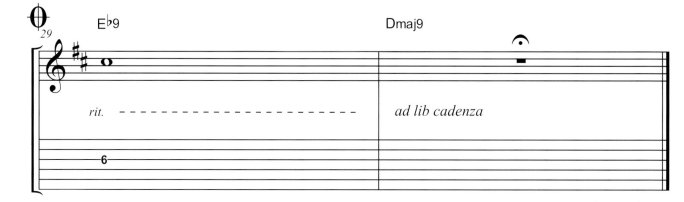

Wake-Up Call – solo

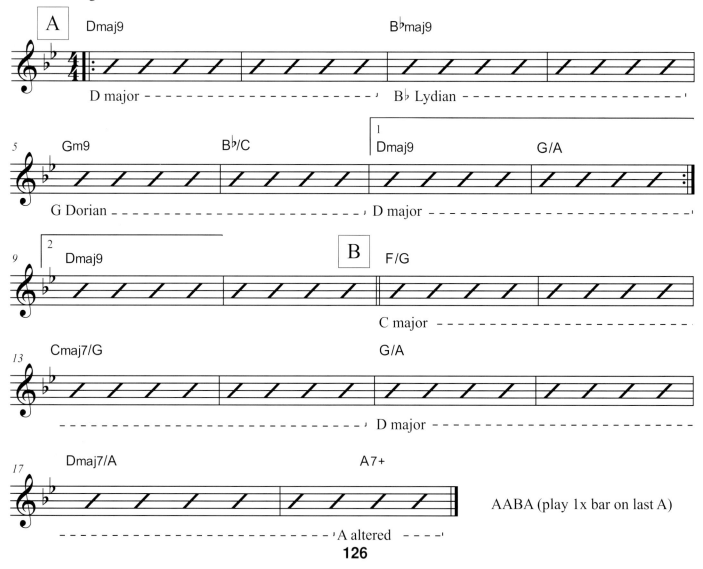

AABA (play 1x bar on last A)

Checkpoint

Swing vs. Straight Eighth Notes

This tune should be played 'straight', i.e. without swinging the eighth notes, giving the tune a contemporary slant. This may take a little practice, but it's much easier when the bass player plays a half-time groove without walking, as in this tune.

Half-time grooves are frequently used to create contrast between different sections of a tune; with the 'B' section often reverting to the familiar walking bass groove. However in this tune the 'B' section uses a dominant pedal to create contrast. Avoiding swing clichés results in a distinctly 'European' (as opposed to 'American') feel.

European jazz was given worldwide exposure by the famous ECM record label in the 70s (the German company was founded in 1969 by **Manfred Eicher**) and was responsible for launching the careers of many famous musicians including **Pat Metheny**, **John Abercrombie**, **Keith Jarrett** and **Dave Holland**. Musicians will often refer to an 'ECM vibe' or 'ECM groove' when a tune is to be played with a European feel.

Arpeggios

The solo chord chart indicates the best scale choice beneath each chord; but in order to explore the ninth sound when improvising you should use the appropriate major/minor seventh arpeggio as your note pool:

Dmaj9   ⟶   F♯min7 arpeggio
B♭maj9   ⟶   Dmin7 arpeggio
Gmin9   ⟶   B♭maj7 arpeggio
B♭/C   ⟶   Gmin7 arpeggio
G/A   ⟶   Dmin7 arpeggio

In the 'B' section use the two scales (and corresponding maj7 arpeggios) as indicated. The final A7♯5 chord lasts for just two beats – you probably won't have time to fit in the altered scale so try squeezing in a few notes from the B♭min/maj7 arpeggio instead (see Chapter 1, figure 1.17).

Since the altered scale is based on the seventh step of the melodic minor scale, the tonic minor arpeggio can always be used a half-step above an altered chord to achieve cool altered tensions.

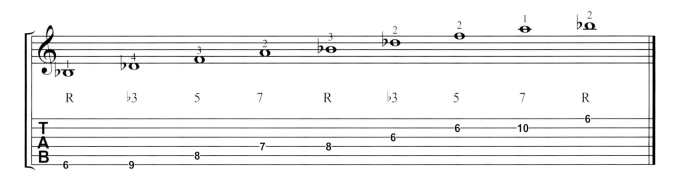

Non-Diatonic Major Sevenths

When confronted with a non-diatonic major seventh chord (i.e. B♭maj7), always use the Lydian mode as your first scale choice (see Chapter 3). Remember that this scale has a raised 4th step (♯11) and you can always use the minor pentatonic down a half-step from the chord's root (i.e. for B♭ Lydian play A minor pentatonic).

Assignments and Improvisation Tips

1. When you are creating a more open soundscape, try to avoid playing too many voicings – a 'four in the bar' swing comp is also a definite no-no!

Instead linger on the full sounding ninth voicings by playing them as block chords or arpeggiating a few notes and letting them ring:

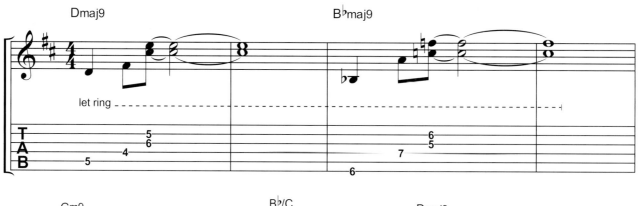

2. Analyse every chord sequence you are confronted with and see if you can spot any shared chord tones. You will often find at least one note in common between chords that might at first seem totally unrelated. These shared notes are invaluable when improvising – you can use them to play a sustained note or repeated lick through the chord change. The example above

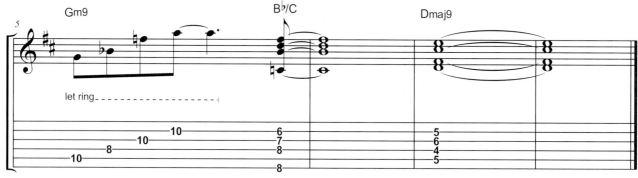

illustrates how, despite the fact that Dmaj9 and B♭maj9 might seem unrelated, they both contain the notes D and A.

3. When you're soloing, try switching between swing and straight 8's – this will add an extra dynamic to your improvising. The best way to learn this technique is to start by practising scales and arpeggios. Set your metronome to half your intended tempo so that you can set it to play on beats 2 and 4 only. Then try practising any scale or mode ascending swing and descending straight.

4. Memorise the chord sequence! The importance of this cannot be stressed enough – you cannot improvise effectively if you are reading the changes. The more tunes you memorise the easier learning new ones will become. Don't forget that you can think through the changes away from your instrument – try to think in roman numerals and not chord symbols!

The Dominant 7th Minor 9th Chord

The minor ninth is an extremely dissonant interval when played on its own; but when added to a dominant seventh chord it creates extra tension for an enhanced 'pull' back home in a perfect cadence.

It's exactly the same as cooking with hot chillies – you wouldn't pick one up and eat it raw, but chop it up and mix it with your food and it adds an exciting dash of spice! Figure 6.14 illustrates the G7♭9 chord in close position voicing, i.e. as stacked thirds, complete with arpeggio.

Fig 6.14 G7♭9 arpeggio and chord

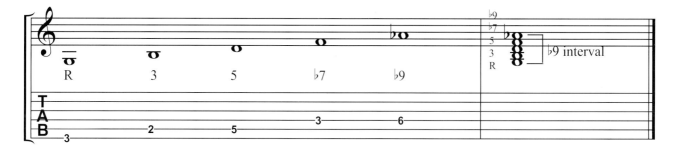

The closest scale that fits the dom7♭9 chord is the Phrygian dominant mode, as demonstrated in figure 6.15. Notice that the parent scale (a dom7♭9 is the mode's tonic chord) adds only two colour tones to the note pool (since there are now five chord tones).

The enharmonic equivalent of the minor sixth is the augmented fifth, so this has been added in parenthesis next to the scale tone.

Fig 6.15 Relationship between G Phrygian dominant and G7♭9

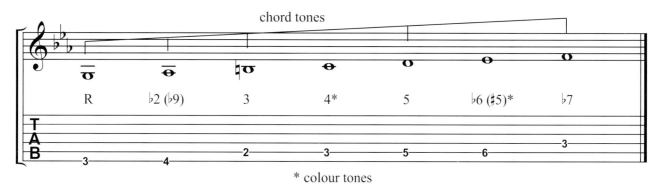

* colour tones

Because the Phrygian dominant is derived from the harmonic minor scale (Chapter 2), you could be forgiven for thinking that the dom7♭9 can only be used in minor cadences. But don't forget that although the major II – V is rarely used in a minor resolution, the minor II – V (i.e. IImin7♭5 – V7♭9) is frequently encountered as a major resolution.

This minor to major relationship has a long history in classical music where it is referred to as the *tierce de Picardie* – and was previously encountered in Chapter 4. The resolution tendencies of the IImin7♭5 – V7♭9 can be clearly seen in figure 6.16 (notice that the ♭9 resolves downwards to the fifth in both instances):

129

Fig 6.16 **Minor II – V – I resolution tendencies**

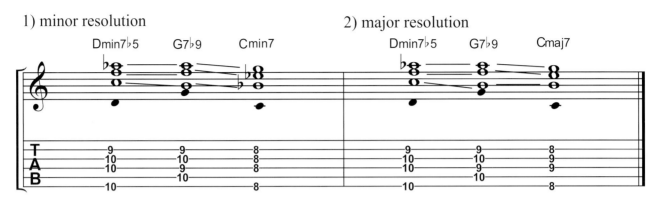

By extending the G7♭9 arpeggio in figure 6.14 above, the full shape one, two octave arpeggio is achieved. The lowest ♭9 interval has been included in this arpeggio to illustrate how the dom7♭9 arpeggio is the same as a diminished seventh arpeggio that starts a half-step above its root:

Fig 6.17 **Two octave G7♭9 arpeggio – shape one**

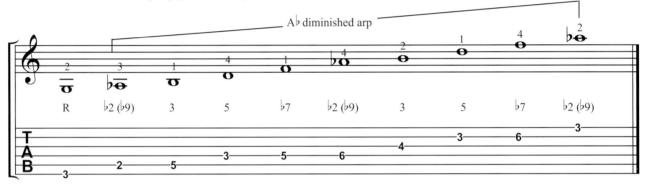

This effectively means that you can play a diminished seventh arpeggio (a symmetrical arpeggio constructed entirely from minor thirds) starting on any of the chord tones of a dom7♭9 apart from the root note (playing a diminished seventh arpeggio from the root would simply create G diminished):

	G	B	D	F	A♭
Chord tones	R	3	5	♭7	♭9
Play arpeggio		B°	D°	F°	A♭°
Tones created			3 5 ♭7 ♭9		

Because the diminished arpeggio is symmetrical (superimposing additional thirds above the four-note arpeggio produces no further chord tones), starting the diminished seventh arpeggio from any of the dominant's chord tones produces the same notes. Aside from being an interesting musical anomaly, this has many useful applications when improvising.

Because of the dom7♭9's close relationship to the diminished arpeggio, the root is often omitted in chord voicings, enabling a four-note diminished shape to be used instead. Figure 6.18 demonstrates how these are used to create five EDCAG guitar voicings:

Fig 6.18 Five four-note G7♭9 'EDCAG' voicings

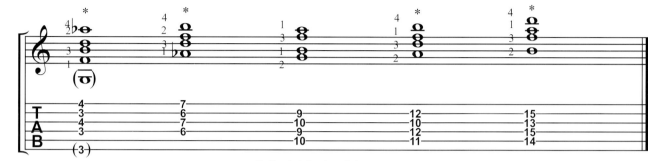

* diminished voicings

The Dominant 7th Augmented 9th Chord

While the dom7♭9 chord has a distinctly jazzy flavour to it that you may not have encountered before, the dom7♯9 is also widely used in blues and rock. In fact you have probably already played it many times, even if you don't refer to it by its overlong official title!

In rock music this is often called the 'Hendrix chord' since it features heavily in many of his famous tunes, the most obvious example being 'Purple Haze'. However this chord pre-dates the late 60s and the birth of heavy rock; it became part of standard jazz vocabulary as early as the 1940s during the be-bop era.

At first examination this chord appears to contain both the major and minor third and it is often (incorrectly) described as a dom7♭10 (the 10th = 3rd + 1 octave). Below is the close position dom7#9 voicing and accompanying arpeggio:

Fig 6.19 G7♯9 arpeggio and chord

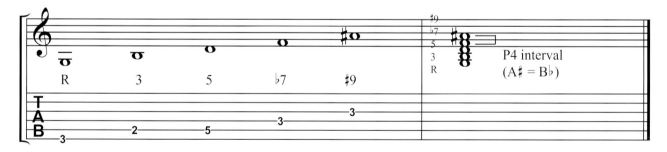

Unusually, the dom7♯9 voicing contains the interval of a perfect fourth between the top two voices. This is because the chord has been created from a 'genetically engineered' mode: the altered scale or Super-locrian mode (created from the seventh degree of the jazz melodic minor scale). Figure 6.20 is a reminder of how the altered scale's fourth degree is enharmonically relabelled as a major third to enable the scale to host a dominant tonic chord (for a deeper explanation of this see Chapter 2).

131

Fig 6.20 The altered scale

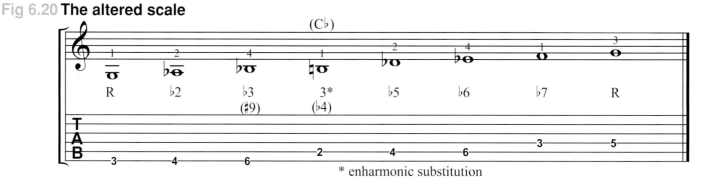

* enharmonic substitution

As before, the one octave arpeggio is extended to create a full shape one 'EDCAG' G7♯9 arpeggio:

Fig 6.21 Two octave G7#9 arpeggio – shape one

As with all of the previous ninth chord arpeggios, only shape one of the EDCAG five shape system is given in this chapter. You should, if you have worked methodically through the book, now possess the skills to create the remaining four arpeggio shapes. Don't forget that you can achieve this very easily by referring to the closest 'parent' scale or mode and simply omitting the 4th and 6th intervals. Because the altered scale is technically a minor scale (see Chapter 2), it requires slightly different

treatment to complete the metamorphosis to a 7♯9 arpeggio. The ♭2nd and ♭6th should be omitted and the ♭5 raised a half-step.

The five EDCAG shapes for G7♯9 are given in figure 6.22. Notice that the root is seldom included in shape one – this prevents the voicing from sounding too 'muddy' particularly when voiced low on the fretboard as in this instance. Shape four is the familiar 'Hendrix shape'.

Fig 6.22 Five four-note G7♯9 'EDCAG' voicings

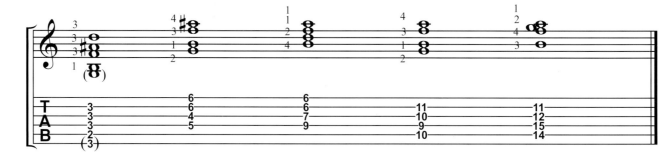

The following tune is inspired by jazz standard 'Out Of Nowhere'. Some chords have been removed (several of the non-diatonic II – Vs in the original sequence have been paired down to a single Vdom9) to allow a full exploration of the shifting dominant ninths when soloing and comping.

'Out Of Nowhere' was written by **Johnny Green** and **Edward Heyman** in 1931 and it has been recorded by countless seminal jazz musicians including **Charlie Parker**, **Django Rheinhardt**, **Joe Pass**, **Kenny Burrell** and many others.

12 Into Somewhere

Phil Capone

♩ = 170 swing

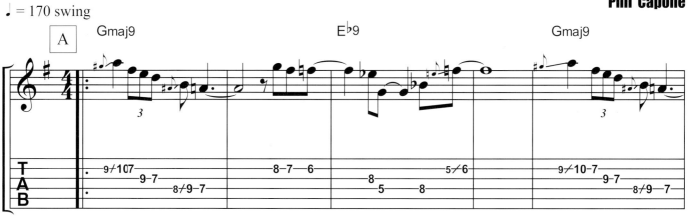

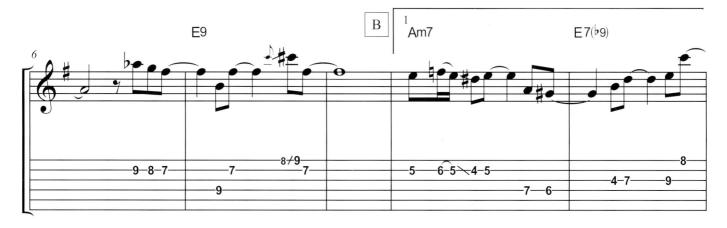

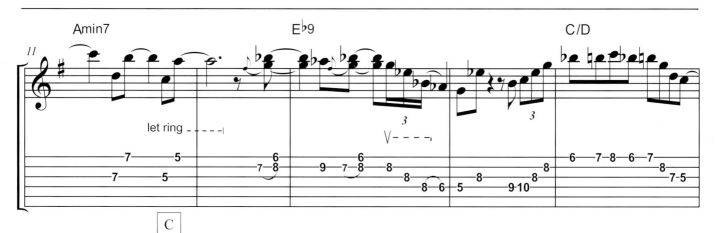

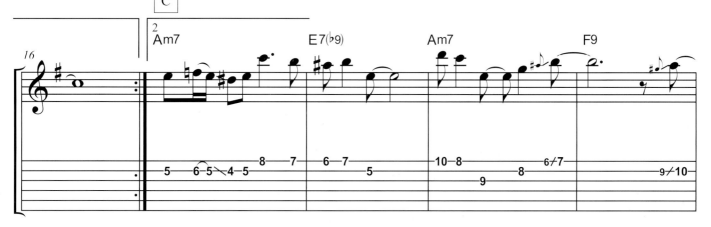

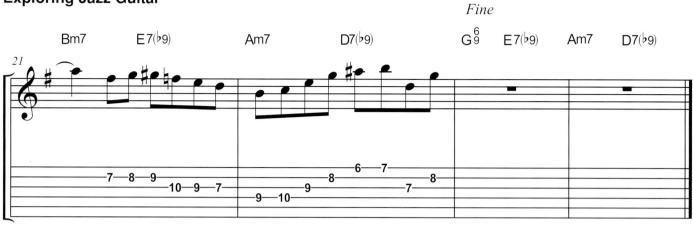

Fine

Solos on form
after last solo *D.C. al Fine*

Into Somewhere – solo

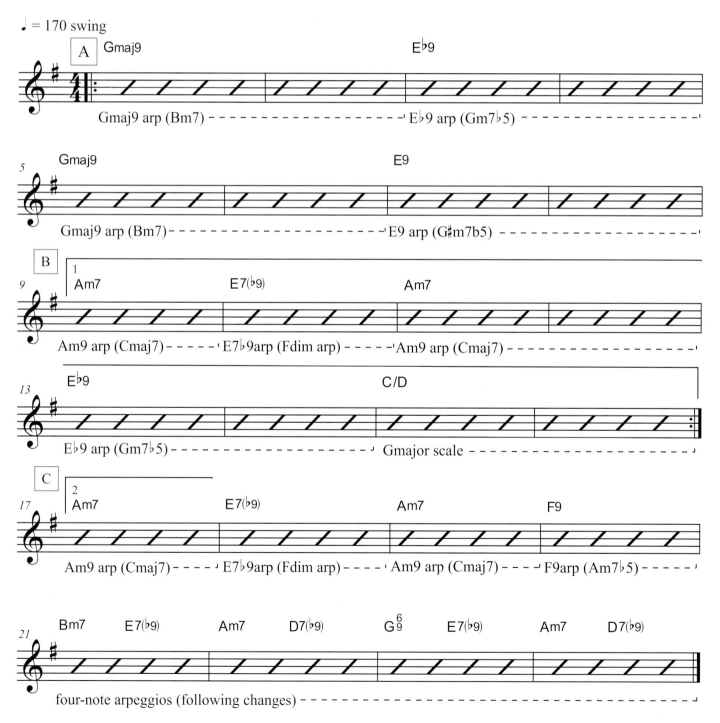

Checkpoint

Song Form

The 32-bar song format used in this tune is a repeated 16-bar section with different first and second time endings. Although not as frequently encountered as the more common 'AABA' 32-bar form, it can be found in many famous standards including 'How High The Moon' ('Ornithology'), 'Here's That Rainy Day', and 'Groovin' High'. This form is best described as 'ABAC': a repeated 'A', a first time ending 'B', and a second time ending 'C'. Each section is eight bars in length with the final section 'C' pushing towards the tune's conclusion.

The last two bars in this form usually feature a turn-around to steer the song back to the start of the chorus. Just as in 'Happy To Be Blue' in Chapter 3 (p. 63), the final turnaround in this tune is omitted to provide a pick-up into the solo.

Below is an example of a typical pick-up phrase. Notice that, although this is played unaccompanied, the phrase is usually conceived as one bar of Gmajor and one bar of D7 – the D7 lick creating tension before the full rhythm section's re-entry at the start of the solo chorus.

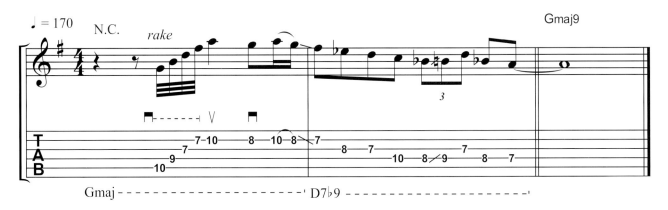

Highlighting the 9th

By chromatically approaching the ninth (i.e. from a half-step below), the quality of the interval is enhanced. This technique is used frequently in the tune; in fact the very first note is the chromatically approached ninth, A, as you can see here.

* chromatic approach of ninth

To heighten the ninth sound when you are soloing, remember to try sliding into it chromatically from the note below. However, although this technique works equally well on min9, dom9 and min9 chords (which all contain a major ninth), it is not so effective when applied to dom7♭9 chords. The minor ninth contained within this chord is already a very strong chord tone and so does not need additional enhancement.

Root Position Comping

To create a more traditional feel for this tune, a 'four in the bar' comp is used on the backing track. The best voicings to use for this style of accompaniment are root position, shape one and four chords. Try to avoid any dissonant voicings that contain minor or major seconds (e.g. min9 and maj9 shape five), these are more suited to creating a 'spacey', contemporary soundscape.

Finally, remember to create a percussive comp by keeping the chords staccato (momentarily releasing the pressure of your fretting hand between each strum of the chord). Don't forget that the swing groove will be enhanced if you slightly accent the chords on beats 2 & 4 (mimicking the drummer's backbeat hi-hat pattern).

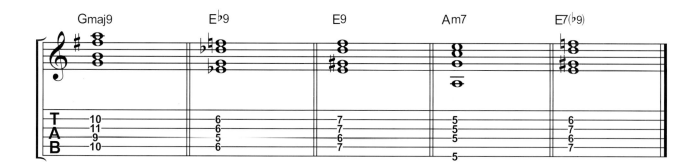

Assignments and Improvisation Tips

1. Turnaround licks. The last eight bars of this tune consist of two sets of turnarounds. Both of the sequences are very similar, the first being III – VI7 – II – V7 and the second a classic I – VI7 – II – V7 turnaround.

When confronted with quick sequences such as this, you have little option but to 'go with the flow' of the changes and play harmonically. If you try and bluff your way through a string of II – V sequences (which is what this effectively is), you are not going to create a convincing solo. Jazz mu-

sicians constantly practise negotiating turnarounds and consecutive II – Vs to enable them to play more freely when improvising. Remember that improvising is 99% perspiration and 1% inspiration!

To help you to start building your own library of III – VI7 – II – V7 licks the 'lick builder' below illustrates some useful approaches to arpeggio practice. Each example starts on a different chord tone – this will empower you to start from any chord note, not just the root.

a) lick starting on root

b) lick starting on third

c) lick starting on fifth

2. When you are practising it pays to keep some kind of recording device handy (this can be a simple dictation machine – you don't need 64-bit quality for jotting down ideas!). In this way you can record new licks as soon as you think of them, transcribe them and then put them into a 'lick scrapbook' that should be revised several times a week. Remember that each new lick should be played in different octaves and different positions on the neck (in each of the five 'EDCAG' shapes) in preparation for transposition to new keys.

3. Always use a metronome – I can't stress this enough! Always use a metronome when you practise. This includes your 'lick builder' practice!

4. The best way to come up with new ideas is to sing them, period. If you can sing a phrase over a III – VI – II – V progression it will not only be musical, but also free from the preconceptions and pattern-based approach that all guitarists fall into when playing the guitar. Your voice is the most important instrument you own, so use it!

Mike Stern used to play a Fender Telecaster until Yamaha built him this Signature Series PAC 1511MS Pacifica model – the two are now inseparable! The guitar features a solid Ash body and maple neck that has a curved 'vintage Fender' radius of 7¼ inches.

7: Time Signatures & Rhythms

The Jazz Waltz

Unlike common time (4/4), the jazz waltz (3/4) has only three beats in the bar, is generally played with 'swing eighths' phrasing, and usually features heavy syncopation. The history of the waltz dates back to early 17th-century Austria and Bavaria, where it started life as a simple folk dance. It has a long history in classical music, and is famously associated with the Austrian composer Johann Strauss, who elevated it from a peasant dance to entertainment for the royalty of the day.

In today's popular music 3/4 time is unfashionable and rarely used, and so it can take a little time to adjust to this unfamiliar metre, particularly when improvising.

3/4 and 4/4 are both categorised as simple time because the metre (or beat) of each bar can only be counted one way, i.e. as three or four beats in each bar. Figure 7.1 below illustrates the differences between 3/4 and 4/4 time.

Fig 7.1 Comparison of 4/4 and 3/4 time

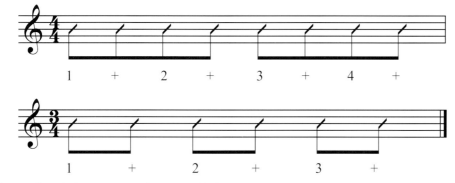

In one bar of 3/4 there are only six eighth notes – which means that two four-note arpeggios will no longer conveniently fit one bar. By extending the octave (i.e. using six notes from a two octave seventh arpeggio) it is simple enough to create a six-note eighth-note grouping. However, many musicians prefer to create harmonic extensions and introduce syncopation into their improvisation by using two triads per bar. In the previous chapter we explored the potential of superimposing arpeggios on the third step of each chord type to create colour tones and/or chord extensions (see Chapter 6). By superimposing the appropriate triad on the third of the chord, interesting lines can be created (especially when mixed with the root position triad):

Fig 7.2 Using double triads

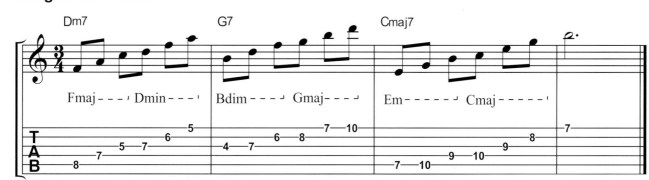

3/4 Comping Rhythms

It's not just improvising that needs a careful re-think either – there are also comping issues! In figure 7.3 the basic jazz waltz comp has been annotated. This is shown complete with bass notes, and sounds cool played fingerstyle (use your thumb for the bass notes and remaining fingers for the chords).

Once you have acclimatised yourself to the groove, try omitting the bass notes and playing just the chords on beat 2 and 3 (don't forget to do this with a metronome!).

Fig 7.3 Basic comp rhythm

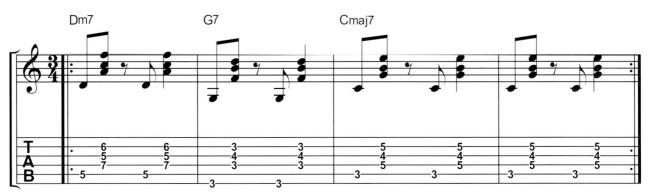

When two chords occur in the bar, the simplest solution is to play them as two dotted quarter notes. This creates a polyrhythm by creating a 'two over three' phrase (a sort of reverse quarter note triplet).

This figure can also be used for breaking up the regular jazz comp – both techniques are illustrated in figure 7.4:

Fig 7.4 Playing 'two in the bar'

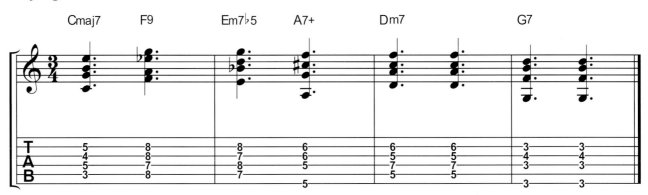

Another characteristic of the jazz waltz is that it can often sound similar to 12/8, i.e. a shuffle groove. This interpretation is only effective when applied to up-tempo tunes such as 'Someday My Prince Will Come'. This tune originally featured on the soundtrack of Disney's 1937 animated movie *Snow White And The Seven Dwarfs*, but only became a jazz classic after being given the **Miles Davis** treatment on his 1961 album of the same name. It's now a fre-

quently 'called' jazz standard (hip jazz-speak, man... in other words it's likely to be called by the bandleader on a gig!).

Up-tempo jazz waltzes can often sound more like 6/8 than 3/4. This ambiguity can be heightened with sparse, melodic ideas that are created by avoiding eighth-note lines. This can be extremely effective, particularly when used over a vamp section:

Fig 7.5 **Long note phrasing**

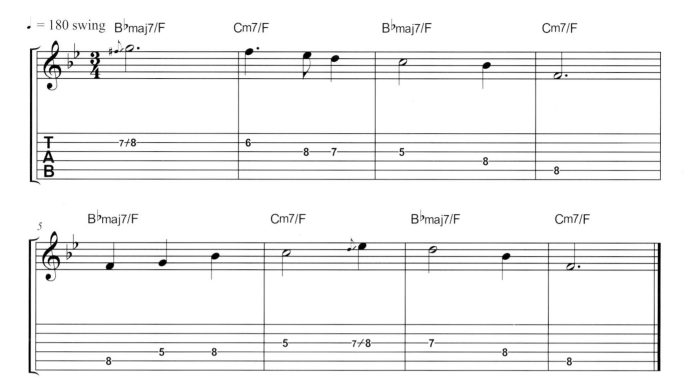

Compound Time

So far all the tunes and examples in this book have concentrated on simple time, i.e. a time signature where the basic beat can only be divided into two parts. The most frequently used simple time metres are 4/4 and 3/4, where the beat is a quarter note. In compound time each beat is a dotted quarter note, which can be divided into three eighth notes. If this is starting to sound over-complex, don't panic!

Since most guitarists cut their teeth on the blues, it's likely that you are already familiar with compound time. The most common compound time is 12/8 – think slow shuffle blues, around 60 b.p.m. That's quite slow, so you'd probably automatically start to tap your foot in eighths, three to the beat. That's what the drummer will be playing on their ride cymbal. Figure 7.6 illustrates the different subdivisions involved in 4/4 and 12/8.

Fig 7.6 **Comparison of 4/4 and 12/8 time**

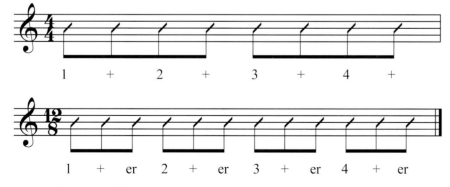

After 12/8 time, the most frequently encountered compound time signature in jazz is 6/8. Just like 3/4, it also contains six eighth notes per bar. However, the principle difference is that 6/8 has a loping

'two' feel, rather than a distinct 'three' groove as found in 3/4. Figure 7.7 overleaf illustrates how these subdivisions compare:

Fig 7.7 Comparison of 3/4 and 6/8 time

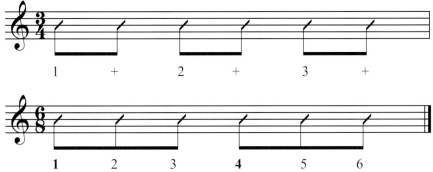

Once again, the late jazz genius **Miles Davis** provides us with the definitive example of a typical 6/8 jazz groove with his tune 'All Blues'. This was originally featured on what many regard as the greatest jazz album of all time, *Kind Of Blue*. Released in 1959, like many Davis albums it marked a new direction in jazz with its modal soundscapes and explorations. Unfortunately there was no guitarist on this album! Interestingly, Davis only regularly featured guitar players in his line-ups from the late 60s onwards. The first album Davis recorded with a guitarist was *In A Silent Way* (1969) and featured the seminal talents of **John McLaughlin**.

6/8 Comping Rhythms

The comping rhythms that we explored earlier in 3/4 can also be used in 6/8, but don't forget that the effect against the groove will be subtly different (e.g. the dotted quarter note pattern loses its polyrhythmic quality in 6/8). However it is more effective, particularly when comping behind a soloist, to use swing phrasing as you would in 4/4.

The principle difference is that in 6/8, eighth notes are played straight and it's the sixteenth notes that are swung (since these provide the offbeats). Figure 7.8 illustrates a comping idea for four bars of G7 (as in the first four bars of 'All Blues'). Notice the dominant chord (D7♯5♯9) in the third bar. As the late great **Joe Pass** would insist, you can always use the dominant of any major, minor or dominant chord when comping or improvising to create extra harmonic movement.

Fig 7.8 6/8 comping rhythms

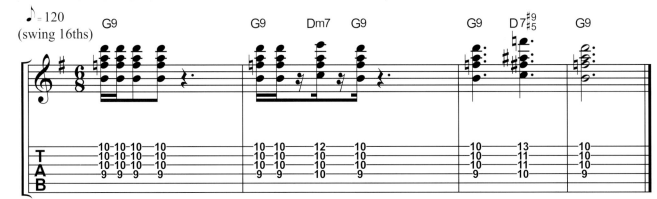

The following tune, 'Three Into Six' is based on the chord sequence of 'Someday My Prince Will Come'. Although written in 3/4, the solo choruses are played with a pseudo 6/8 feel (e.g. with the bass walking). Effectively this means that two bars of 3/4 become one bar of 6/8 while the harmonic rhythm remains the same (i.e. the chords change at the original pace).

13 Three Into Six

Phil Capone

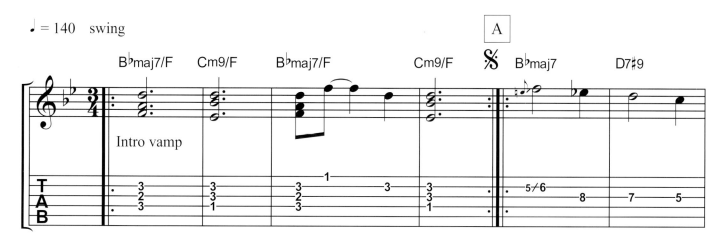

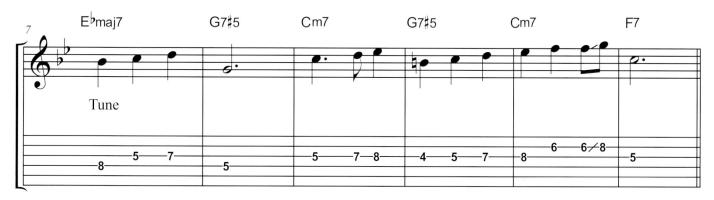

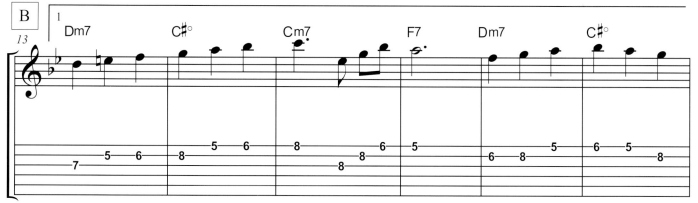

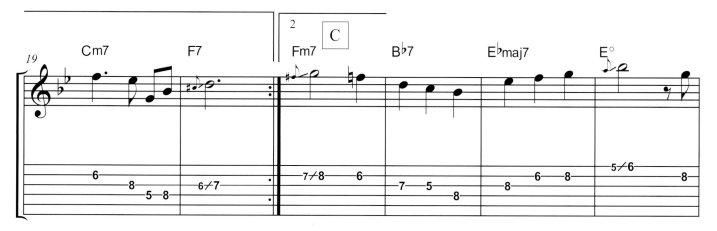

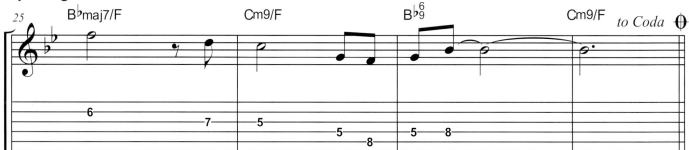

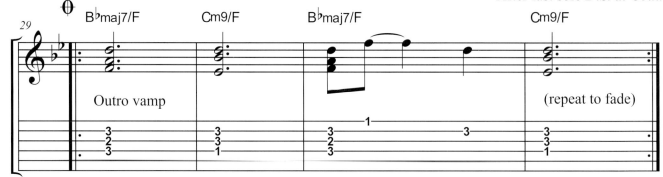

Three Into Six – solo

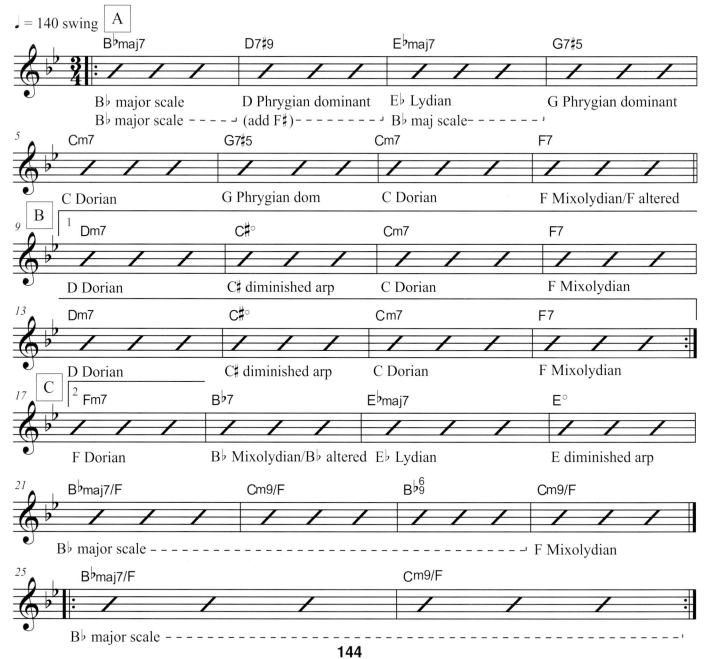

Checkpoint

Intro & Outro Vamp

Vamps are sometimes played before the first and after the last statement of the 'head' (i.e. the tune). They are generally improvised (i.e. not part of the tune) and often based on a dominant pedal (the root of the V chord in the key), with alternating tonic/dominant voicings superimposed on top. Normally the instrument that plays the 'head' will also improvise over the vamp. The use of a vamp at the beginning and end of a tune gives the arrangement a cyclic quality that the usual head-solos-head arrangement doesn't.

In this tune the tonic chord and IIm9 chord (remember this is a close relation of V7) are superimposed over the pedal to create a suspended dominant texture. This is the same as the dominant eleventh vamp we studied in Chapter 6. The tonic major (B♭) is the most effective scale to use when improvising. You can also use the example from figure 7.5 earlier in this chapter to start your intro.

Song Form

'Three Into Six' is based on a 32-bar 'ABAC' song form. This structure was also used in 'Into Somewhere' in the previous chapter (p. 133). However the slower tempo, 3/4 time signature, use of the vamp and the unusual opening chord sequence all contribute to making this arrangement sound very different.

When you're learning a new standard, before you attempt to work it out on your guitar or reach for that 'fake book', try listening to an early recording of the tune (preferably with vocals). Try figuring out the form of the song in your head as you listen to the root movement; in this way you will be learning the song in the traditional way, by using your ears! This is a far more effective method than reading the tune from a fake book – you can always use this later to tie up any melodic loose ends and gain tips on alternate harmonisations.

Dealing With Unusual Chord Progressions

The opening four bars use seemingly unrelated chords to create a climbing sequence. Closer examination will help you to understand each chord's function and enable you to improvise over the sequence more effectively. In the example below you can see that in the first three bars, only the F♯ of the D7♯9 chord is a non-diatonic note. This gives you two options: 1) treat the chords modally, applying a scale to each chord as indicated; 2) alter the tonic scale to incorporate any non-diatonic notes contained in the sequence as shown in the second row of options (notice the use of the E♭ maj9 voicing that maintains the F pedal note as the top voice).

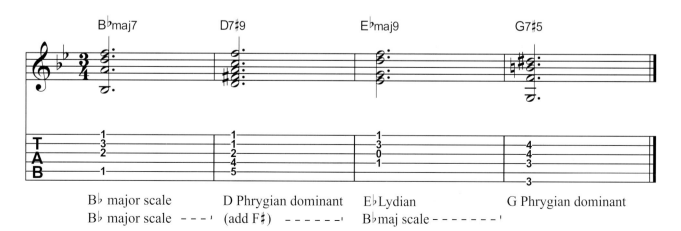

Altering the tonic scale to reflect non-diatonic chords in this way is the 'old-fashioned' approach, and much closer to how jazz musicians would have originally 'thought' when improvising. This method is essentially more melodic, since you are 'thinking' in the tonic key. By contrast, the modal approach treats each chord as an individual pocket of harmony; every chord type is allocated with its own specific mode(s). The downside of this technique is that it can result in a mish-mash of unrelated phrases blasted over each chord with no connecting ideas, which does not create an appealing solo! The most interesting aspect of both techniques is that they actually provide identical note pools as you can see below:

B♭ major (change F to F♯)	
D Phrygian dominant	D – E♭ – F♯ – G – A – B♭ – C
B♭ major	
E♭ Lydian (diatonic mode IV)	E♭ F G – A – B♭ – C – D

Since both approaches generate the same notes, we can deduce that the important element is actually the philosophy behind each improvisational approach. Neither is correct nor incorrect since both systems produce the same note pool – it is how you will be 'thinking' that is important. Ideally you should use a combination of both approaches to achieve the ultimate results. In this way you will gain the best of both worlds: melodic sensibility with natural phrasing across the changes, plus modal intellectuality that allows the individual character of each chord to be emphasised if desired.

Assignments and Improvisation Tips

1. Learn the changes! I keep 'banging on' about this, but it is really crucial to creating an interesting and 'liberated' improvisation. If you have studied the chord sequence you will have understood where all the natural tension and release points occur, and you will be able to reflect this in your solo. However if you are simply reading the chords off a sheet when you improvise then you won't be thinking ahead – you will be constantly 'chasing' the harmony rather than anticipating it.

2. You can use a diminished arpeggio or diminished scale starting on the diminished chord's root note (see Chapter 5). Don't forget that you can start your scale or arpeggio on any of the chord tones (i.e. in rising minor thirds).

3. It's important to tackle those 'difficult to improvise over' sections head on. If you have any kind of 'looping' equipment handy (e.g. effects pedal, headphone amplifier, computer software), then use it when you practise. Just record a short section of the chords, say four bars, loop it and jam over the top. Looping pedals are now available as compact, relatively inexpensive, units and are extremely handy tools for developing your improvising skills.

The Bossa Nova

The bossa nova evolved in Brazil during the late 1950s, and quickly became one of the most popular jazz styles of the day. An infectious blend of Brazilian samba rhythms and cool jazz harmony, this new music heralded hope for jazz musicians as audiences and record sales were in decline by the early 60s.

One of the important pioneers of this style was Brazilian guitarist/pianist and composer **Antonio Carlos Jobim**. He wrote many bossa nova standards including 'The Girl From Ipanema', 'Wave', 'How Insensitive' and many others. However it was jazz guitarist **Charlie Byrd** who was largely responsible for popularising the bossa nova style. Byrd had been fascinated by the new music while touring South America and his subsequent album *Jazz Samba*, recorded with **Stan Getz**, became an instant hit on its release in 1962.

Traditionally, the bossa nova is played on a nylon string, or classical guitar – perfect for creating smooth comping textures and gentle improvisations. This doesn't mean you can't play it on an electric; it can sound just as cool as long as you use a mellow jazz 'clean' tone. Throughout his career, fusion maestro **Pat Metheny** has recorded many Latin-flavoured tunes on his trademark Gibson ES175.

Unlike most jazz styles (where the saxophone and piano outrank the guitar), the guitar is an integral part of the bossa nova. In fact, many of the early recordings of the style were performed as simple guitar and vocal arrangements. Traditionally this accompaniment is played fingerstyle; it's well worth learning the rhythm this way first – not only will you find the technique invaluable in a duo situation, you'll also gain a deeper insight of the rhythm. In an ensemble situation, you simply omit the bass notes and play the chords with a pick.

Figure 7.9 illustrates two examples of the bossa rhythm, the first is the original and simplest form, and the second features additional syncopation. The bass notes in both examples are achieved by alternating your 1st finger between the 5th and 6th strings. Don't forget that Latin music is played 'straight', so don't swing those eighths, man! Aim for a lilting, swaying groove, making sure those bass notes are played right on the beat.

Fig 7.9 Bossa nova comp

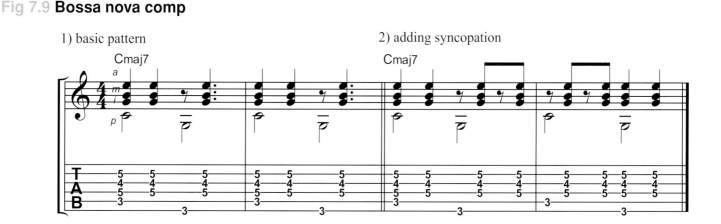

The second example in figure 7.9 is a two-bar rhythmic pattern. Most chord changes occur one per bar, so the chord change in the second bar must be anticipated before the bass note as demonstrated in figure 7.10:

147

Fig 7.10 Comping with 'one per bar' changes

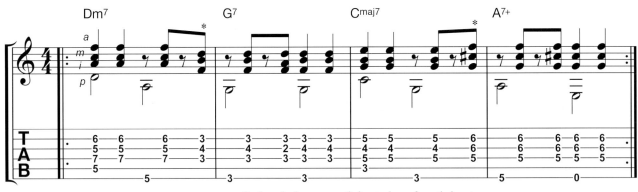

* chord change anticipated on fourth beat

Frequently 'two per bar' changes will be encountered, particularly during turnaround sections. These can be especially tricky since it's important not to disrupt the flow of the bossa rhythm with clumsy or delayed changes. Figure 7.11 illustrates a bossa 'two per bar' turnaround with the chord anticipations occurring at the end of the first bar and halfway through the second. It's often best to practise the upper part of the comp (i.e. the chords) separately and add the bass notes once you're fluent.

Fig 7.11 Comping with 'two per bar' changes

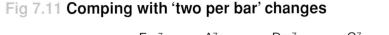

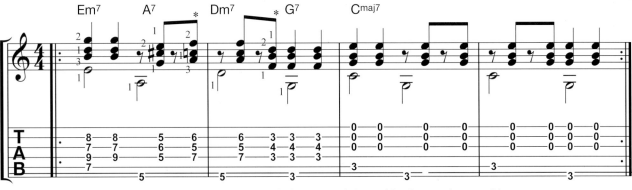

* chord change anticipated in first and second bar

The Jazz Samba

The samba is an Afro-Brazilian music that originated in Rio de Janeiro during the early 20th century; it still reigns as one of the most popular styles of music in Brazil to this day. The traditional Samba is reliant on the use of percussion and heavy syncopation; even the bass will frequently anticipate chord changes half a beat early. The jazz samba is really an approximation of this music rather than an authentic Latin style. Nonetheless it retains the cut-time (two beats per bar) metre and fast tempos of the original – creating fiery, exhilarating grooves that are fantastic for soloing.

Cut-time is a term used to describe music written in 2/2 time, i.e. two half-note beats per bar. A bar of 2/2 contains exactly the same note values and subdivisions as a bar of 4/4, it's just generally played at a faster tempo – using half-notes as the metre makes counting time easier. Because each beat requires a subdivision of four to create four eighth notes, it should be counted in exactly the same way as sixteenth notes in 4/4 time (using 'e', '+' and 'er' to vocalise the subdivision). Figure 7.12 opposite illustrates the similarities and differences between 2/2 and 4/4.

Fig 7.12 Comparison of 4/4 and 2/2

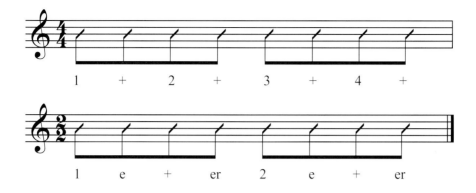

In Brazil the 'samba' is a carnival event performed by a collective of musicians and dancers; it's a lively, intense music that works best in a group setting. With its heavy reliance on percussion, the samba demands a 'busy' rhythm section to bring it to life. So in contrast with the laid-back bossa nova comps above, the rhythms annotated in figure 7.13 are most effective in an ensemble setting and should be played with a pick.

Don't forget that the samba is a fast, 'cut-time' (2/2) rhythm, so set your metronome to give you a half-note pulse (around 60 b.p.m. to begin with) and make sure you tap your foot two times (not four!) per bar. It's also important to maintain a constant alternate strumming pattern throughout – this will help you to keep in time and achieve a strong, driving comp.

Fig 7.13 Samba comping rhythm

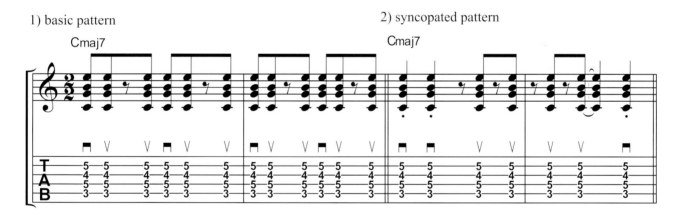

Double Stop Comping

Double stop comping involves sounding two chord notes (usually the third and fifth) against a descending/ascending line on the fourth string. This pattern is frequently used by guitarists, either as an intro riff or comping pattern, and is derived from a montuno piano vamp originally used in Cuban and salsa music. Normally the double stop is played on the second and third strings where a minor third interval can be played by simply barring across the strings. This riff is extremely effective when used over a static minor chord or an unresolved, repeating II – V sequence. Figure 7.14 demonstrates the riff within the context of a repeated II – V sequence in G major. It could also be played over an A minor chord, with the chromatic line descending to the major sixth interval. To achieve a strong groove, use alternate picking throughout (your picking hand should move constantly – just lift it off the strings to 'play' the rests).

149

Fig 7.14 Double stop 'montuno style' comp

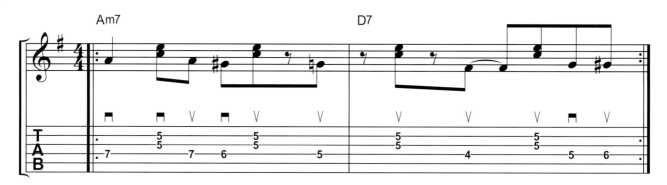

When confronted with a static major chord, this pattern can be easily adapted as shown in figure 7.15. Alternating between the major 7th and 6th of the chord creates the lower notes of this vamp:

Fig 7.15 Static major comp

An interesting contrast is created when 'Latin' and 'swing' grooves are used in the same tune. This works well with 'AABA' structures, where the 'A' is played 'Latin' (which can be bossa or samba depending on the tempo), and the 'B' is played 'swing'. Standards such as 'On Green Dolphin Street', 'Caravan', 'Mambo Inn' and 'Nica's Dream' are favourites for this treatment. The solo choruses can mirror the 'head' and alternate between Latin and swing, or simply stick to a Latin groove until the end of the solo section.

The following tune contains both Latin and swing sections during the head and solos, and is ideal for practising all of the Latin rhythms we have explored in this chapter. The shift between Latin and swing may sound complicated, but after a little practice you will soon find yourself changing effortlessly between them.

Phil Capone

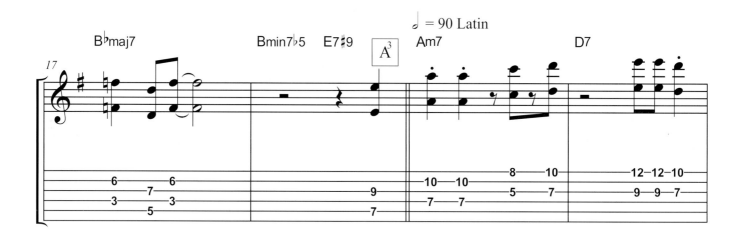

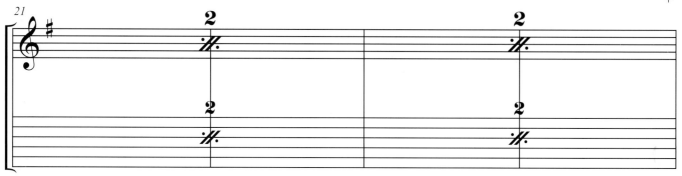

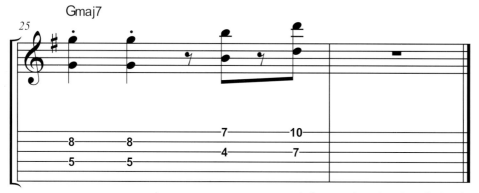

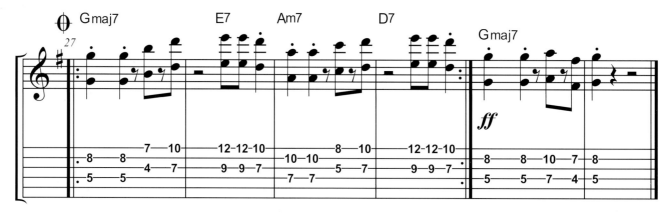

The Latin Quarter – solo

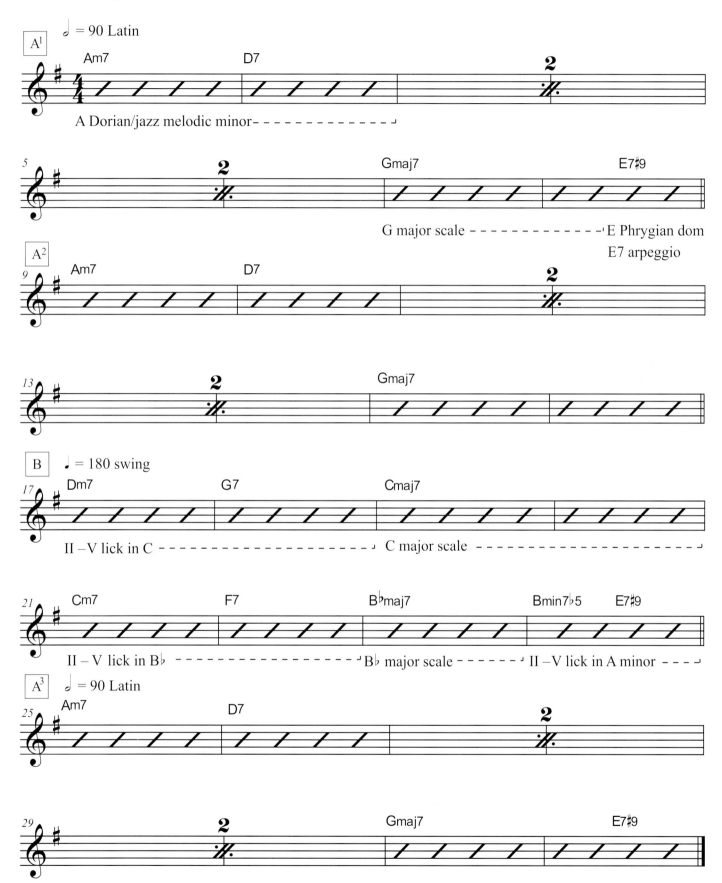

Checkpoint

Song Form

By now you should be quite familiar with the 'AABA' song form. The difference here is that the 'A' section is played with a samba groove, while the 'B' section is played swing time. If it's written on a chart at all (on a gig, it's normal for the bandleader to tell the musicians when a Latin tune has a swing section), it is only indicated by the words 'Latin' or 'swing' at the start of the appropriate sections. Although the tempo doesn't actually change between sections – it simply moves from cut-time (2/2) to common time (4/4) – tempo indications have been added to remind you to 'feel' each groove appropriately. In other words you should be tapping your foot to a half-note 90 b.p.m. pulse in the samba sections, and to a quarter-note 180 b.p.m. pulse in the swing sections.

Octaves

This isn't the first tune that you've encountered octave lines in; they were also featured in 'Happy To Be Blue' (Chapter 3, p. 63), 'Hitting The Changes' (Chapter 4, p. 83) and 'Sunnyside Up' (Chapter 5, p. 104). However as 'The Latin Quarter' is played at a bright 180 b.p.m., you will need to keep your octave 'chops' in tip-top shape to play this tune cleanly.

So let's review a few octave tips and tricks. Remember that octaves should not be fingerpicked, but played simultaneously with your thumb (the original **Wes Montgomery** technique), or a pick (back off your guitar's tone control to keep the sound mellow). Playing them in this way achieves a much hipper and more rhythmical sound; the downside is that you have to damp the open strings very carefully. The position of your 1st finger is crucial – by laying it flat across the strings you will be able to use the tip and side of your finger to damp all the surrounding strings while simultaneously fretting the lower octave.

Don't forget to use your 1st and 4th fingers to play octaves where the higher note is on the 1st and 2nd strings, and your 1st and 3rd fingers where the higher note is on the 3rd and 4th strings. The example below annotates the tricky 'B' section of 'The Latin Quarter' with correct fingering – this is especially important during the quick jump across the strings at the end of each phrase. You may find it helpful to visually concentrate on just the upper note – as long as your fingering is correct the lower octave should take care of itself! Notice that the second phrase is identical to the first; simply shift it down two frets.

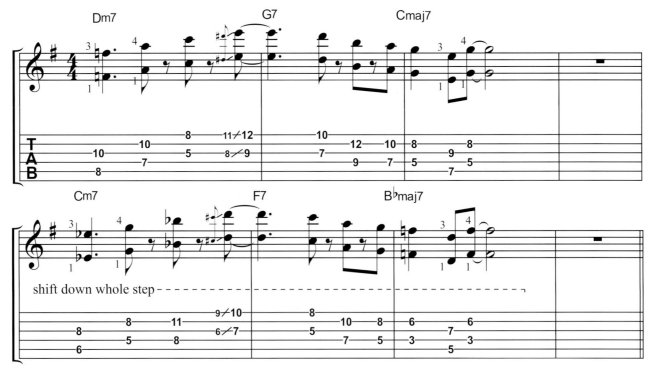

Latin To Swing

Practise moving between the Latin and swing feels with a metronome before you play with the backing track. This will ensure that you have fully internalised the contrasting grooves and help you to achieve a confident and musical delivery. Previously we have practised swing grooves with the metronome ticking away on beats two and four. However because the 'A' section is cut-time Latin, you will need to practise both sections against a half-time click on beats one and three. This is less conducive to conjuring up a swing backbeat so the swing groove will come entirely from you! Try and imagine a hi-hat on the backbeat during the swing sections – this will help you to generate the swing groove.

Double Stop Comp

The double stop 'montuno' vamp can be used throughout the 'A' sections in the tune and the solo choruses. The examples given in figure 7.14 and figure 7.15 earlier in the chapter will work perfectly. However you will need to adapt the second example to include the E7♯9 chord in the first time bar:

Don't use the motuno vamp exclusively – you should also incorporate the jazz samba comps illustrated in figure 7.13. All of these rhythms are improvised by Latin musicians, they are never notated – so they are not set in stone! Feel free to adapt them to create your own variations, but only try this once you have fully mastered the original rhythms.

Assignments and Improvisation Tips

1. Memorise the rhythms. The best way to learn anything is to do it 'little and often'. You will internalise these rhythmic patterns much more effectively if you clap/tap/sing them away from the guitar. Why not take time out to tap a couple of rhythms when the commercials come on TV, when you're stuck in a traffic jam, or simply doing chores!

2. Try anticipating the changes between Latin and swing – don't be simply 'dragged along' by the rhythm section! You should also practise changing from Latin to swing with the metronome alone. You don't have to play the full arrangement, just use the II – V vamp of the 'A' section to start with. Don't forget that you will need to imagine the hi-hat backbeat to give you a half-note click on beats one and three:

(play each section 4 times)

3. As indicated on the solo chart, you can use the A jazz melodic minor scale over the Am7/D7 vamp. Although the G♯ (natural seventh) technically clashes with the G (flattened seventh) of the Am7 chord, you can create some very cool licks by using the G♯ as a chromatic approach note or as the lower note of an encirclement. The first example below shows the G♯ used as a chromatic approach note, 'pulling' up to the root from a half-step below it. In the second example, the G♯ is the lower chromatic note in an encirclement figure (encirclement means playing the note above and below the target note to highlight it).

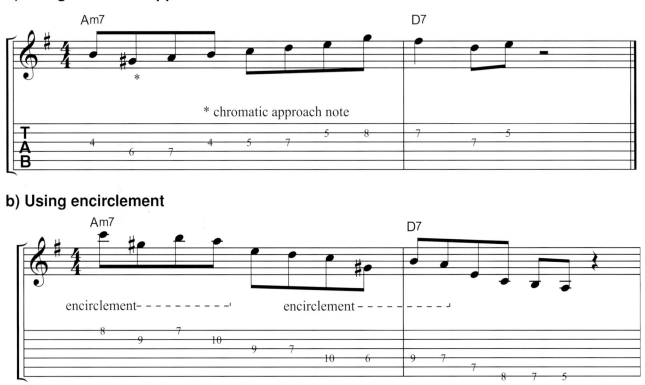

a) Using chromatic approach

* chromatic approach note

b) Using encirclement

4. Try shifting II – V – I ideas down a whole step. It is a common mistake of many musicians to assume that any kind of repetition is a bad idea. In fact the exact opposite is true; for the listener, repetition actually creates a more interesting improvisation. Repeating ideas will give your solo more structure and melodic unity, thus avoiding the dreaded collection of unrelated licks that many inexperienced improvisers use to create a solo. So when you're presented with the opportunity to simply transpose an idea and repeat it, note for note, as in the 'B' section of this tune, grab it with both hands and milk it!

8: Turnarounds & Rhythm Changes

The I – VI – II – V Progression

The I – VI – II – V progression has already featured in a couple of the tunes in this book as a 'turnaround' sequence. Turnarounds are generally no more than two bars long (i.e. two beats per chord), and occur in the last two bars of a chorus. Their principle function is to push the harmony back to the start of the progression, while simultaneously creating some harmonic interest. A turnaround is seldom written into a chart, and is usually improvised 'on the fly' by the rhythm section.

Because there is no melody note to consider, turnarounds can be entirely diatonic, or they can contain nothing but altered dominants – so it is important that you are fully aware of the harmonic

possibilities. Sometimes you will be free to dictate the harmony, and sometimes you will need to follow the bass player's root movement, or the pianist's comping. The old adage 'what you don't know, you can't hear' is certainly true in this instance. By studying all of the harmonic variations (and training your ear to recognise them), you will be well equipped to deal with any turnaround sequence.

The original I – VI – II – V progression is entirely diatonic and so contains no secondary dominants. Because of the close relationship between chord I and VI (VI is the relative minor of I), the diatonic sequence could be considered as one bar of a I chord followed by a II – V. Figure 8.1 illustrates the progression using four-note seventh chords:

Fig 8.1 The diatonic I – VI – II – V progression

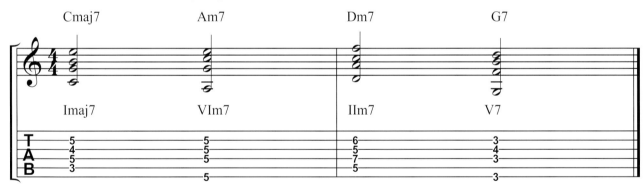

Since the diatonic turnaround contains no notes outside of the key, it would be theoretically possible to solo over the progression using only the parent major scale. However by disregarding the constantly changing pattern of chord and colour tones, this would not create a particularly convincing or musical improvisation.

So to familiarise yourself with these changing chord tones, the sequence should be practised in three stages. Start with the guide tones approach using

mainly half notes (this produces surprisingly melodic results) as demonstrated in figure 8.2(a). In figure 8.2(b) ascending and descending four-note arpeggios (notice the stepwise resolution to the next chord tone) are used against each chord. Finally, figure 8.2(c) introduces encirclement (this can be diatonic or non-diatonic) and chromatic approach notes to heighten each chord change.

157

Fig 8.2(a) I – VI – II – V practice techniques – guide tones

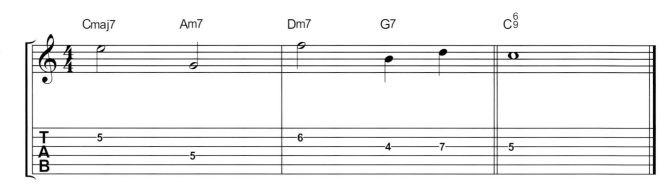

Fig 8.2(b) I – VI – II – V practice techniques – four-note arpeggios

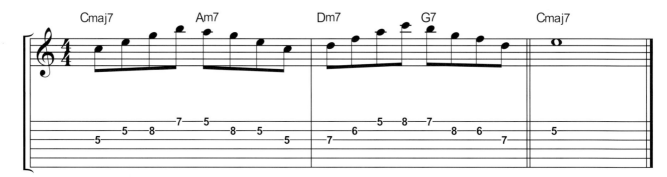

Fig 8.2(c) I – VI – II – V practice techniques – adding encirclement and chromatic notes

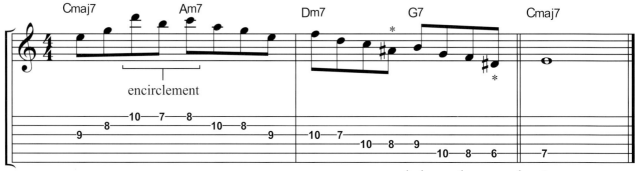

* chromatic approach notes

Introducing Non-Diatonic Chords

Usually the first chord to be 'tweaked' in a I – VI – II – V progression is the VI chord. Changing this chord into a functioning secondary dominant introduces additional tension into the sequence. So our progression becomes I – VI7 – IIm7 – V7 – a sequence now containing two perfect cadences as you can see in figure 8.3. Notice that the fifth of each chord has a solid notehead since it exerts no resolution tendencies.

Fig 8.3 Resolution tendencies of double perfect cadence

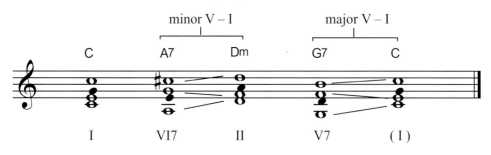

The inclusion of the VI7 chord, where it now functions as the dominant of chord II, should be reflected in the soloist's improvisation. In dealing with the chord sequence of 'Three Into Six' in the previous chapter (p. 143), we discovered that there are two basic paths that an improviser can follow when dealing with non-diatonic chords. The first is to simply alter the relevant tonic scale tones to accommodate the chord; the second is to apply the notes of the relevant mode. Although the modal approach is not particularly useful when dealing with a series of chord changes, it is still important to understand which mode relates to each chord. This will enable you to apply the appropriate extensions/colour tones when comping or improvising.

Because VI7 is functioning as the V7 of a minor chord, the first scale choice would be the Phrygian dominant derived from the fifth degree of the harmonic minor. By also altering the tonic scale to incorporate the raised third of the VI7 chord you can see that two subtly different modes are generated:

C major (C to C♯) ⟶ (A-B-C♯-D-E-F-G) = D melodic minor

A Phrygian dominant ⟶ (A-B♭-C♯-D-E-F-G) = D harmonic minor

The scale generated by altering the tonic major scale is actually the fifth mode of the jazz melodic minor, often called the Mixolydian ♭13 since it is the same as the Mixolydian mode with a minor sixth instead of a major sixth (remember that extensions and colour tones are applied as compound intervals hence the sixth is reinterpreted as a thirteenth).

So to summarise, when adding colour tones to chord VI7 when comping or improvising, the ninth can be major (diatonic) or minor (non-diatonic). Adding a minor ninth (i.e. A7♭9) will create a darker chord progression with a heightened 'pull' to the minor II chord. Figure 8.4 illustrates both chord types with their accompanying modes. Don't forget that A Mixolydian ♭13 is simply the C major scale with the root sharpened. Interestingly, although the A9 chord and accompanying mode are more diatonic than A7♭9 and the Phrygian dominant, it is the latter chord and mode that sounds more 'inside' when used in a I – VI7 – II – V7 sequence. This is because the Phrygian dominant is usually the first scale choice in any minor perfect cadence.

Fig 8.4 **Scale and chord choices for chord VI7**

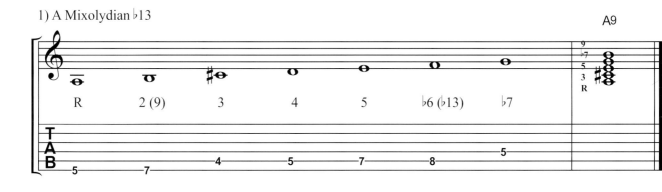

1) A Mixolydian ♭13

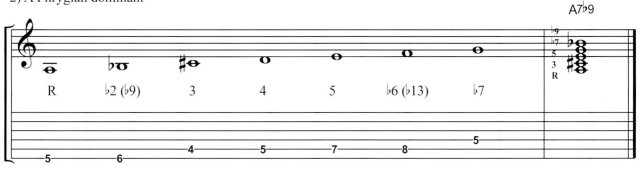

2) A Phrygian dominant

In a quick moving set of changes there's simply not enough time to apply modes to each chord. However, armed with the information above, you are now free to experiment by adding ninths to the VI7 and V7 chords using an arpeggio-based approach. In figure 8.5, the first example incorporates the major (diatonic) ninth in an arpeggio lick. Apart from the C♯, all the other notes are diatonic to C

major. The second example flattens the ninth over the A7 chord, creating a smoother lick that moves effortlessly through the changes. Notice that the ninth of the G7 has also been flattened, mirroring the treatment of the VI7 chord. Remember that you can always add non-diatonic tensions in a perfect cadence that is returning 'home' to the tonic chord.

Fig 8.5 **Adding 9ths to the VI7 arpeggio**

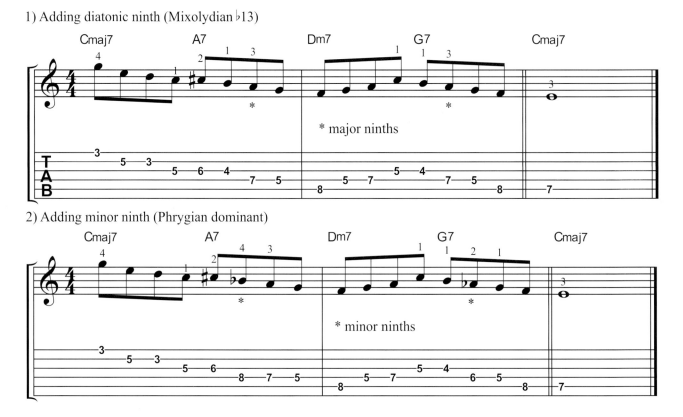

Changing Chord II To A Secondary Dominant

Now that the VI chord has been changed to VI7, the next chord to receive the secondary dominant treatment is chord II, transforming the sequence into a I – VI7 – II7 – V7 progression. Every chord (apart from the tonic major) is now a dominant seventh, creating two sets of chromatic lines between the three dominant chords (figure 8.6): C♯ – C – B and G– F♯ – F. The A7 and D7 are still described as functioning secondary dominants despite the fact that each resolves to another dominant chord instead of a major or minor seventh.

Fig 8.6 **Chromatic lines introduced by II7**

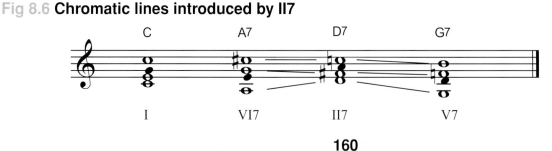

The chromatic resolutions in the sequence make it quite easy to create interesting chromatic phrases. By incorporating chromatic descending guide tones or, more adventurously, a series of chromatic encirclements (figure 8.7), some very hip-sounding licks can be created:

Fig 8.7 Using chromatic encirclement in the I – II7 – VI7 – V7 progression

Using the 'adjusted tonic scale' and modal approaches to improvising over the II7 chord will produce the same results. The Mixolydian mode should be your first choice for improvising over any secondary dominant chord, whether functioning or non-functioning, unless it is resolving to a minor chord.

By applying the mode to our II7 chord, you will be able to see exactly what extensions can be applied to the chord when improvising or comping through a quick moving I – II7 – VI7 – V7 sequence. Notice that the major ninth is the appropriate extension to add to the chord:

C major (F to F♯) ⟶ (D-E-F♯-G-A-B-C)
                              D Mixolydian

Fig 8.8 Scale and chord choices for chord II7

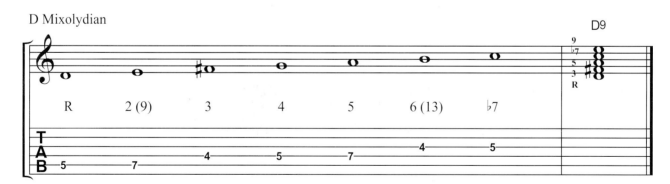

The only scale tone that has to be treated with care in the Mixolydian mode is the 4th interval. This should be used as passing note only – lingering on this interval creates dissonance when sounded against the major third (F♯) of the D9 chord.

Replacing Chord I with Chord III

Because the principle job of the I – VI – II – V sequence is to steer a tune back to the tonic chord, it is sometimes desirable to substitute chord I for chord III. This creates a more interesting sequence and also 'saves' the tonic chord for the resolution at the end of the turnaround.

Back in Chapter 3 we learnt that building a chord on the third step of the major scale created a minor seventh chord (see Chapter 3, figure 3.5 for all seven diatonic major chords). The relationship between chord Imaj7 and IIImin7 was also explored from an improvisational perspective in Chapter 3 (using the minor pentatonic over a major chord), and Chapter 6 (creating ninth chords). Figure 8.9 illustrates the similarity between the two chords – the Emin7 could be viewed as a first inversion (i.e. the third in the bass) major ninth (Cmaj9/E).

Fig 8.9 The relationship between IImin7 and Imaj7

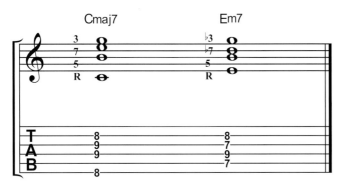

Substituting chord III creates a greater sense of harmonic movement since it now comprises two II – V sequences:

Fig 8.10 The III – VI7 – II – V7 sequence

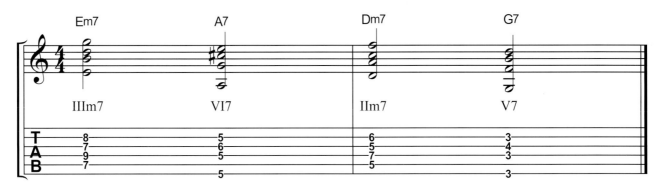

By indulging in a little more harmonic 'tweaking' the sequence can be transformed into a minor II – V followed by a major II – V. Although this is technically 'less diatonic' than the previous sequence, it creates a more colourful and 'jazzy' progression:

Fig 8.11 Enhancing the minor qualities of III – VI7

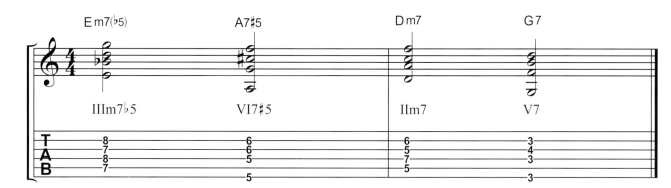

Since it can be approached as two independent II – V progressions instead of four separate chords, this sequence is somehow easier to create flowing lines over than a regular I – VI – II – V. The first example in figure 8.12 illustrates a more conventional arpeggio approach to the sequence. Notice the use of the diminished arpeggio over A7♯5 to create a flat nine lick, and the addition of the flat nine over the final V7 creating a stronger pull 'home'. The second example takes a modal approach, treating the minor II – V as one bar of a minor V7 (don't forget that you can always ignore the II or the V chord) and using the altered scale over the final V7 to create maximum tension before resolving stepwise to the third (E) of Cmaj7.

Fig 8.12 Treating the sequence as a double II – V progression

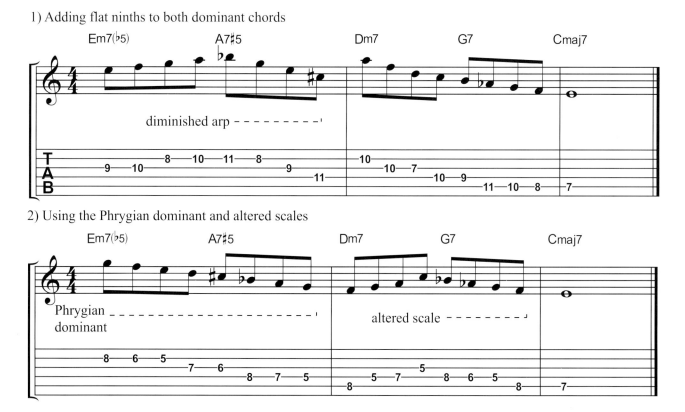

We're not done tweaking the I – VI – II – V sequence yet! Now that we've explored the possibilities of replacing the turnaround's I chord with a III chord, let's see what happens when we change both the II and the III chord into functioning secondary dominants...

Using III7 To Create A Series Of Dominant 7ths

Earlier in the chapter we introduced II7 to add a third dominant seventh chord to our turn-around sequence. By changing the III chord to a non-diatonic secondary dominant, a progression consisting entirely of dominant sevenths is produced. Figure 8.13 highlights the chromatic lines inherent in this progression:

Fig 8.13 Chromatic lines introduced by III7

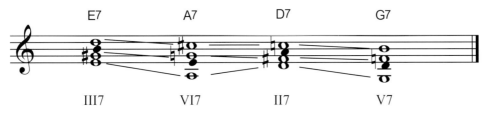

Using our traditional (alter the tonic scale to fit) and modern (modal) approaches to create a note pool for our III7 chord once again produces the same scale:

C major (G to G♯) ⟶ (E-F-G♯-A-B-C-D)
E Phrygian dominant

Because the E7 chord is resolving to a 'minor' dominant (i.e. diatonic to D minor), the Phrygian dominant is the first scale choice for this chord.

Cross-referencing applied modes with the 'altering the tonic scale to fit' approach is a great way to check that you are applying the appropriate mode. Figure 8.14 revisits the lick that was used to create chromatic encirclement over the I – VI7 – II7 – V7 in figure 8.7 earlier. By changing the first three notes to highlight the third (G♯) of the E7 chord, it can easily be modified to fit the III7 – VI7 – II – V7 progression (it's worth remembering that by making slight adjustments you can make your favourite licks work over many different sequences):

Fig 8.14 Using chromatic encirclement over a III7 – II7 – VI7 – V7 sequence

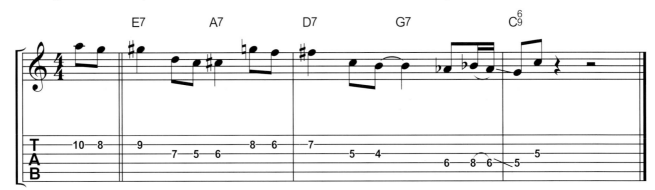

The following tune is based on the chord progression of **George** and **Ira Gershwin**'s timeless standard 'I Got Rhythm'. The chord sequence is commonly referred to as 'rhythm changes' since it has been 'borrowed' and used in countless tunes since the 1930s to the present day. Famous tunes that have been written over this sequence include **Charlie Parker**'s 'Anthropology', **Horace Silver**'s 'Room 608' and contemporary fusion guitarist **Mike Stern**'s 'Good Question'. 'Rhythm Changes' is the benchmark chord progression that every jazz musician needs to master, and it is frequently called on gigs and jam sessions. As you will see, the progression is based on an entire sequence of turnarounds and so provides a challenging improvisational workout.

15 The Twister

Phil Capone

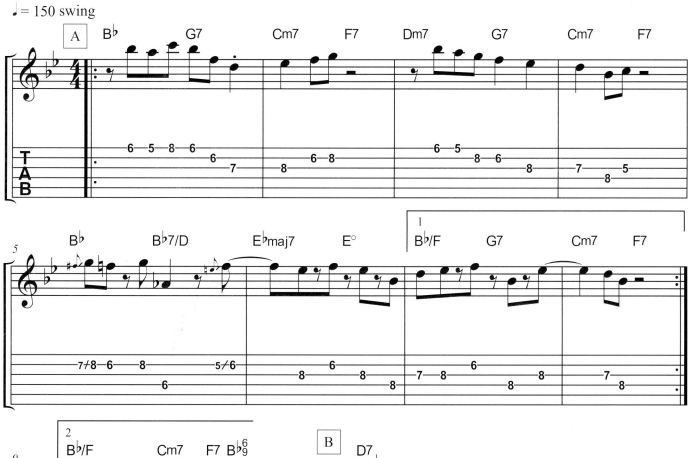

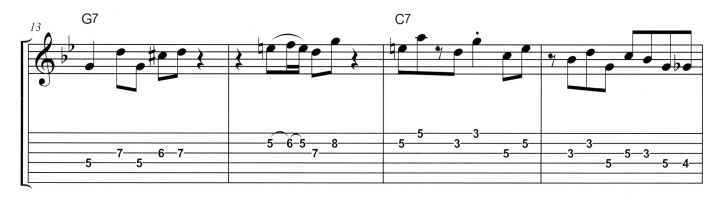

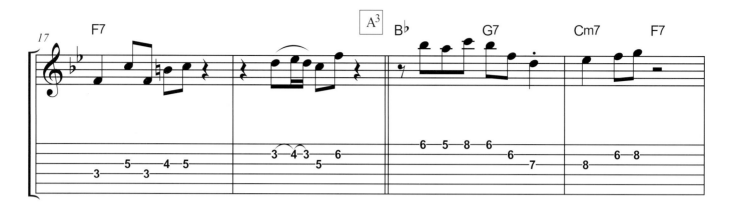

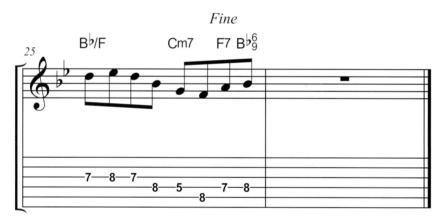

After last solo *D.C. al Fine*

Checkpoint

Historical Perspective

The original chords of **George Gershwin**'s 'I Got Rhythm' have been tweaked and substituted by many great players over many decades. There has always been a compelling fascination about playing over rhythm changes – **Charlie Parker** is said to have practised this sequence in every key. Along with the 12-bar blues, it remains the most common chord progression for a jazz musician to practise, and countless players have obsessed about creating ever more adventurous and fluent improvisations over this challenging progression.

Since there are many different ways to play rhythm changes, the chords in this version have been kept as authentic as possible while remaining hip to the most frequently used changes. Although we will consider a few obvious substitutions, there would be no point in compiling an endless list of possible alternative chords; the best way to learn new harmonisations is through listening to the recordings of the great players and playing with other musicians. Once you have become familiar with the basic changes, you will find that learning alternative substitutions won't be a big deal.

The Twister – solo

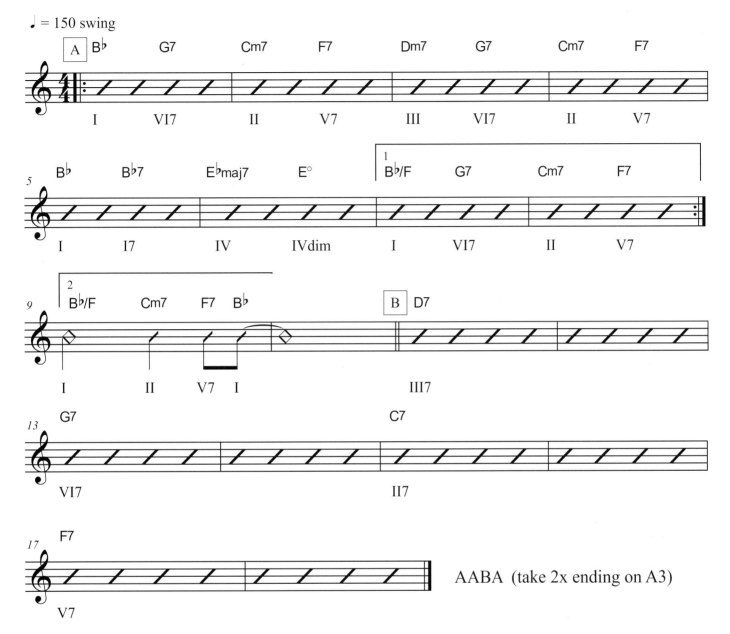

AABA (take 2x ending on A3)

Song Form

'The Twister' is constructed using an 'AABA' 32-bar song form, usually with a first and second time end-ing. The entire chord sequence is nothing more than a series of turnarounds in the tonic key; these can be broken down into three simple sequences:

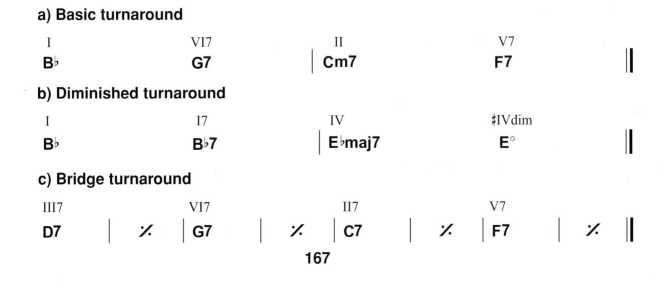

a) Basic turnaround

I		VI7		II		V7	
B♭		G7		Cm7		F7	

b) Diminished turnaround

I		I7		IV		♯IVdim	
B♭		B♭7		E♭maj7		E°	

c) Bridge turnaround

III7			VI7			II7			V7		
D7		✗	G7		✗	C7		✗	F7		✗

167

The basic turnaround above is the primary component of the 'A' section. It is repeated in bars 3 and 4 (with chord III being substituted for chord I) and again in bars 7 and 8 (where chord I is generally played with the fifth in the bass).

The diminished turnaround is a familiar sequence in older standards and many blues tunes, and it's actually very similar to the basic turnaround – E♭ maj7 (IV) is the relative major of Cm7 (II) so it performs the same harmonic function. The E diminished (♯IVdim) exerts a strong pull 'back home' to the I chord just as the F7 (V) does, and so it is also performing an identical harmonic function. For this reason many players will superimpose a I – VI – II – V lick directly over the diminished turnaround. This means that the 'A' section could be conceived as a basic turnaround repeated four times.

The bridge sequence creates the illusion of modulation when it hits D7. However it is no more than III7, the first chord in yet another turnaround – this time using a sequence of dominants to pull back to the tonic. Notice that the change in harmonic rhythm creates the contrast, since each chord in the sequence lasts for two bars instead of just two beats.

Snakes and Ladders

There are many twists and turns in the rhythm changes progression, and just as the bucking bronco will easily throw the wannabe rodeo star, so the inexperienced improviser is unlikely to 'hang on' to this sequence for too long.

The most important thing to remember is to keep track of where you are – the 'A' section can easily sound like an endlessly repeating turnaround; it is very easy to get lost. Don't worry too much about clashing substitutions or chord extensions when you are improvising either. As long as you are sticking to the changes and hitting the key resolution points, you will produce a convincing solo. It's actually cool to superimpose substitutions when the rhythm section is just playing regular changes – it adds exciting tensions and that's what jazz is all about.

The example below illustrates a hypothetical scenario with two seemingly conflicting sets of changes used by an accompanist and an improviser. Essentially these are two separate routes with occasionally crossing paths, but eventually arriving at the same destination:

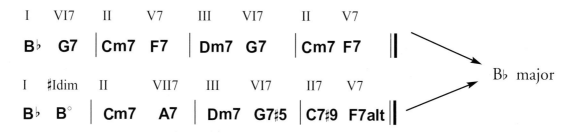

The top line of chords represents the accompanist's conservative interpretation of the changes (always keep it simple when comping – don't push the soloist around); the second line represents how an improviser might 'think' as they 'blow around the changes'. The B diminished chord in the first bar is simply functioning as G7♭9 (remember that the diminished arpeggio can be used on any of the dominant's chord tones apart from the root – in this case it starts on the major third).

The A7 at the end of the second bar is functioning as the dominant of Dm7. Although a lick based on A7 will clash with the underlying harmony it adds momentum by pushing the solo towards the Dm7 at the start of the next bar. The improviser 'thinks' of the remaining three chords as dominants with extensions, so creating additional tensions before the resolution to the tonic chord in bar five.

Assignments and Improvisation Tips

1. Sing the root movement. This is the best way to internalise the sequence and will also help you to get a good overview of each eight-bar section. In fact, why not go the whole hog, add a metronome backbeat on beats 2 & 4, and sing through the full 'AABA' cycle – you'll find this an invaluable warm-up to practice.

2. The major pentatonic can be used to improvise over the 'A' section. The original 'I Got Rhythm' tune was a simple, pentatonic-based melody. Kicking off your solo with a few nicely phrased pentatonic ideas will not only sound cool, but will also allow you to build the harmonic complexity of your improvisation from a simple starting point:

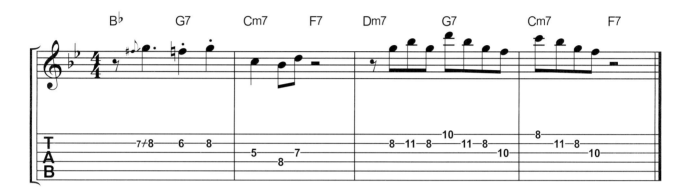

3. You can create cool bluesy vibes by superimposing the B♭ blues scale or the B♭ minor pentatonic at any point in the 'A' section. However don't use them exclusively – otherwise you'll just sound like a rock guitarist trying to play jazz! The example

below illustrates how bluesy licks can be applied throughout the 'A' section. Notice the use of the D natural (major third), which subtly reaffirms the major tonality at strategic points:

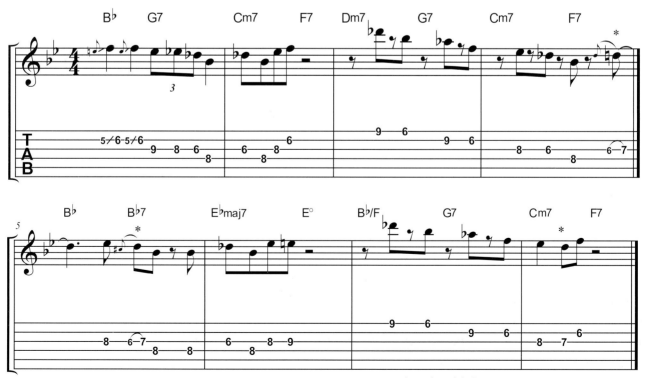

* major third

169

3. Back in Chapter 5 we saw how the C jazz melodic minor scale could be played a fifth above a dominant seventh to create F9♯11 colour tones. The scale created from the fifth step of the jazz melodic minor is called the Lydian dominant mode since it shares the ♯11 (♯4) interval with the Lydian mode but also has a ♭7 degree:

Lydian mode:

1 - 2 - 3 - ♯4 (♯11) - 5 - 6 - 7

Lydian dominant mode:

1 - 2 - 3 - ♯4 (♯11) - 5 - 6 - ♭7

It's best to think of this mode as the Mixolydian with a raised 4th step. Wherever the Mixolydian works, the Lydian dominant will work too, and will add an extra *frisson* of harmonic excitement with its dark ♯11 colour tone. The 'B' section of rhythm changes becomes hipper and more 'bop' sounding if you use the Lydian dominant over each dominant chord. The example below shows a D Lydian dominant lick played over the D7 and a G Lydian dominant lick played over the G7 in the first four bars of the bridge:

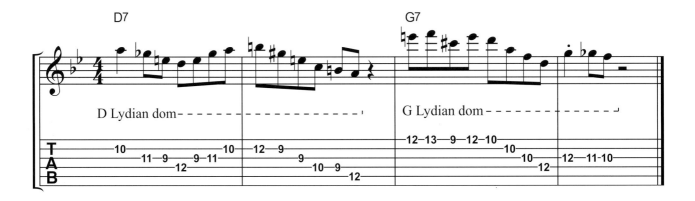

Charlie Christian playing his Gibson ES-150, a guitar so closely associated with him that it became known as the 'Charlie Christian' model.

The Minor I – VI – II – V Progression

The minor I – VI – II – V has exactly the same root movement as its major cousin, but generally employs a single dominant, the primary dominant seventh (V7). This is because the VI chord is rarely changed to a secondary dominant. If the VI chord were changed to a dominant, it would resolve onto a minor7♭5 (II) chord – a chord that does not calm the tensions of the dominant as satisfactorily as a minor7 chord (as in the major VI7 – II sequence).

It is however acceptable to change both the VI and the II chords to secondary dominants, and we will be exploring this possibility a little later on. In figure 8.15 below the 'diatonic' sequence is annotated. I'm using the term 'diatonic' in this way because, as with many minor key scenarios, there is no principle minor scale, and the sequence in fact has two parent minor scales:

Fig 8.15 **The minor I – VI – II – V progression**

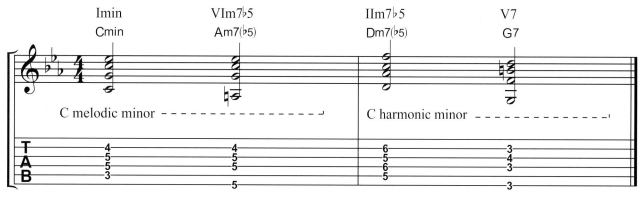

By using the VI chord from the melodic minor scale (Amin7♭5), the root movement of the minor turnaround retains the forward motion quality of its major equivalent. If the progression were kept entirely diatonic to the harmonic minor scale, the VI chord would actually be a half-step lower (the sixth step of this scale is minor), and a major seventh (static) chord would be produced. Although this is still a useful sequence, it doesn't have the strong root progression of the standard minor turnaround since the cycle of fifths movement between the last three chords would be missing.

As you can see from figure 8.15, it would be possible to just play C melodic minor through the first bar and C harmonic minor during the second. As we've discovered before, a scale-based approach to a busy chord sequence just doesn't work.

What you should be constantly aiming for in your solos is an equally strong statement of the underlying harmonic movement as the chords themselves provide. Let's revise the three techniques we used to practise the diatonic major turnaround earlier in this chapter. Figure 8.16 (overleaf) demonstrates the guide tone approach, arpeggio approach and finally the use of encirclement when improvising around the minor I – VI – II –V progression:

Fig 8.16 Minor I – VI – II – V practice techniques

1) Guide tones

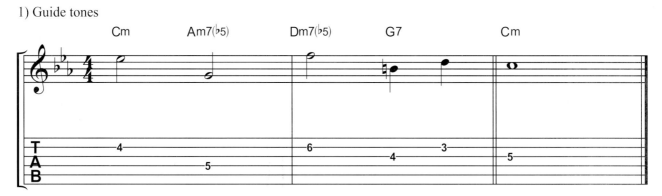

2) Four-note arpeggios

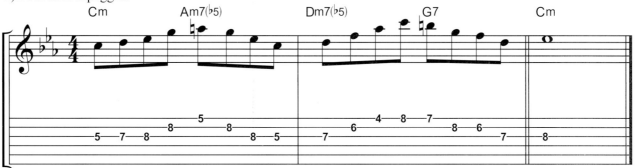

3) Adding encirclement and chromatic notes

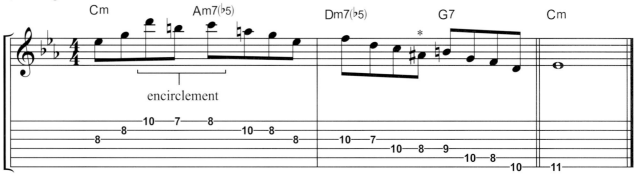

* chromatic approach note

Substituting Secondary Dominants On VI & II

To add extra spice to the minor turnaround, particularly when it has no accompanying melody (i.e. at the end of a chorus), the VI and II chords can be changed to secondary dominants. To ensure the texture of the turnaround remains 'dark' and in keeping with the minor tonality, altered scale tensions are generally added to each dominant seventh.

Figure 8.17 illustrates two examples of this, the first descending to the VI chord from C minor and adding one extension per chord, the second rising to the VI chord and adding two extensions per chord. Notice the use of Cm7 and Cm9 as tonic minors which creates a modal tonality (the tonic minor of the harmonic and melodic minor scales would be a min/maj7):

Fig 8.17 Adding secondary dominants with extensions

1) Descending to VI with single extension per chord

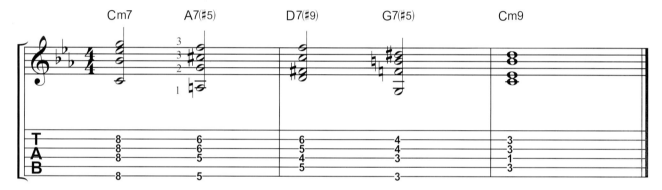

2) Ascending to VI with double extension per chord

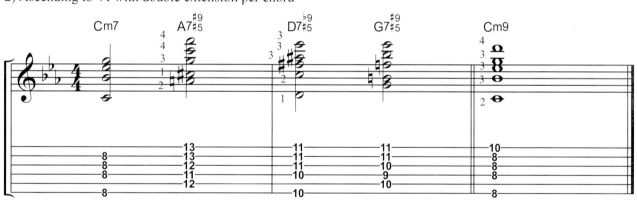

Our minor turnaround has now been 'spiced up nice and strong' yet loses none of its minor tonality. Adjusting the minor scale to fit non-diatonic chords is not a particularly effective tool in this scenario. Firstly, even the basic turnaround demands two scales, and secondly, since altered tensions have been applied throughout, it makes more sense simply to apply the altered scale to each chord.

When playing over dense harmonies such as these, the most effective lines can sometimes be created

with just a few notes from the minor pentatonic (particularly at slower tempos) – just let the chords do the work for you! Figure 8.18 (overleaf) illustrates two approaches, the first applying the altered scale, and the second using only the C minor pentatonic scale:

Fig 8.18 **Applying altered tensions to Im7 – VI7 – II7 – V7**

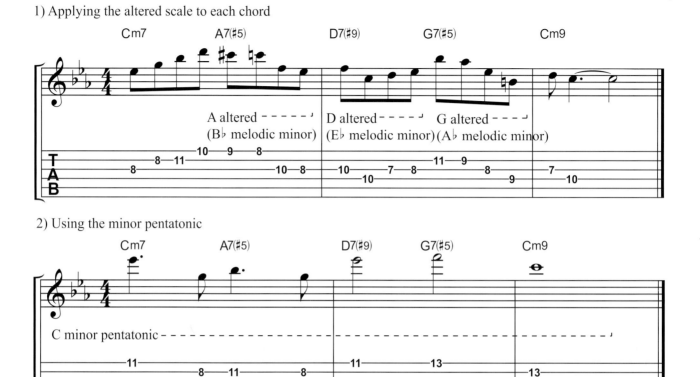

1) Applying the altered scale to each chord

2) Using the minor pentatonic

Just as 'rhythm changes' tunes are constructed from a series of major turnarounds, many minor tunes are also based on the minor I – VI – II – V sequence. Popular standards such as 'Softly As In A Morning Sunrise', 'Lullaby of Birdland' and 'Moanin'' are all constructed from the minor turnaround.

Tunes that contain static tonic minor chords (i.e. lasting for two or more bars), such as 'Summertime' or the minor blues progression, will often have additional turnarounds added. This creates greater harmonic movement and provides the improviser with a more challenging chord sequence.

Our final tune is a minor turnaround workout in C minor based loosely on the changes of 'Softly As In A Morning Sunrise'. Since the bridge modulates to the relative major, you will also be able to incorporate the major turnaround ideas that we explored earlier in the chapter.

Phil Capone

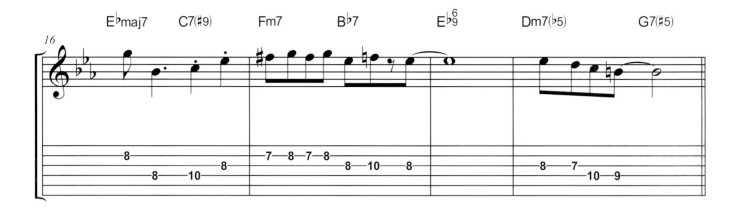

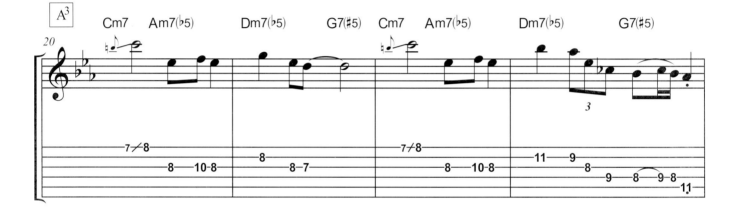

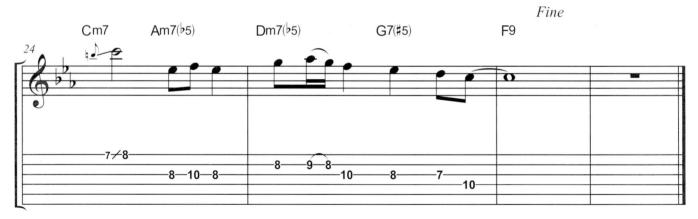

After last solo *D.C. al Fine*

Checkpoint

Song Form

Just like the previous tune, this song is also based on the popular 'AABA' song form. There is no generic term to describe a tune based on the minor turn-around, and the sequence doesn't offer the same endless harmonic possibilities as its major equivalent.

However it is still a challenging sequence, and demands a high level of harmonic awareness and spontaneous melodic creativity from the soloist.

Modulation Points

The 'B' section is preceded by a major II–V that 'announces' the modulation to the relative major key, E♭.

Minor Detail – solo

Mirror this in your improvisation by leading into the bridge with an E♭ II – V lick. Remember that you can always 'think' in terms of the II or the V chord alone.

The first example overleaf demonstrates the use of a diminished arpeggio over the Fm7/B♭7, ignoring the Fm7 and creating a bar of B♭ 7♭9 tensions.

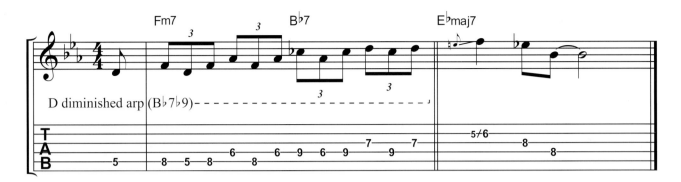

Similarly, the return to the 'A' section is preceded by a minor II – V. Again, reflect this in your solo:

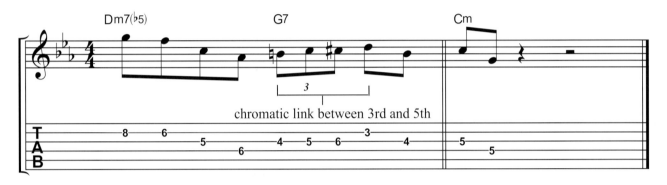

Hybrid Turnarounds

The second turnaround of the bridge starts on chord III – something we looked at earlier in the chapter. However, in this case the III chord is a minor7♭5 chord. This creates a double II – V sequence where the first II – V is minor and the second is major. If you use the guide tone or encirclement approaches then this will sound very similar to a regular III – VI – II – V. However, by ignoring the minor7♭5 chord and using the Phrygian dominant over the C7, the dominant tensions are highlighted. This creates a more dramatic resolution to the Fm7 (II) and helps to break up the repetitive nature of the linked turnarounds.

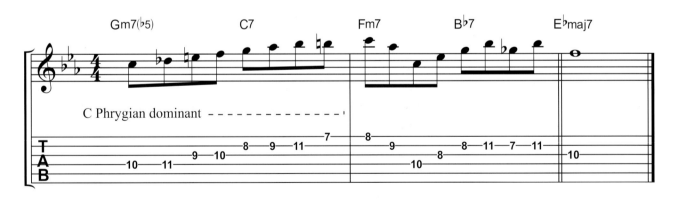

Assignments and Improvisation Tips

1. Practise comping using only guide tones (3rds and 7ths). These can be played on the middle strings (3rd and 4th), but also work well on the higher (2nd and 3rd strings) and lower (5th and 6th strings). These simple, double stop chord voicings are extremely effective for comping through fast moving changes and will not add colour tones that might conflict with the soloists note choices.

2. Start simple. Remember that you can always omit chords and break a sequence down into its simplest form. Sometimes thinking this way when improvising is the best way to create melodic licks. In the example below, related chords are omitted leaving the skeleton sequence of I – V. Since the Am7♭5 will still be present in the sequence (even if you're not playing it), only a minor scale that contains a diatonic VIm7♭5 chord can be used. Both the C jazz melodic minor and the C Dorian scales can therefore be used over the first bar. Remember that the Phrygian dominant should be your first choice for a minor primary dominant. However if you desire darker vibes then the altered scale will deliver!

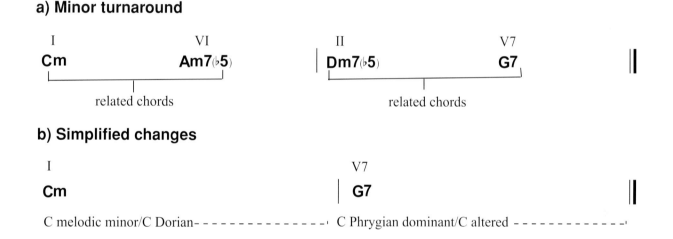

a) Minor turnaround

I	VI	II	V7
Cm	Am7(♭5)	Dm7(♭5)	G7

related chords   related chords

b) Simplified changes

I	V7
Cm	G7

C melodic minor/C Dorian - - - - - - - - - - - - - - ' C Phrygian dominant/C altered - - - - - - - - - - - - '

3. Whatever approach you use when improvising, don't ignore the most fundamental and important asset – your voice. Play the minor turnaround on your guitar and try singing some ideas; this is the most effective way to come up with original licks. To improve your ear, try reversing the process – sing what you play on the guitar. The more you can internalise your soloing (i.e. hear the notes in your head before you play them), the quicker your improvising skills will develop. For inspiration check out just about any recording by the outstanding jazz guitarist **George Benson**. Mr Benson can simultaneously sing what he is playing on the guitar, and has made the technique his trademark.

4. The accompanying CD will provide you with an invaluable resource for developing and honing your playing skills. However don't forget to practise just with a metronome too! Set it to 'click' on the backbeat (beats two and four) when playing a swing groove.

Joe Pass with his famous 1962 Gibson ES-175, which he played almost exclusively between 1963 and 1980. Legend has it that when Pass left rehab in the early 60s he was playing gigs with a borrowed solid-bodied electric and a wealthy fan bought Joe this guitar brand new for his birthday!

Conclusion

Congratulations!

By working through this book methodically you will have improved your fingerboard geography, sight-reading facility, picking technique, chord vocabulary, scale resource, sense of rhythm, aural skills and will possess a working knowledge of jazz harmony. No mean feat.

To achieve all of this with a 'virtual' teacher (that's me!) takes self-motivation and dedication – essential qualities that you will need to become a good jazz guitarist. You now have all of the necessary skills to start playing jazz and developing your own style.

Don't worry about avoiding clichés (all the great players embrace them), take them apart and analyse them (a cliché becomes a cliché because it's effective and succinct). Search out as many jazz recordings as you can (the Suggested Listening section will help) and go to as many gigs and jam sessions as possible.

Many players (including myself) keep a 'lick diary' of all the bits and pieces that they've transcribed. This way the material can be regularly reviewed (keep the diary next to your guitar). The assimilation process should involve practising each 'jazz soundbite' (this could be a lick, chord voicing or a comping phrase) in each of the five 'EDCAG' positions, followed by a 'take it through the keys' workout (this is most effective when you remain in the same neck position).

So don't stop now – if you've made it this far then there's no reason why you shouldn't ultimately achieve a professional playing standard. There will be times when it feels like you've 'plateaued out' and you just can't seem to make progress any more. This happens to all of us at sometime or another. Try listening to the recordings that got you into jazz in the first place, or go and check out a gig. Inspiration will return, don't worry.

Some of the topics that you will need to consider for further study are:

Comping with walking bass lines
Solo jazz guitar techniques (there are many books written on this topic alone)
Chord substitutions (including ♭5 substitution)
Advanced pentatonic improvisation
Rhythmic groupings
Thirteenth chords
'Giant Steps' improvisation
Studying all of the melodic and harmonic minor scale modes
Quartal harmony
Extended use of chromaticism
Rootless chord voicings
Full analysis of 'slash' chord types
Conversion of regular chords to 'slash' chords and vice versa
Diminished scale (including extensions and intrinsic major triads)
Using 'straight eighth' phrasing over a swing groove
Sixteenth-note licks
Superimposing changes over a static chord vamp (for improvising)
Improvising at fast tempos

To help you with your quest why not invest in some of the excellent books and DVDs that are available today. Check out Barry Galbraith's Guitar Solos (vols 1 & 2 – Mel Bay Publications) or Guitar Comping (part of the Jamey Aebersold series), and Joe Pass's Guitar Style or Guitar Chords (both Mel Bay Publications). These books offer a concise and invaluable insight into the harmonic approach of two geniuses of the jazz guitar. And don't forget that the entire Jamey Aebersold 'play-a-long' series (there are now well over a hundred titles) are fantastic for learning tunes and practising your improvising.

Finally there are some excellent DVDs available (check out the *Hot Licks* Videos series) by many legendary players: **Joe Pass**, **Emily Remler**, **Martin Taylor**, **Mike Stern**, **George Benson** et al. Get them on your 'wish list' now!

Suggested Listening

Learning To Listen

Listening is a vital element of playing jazz; it provides us with inspiration and also helps us to speak the language of jazz more fluently. But where do you start? There are a bewildering number of styles covered by the generic term 'jazz'.

The following list is designed to highlight each era's key players, and provide you with a condensed snapshot of jazz guitar history. Essential CDs that deserve a place in any self-respecting jazz guitarists' collection are included! To become a fully rounded jazz musician, it's essential that you become ac-

quainted with each stage of the music's evolution. As a student of the Guildhall School of Music some years ago, the jazz history lectures by **Ian Carr** (jazz trumpeter, bandleader, jazz educator and biographer) had a lasting impact on me. Ian is a firm believer in the importance of a good historical perspective; it helps to keep us all moving forward as players. At some time or another every musician hits a brick wall and finds themselves stagnating; by re-examining the music of the great pioneers we can often find the inspiration we need to get back on track and keep moving forward.

The Pioneers: 1920s

In his short life, **Eddie Lang** (1902–1933) established himself as the earliest jazz guitar virtuoso, playing single-line improvisations in the style of a horn player. His famous duets with guitarist **Carl Kress** and violinist **Joe Venuti** are astonishing reminders of just how good a player Eddie was. Without **Eddie Lang**, many historians believe there would have been no **Django Rhienhardt**.

Eddie Lang – A Handful of Riffs (originally released 1929, re-released in 1997 on the Living Era label)
Eddie Lang & Joe Venuti – The New York Sessions 1926–1935 (remastered and re-released on the JSP label in 2003)

Carl Kress (1907–1965) and **Eddie Lang** were the undisputed fathers of jazz guitar. While Lang concentrated on developing his single-line approach to improvisation, Kress pioneered the art of chord soloing. His recordings with **Eddie Lang** and **Dick Mcdonough** are widely regarded as the finest examples of jazz guitar duets.

Eddie Lang/Carl Kress/Dick Mcdonough – Pioneers of Jazz Guitar 1927–1939 (released on the Retrieval label in 2000)

The Swing Era: 1930s/40s

Django Rheinhardt (1910–1953) was a self-taught gypsy guitarist. At just eighteen years old, he was involved in a caravan fire that left his left hand and right side of his body badly burned. This left the young Django with the use of only two left hand fingers – enough to make most people forget their

dreams of becoming a professional guitarist. But while spending eighteen months convalescing, he developed a system of soloing using his remaining index and middle fingers. When you listening to Django's recordings you will marvel at the level of fluency he achieves, an incredible example of human persistence triumphing against all odds. One of the few European musicians to have an impact on the early evolution of jazz, no jazz guitar collection would be complete without at least one of his CDs.

Django Rheinhardt – Djangology (double CD released on the Recall label in 2000)
Django Rheinhardt – The Best of Django Rheinhardt (released on the Blue Note label in 1996)

Charlie Christian (1916–1942) was the first player to 'go electric' and consequently revolutionised the role of the jazz guitarist. He simultaneously paved the way for the electric blues and rock 'n' roll guitarists that would follow in his wake. Finally the guitar was capable of competing with horn players for a slice of the soloing cake. Christian shot to stardom in the **Benny Goodman** Orchestra, whose ranks he joined in 1939. His horn-like, single-line

Bop-Bop: 1940s/50s

Barney Kessel (1923–2004) was one of the most important electric players immediately to follow in **Charlie Christian**'s trailblazing footsteps. He recorded with **Charlie Parker** in the late 1940s and became famous for his 1950s trio recordings with **Ray Brown** (bass) and **Shelly Manne** (drums). Later in the 60s he became the most 'in-demand' session guitarist in the USA, recording on film scores and pop songs alike. Kessel refined the electric jazz guitar sound and coined many of the phrases that we now consider clichés.

Barney Kessel – Kessel Plays Standards (fifties recording re-released on Original Jazz Classics, 1991)
Barney Kessel, Ray Brown & Shelly Manne – Poll Winners Three! (another fifties classic also re-released

Pop Jazz – Latin, Funk & Wes: The 1960s

Charlie Byrd (1925–1999) is most famous for spearheading the 1960s bossa nova movement with saxophonist **Stan Getz**. While 'serious' jazz was becoming more experimental, Byrd stayed mainstream by introducing the new easy listening style

improvisations continue to inspire players to this day. His licks stand the test of time and still sound cool in a contemporary setting – incredible when you consider how long ago he recorded them. Essential listening.

Charlie Christian – The Original Guitar Genius (big value 4 CD boxed set released on Proper, 2005)

Freddie Green (1911–1987) held the rhythm guitar chair in the **Count Basie** Orchestra for almost fifty years. His 'four in the bar' comping style remains peerless. You won't learn how to play blistering licks by listening to Green (he rarely played solos at all), but you will learn how to play tasteful, swinging rhythm guitar.

Count Basie – April in Paris (remastered original recording from 1955 re-released on the Verve label in 1999. Green is clearly audible on every track)

on the Original Classics label in 1992)

Tal Farlow (1921–1998) was the quintessential reluctant jazz guitar hero; he despised touring and recording and in later life only performed near his hometown on the USA's East Coast. He initially found fame with the **Red Norvo** Trio in the late 1940s. Famous for his melodic bop-style improvising technique, lush chord voicings and the pioneering use of artificial harmonics when soloing.

Tal Farlow – The Swinging Guitar of Tal Farlow (originally released, 1957, re-released Verve, 1999)
Tal Farlow – Chromatic Palette (a beautiful trio recording from 1981, re-released in 1994 on the Concord Jazz label)

to the USA. During his 40-year career he recorded many outstanding albums.

Stan Getz & Charlie Byrd – Jazz Samba (originally released 1962, remastered/re-released, Verve, 1999)

Grant Green (1935–1979) is considered by many to have paved the way for the success of both **Wes Montgomery** and **George Benson** . Green's uncomplicated, melodic playing style won him many fans. He is also widely recognised as being the pioneer of jazz-funk with his grooving, funk-influenced albums of the late 1960s.

Grant Green – Green Street (originally released in 1961, re-released by Blue Note in 2002)
Grant Green – Green Is Beautiful (originally released in 1970, re-released by EMI in 1994)

Wes Montgomery (1925–1968) is arguably one of the most important post-**Charlie Christian** jazz guitarists. Interestingly, Christian was also one of Montgomery's biggest heroes. Wes's lyrical, intensely melodic improvisations, fast octave licks, and thumb technique (which gave him his trademark, mellow tone), make him one of the smoothest and coolest guitarists in the history of jazz. He was widely criticised for 'selling out' in the mid 1960s when he released a series of collaborations with arranger **Don Sebesky** and producer **Creed Taylor**. These brilliantly conceived, but nonetheless homogenised, recordings are not to everyone's taste, however they established the 'smooth jazz' sound that is still copied to this day. Containing both standards and pop songs of the day, and featuring lush string arrangements, the albums were an instant success. Wes consequently became the most famous jazz guitarist in the world for three years before his untimely death from a heart attack at the age of 43.

Wes Montgomery – The Incredible Jazz Guitar Of Wes Montgomery (originally released in 1960, re-released on the Concord label in 2006)
Wes Montgomery – Bumpin' (originally released in 1965, remastered and re-released on Verve, 1999)

Fusion – Joe's Duets With Ella & Pat: 1970s

Miles Davis was said to have been a big fan of **Jimi Hendrix**, and in the late 1960s he electrified his band, augmenting it with a young guitarist from England, **John Mclaughlin** (born 1942). McLaughlin is featured on Miles' albums *In A Silent Way* (1969) and *Bitches Brew* (1970). He left the Miles Davis Group to form his own band The Mahavishnu Orchestra and, as they say, the rest is history. McLaughlin's sound was distorted and loud, he played through a Marshall stack using solid-bodied guitars. His fiery, machine gun licks influenced an entire generation of guitarists. Guitar-led, jazz-rock fusion would dominate the jazz scene for the rest of the decade.

The Mahavishnu Orchestra with John McLaughlin – The Inner Mounting Flame (originally released in 1971, remastered and re-released on the Sony Jazz label in 1999)
The Mahavishnu Orchestra with John McLaughlin – Birds of Fire (originally released in 1973, remastered and re-released on the Sony Jazz label, 2000)

Joe Pass (1929–1994) was arguably the greatest solo jazz guitarist in the history of the instrument. Joe had enjoyed a successful career since the 1960s, and had been a sideman for many famous vocalists including **Frank Sinatra**, **Sarah Vaughan** and **Johnny Mathis**, but his collaborations with **Ella Fitzgerald** during the 1970s and 1980s are widely regarded as his best recordings. These influential, incredible albums redefine the art of guitar accompaniment – Joe makes the instrument sound like a full band.

Ella Fitzgerald with Joe Pass – Take Love Easy (originally released in 1973, re-released on the Pablo label in 2005)
Ella Fitzgerald and Joe Pass – Easy Living (originally released in 1986, re-released on Pablo, 2006)

Pat Metheny (born 1954) is one of the most commercially successful jazz guitarists ever, achieving the rare feat of notching up huge record sales (to a cross-over audience) while still remaining a critically acclaimed and hugely respected musician. His liquid phrasing, country-flavoured acoustic work and use of guitar synthesizers are legendary, and have earned him a huge worldwide fan base. Metheny has recorded with many artists but is most famous for his Pat Metheny Group recordings with long-time collaborator, pianist and composer **Lyle Mays**.

Back To Basics: 1980s – Present Day

Pat Martino (born 1944) recorded many ground-breaking and hugely influential albums throughout the 1960s and 1970s. In 1980, after receiving surgery for a brain aneurysm, he suffered from severe amnesia and apparently had no recollection of his distinguished career as a jazz musician. With the help of friends, his recordings, and unbelievable determination, Pat rediscovered his talents. His return to the jazz arena was marked by his 1987 release *The Return*. Martino's pioneering approach to improvisation (using only minor scales) and his incredible sixteenth-note phrasing are legendary.

Pat Martino – Live At Yoshi's (an outstanding live album released in 2001 on the Blue Note label)
Pat Martino – Remember (a tribute to **Wes Montgomery** released in 2006 on Blue Note)

Jim Mullen (born 1945) achieved worldwide fame during the 1970s and 1980s with the jazz-funk band Morrissey/Mullen (featuring the late tenor saxophonist **Dick Morrissey**). Mullen established himself as a solo artist during the late 1980s and returned to a more straight-ahead jazz setting with his 1996 standards album *We Go Back*. In recent years he has concentrated on touring and recording with his own band The Organ Trio – influenced by **Jimmy Smith**'s classic Hammond organ trio sound.

Jim Mullen – We Go Back (released in 1996 on EFZ
The Organ Trio – Way Of Life (released in 2002 on the Flamingo Records label)

Emily Remler's (1957–1990) tragically short career spanned just under a decade; in this brief time she recorded an incredible ten albums. Ignoring the fusion that dominated the 70s, Emily spearheaded a new generation of jazz guitarists who returned to a more straight-ahead style, with a traditional 'clean' jazz sound. Although strongly influenced by **Wes**

Pat Metheny Group – Pat Metheny Group (originally released in 1978, re-released on ECM, 1988).
Pat Metheny Group – Still Life Talking (originally released in 1987, re-released on Geffen, 1993).

Montgomery and **Pat Martino**, she created her own unique style that was fluent and melodic. In addition to her own compositions, she also recorded many popular jazz standards, often reworked and re-harmonised to create fresh interpretations. Because she avoided the guitar sounds that were in vogue at the time, her recordings have a timeless, classic quality. A highly recommended player.

Emily Remler – Take Two (originally released in 1982, and re-released on Concord, 1992)
Emily Remler – East To Wes (originally released in 1988 on the Concord label)

English guitarist **Martin Taylor** (born 1956) is one of the greatest guitar talents on the jazz scene today. Equally proficient at playing solo jazz guitar (fluently playing melodies, bass lines and chords simultaneously), acoustic Django-inspired gypsy jazz, swinging blues, or straight ahead hard bop, Taylor shot to stardom as **Stephan Grappelli**'s guitarist in the 1980s. He's a highly respected musician and has collected a string of awards (including an MBE 'For Services To Music'). **Pat Metheny** describes him as 'one of the most awesome solo guitar players in the history of the instrument. He's unbelievable'. So check him out!

The Martin Taylor Quartet – Change Of Heart (released on Linn Records in 1991)
Martin Taylor's Spirit of Django – Spirit Of Django (released on Linn Records in 1994)

Don't forget that this list is not intended to be exhaustive. There are many fine players that have been left out for no other reason than space limitations – this is just a reference point to get you listening to a few of the most influential jazz guitarists recordings. Listen to jazz shows on the radio – many of my best 'discoveries' have been made this way. Good luck!

Index

CD Track Listing

How To Use This CD

Guitar accompaniment is panned to the left while the tune is panned right throughout the CD – to remove the accompaniment set your hi-fi's balance control to pan hard right or left respectively (if you have a 'mono' button, you can use this to send the resulting signal to both speakers). Where the melody is doubled on keyboard, this has been left 'centre stage' to produce an authentic sounding mix.

Some of these tracks have piano or organ accompaniment – in this case the comp is not panned. This is to allow you to practise comping simultaneously with a keyboard player – a scenario that is frequently encountered 'on the gig'.

The number of solo choruses varies with each song; slow tunes may have just one chorus (as they would on a gig), whereas up-tempo tunes will often contain as many as four solo choruses. Practise comping along with the track first – this will help you to learn the chord sequence and also help to clarify the song's geography.

CD Recording Credits

Guitars, keyboards, midi sequencing and loop editing – Phil Capone

Acoustic and Electric bass – Mike Edmunds

All the electric guitar parts were recorded on a 1981 Gibson ES-175 played through a 1979 Fender Champ combo. No effects were used, just a dash of reverb in the final mix.